The Red River Campaign of 1864
and the Loss by the Confederacy
of the Civil War

ALSO BY MICHAEL J. FORSYTH

*The Camden Expedition of 1864 and the Opportunity
Lost by the Confederacy to Change the Civil War*
(McFarland 2003; paperback 2008)

The Red River Campaign of 1864 and the Loss by the Confederacy of the Civil War

MICHAEL J. FORSYTH

McFarland & Company, Inc., Publishers
Jefferson, North Carolina, and London

The present work is a reprint of the library bound edition of The Red River Campaign of 1864 and the Loss by the Confederacy of the Civil War, *first published in 2002 by McFarland.*

LIBRARY OF CONGRESS CATALOGUING-IN-PUBLICATION DATA

Forsyth, Michael J., 1966–
 The Red River Campaign of 1864 and the loss by the Confederacy of the Civil War / by Michael J. Forsyth.
  p. cm.
 Includes bibliographical references and index.

 ISBN 978-0-7864-4499-1
 softcover : 50# alkaline paper ∞

 1. Red River Expedition, 1864. 2. Louisiana—History—Civil War, 1861–1865—Campaigns. 3. Arkansas—History—Civil War, 1861–1865—Campaigns. 4. United States—History—Civil War, 1861–1865—Campaigns. I. Title.
 E476.33.F67 2010
 973.7'36—dc21   2001044439

British Library cataloguing data are available

©2002 Michael J. Forsyth. All rights reserved

No part of this book may be reproduced or transmitted in any form or by any means, electronic or mechanical, including photocopying or recording, or by any information storage and retrieval system, without permission in writing from the publisher.

Cover images: (clockwise from upper left) Major General Richard Taylor; Rear Admiral David D. Porter; Major General Nathaniel P. Banks; Lieutenant General Edmund Kirby Smith; flags ©2010 ClickArt

Manufactured in the United States of America

McFarland & Company, Inc., Publishers
 Box 611, Jefferson, North Carolina 28640
 www.mcfarlandpub.com

To soldiers, who bear the brunt of all decisions
made by their leaders—good and bad.

Acknowledgments

When writing of any magnitude is undertaken there are inevitably people who assist the author in completing the project. I am certainly indebted to many and take this small space to thank them for their contributions, support, and assistance.

Up front, I must recognize my wife Maryellen and our children, Andrew and Ashley. I spent many hours daily with books strewn from one end of our house to the other. I am sure my disposition was not always pleasant, but through all this my wife supported everything I did, as she has done for eleven years. My children made sacrifices as well, as Dad was not always accessible to play baseball or dollhouse. Thank you to you three for always being there for me.

Next, I would like to thank Dr. Stanley Hilton for his advice and encouragement. When I began this project, I doubted whether I could really do it. "Doc," however, told me and the other students in our program not to become wrapped up in minutiae. He told us to simply "write history and tell a story." That simple piece of advice kept me focused on telling a story, which is what I love to do.

I have to thank Mr. Scott Dearman Jr. and Mr. Steve Bounds, rangers at the Mansfield State Commemorative Area in Louisiana. Scott and I trekked all up and down central Louisiana taking pictures and walking the battlefields of the Red River Campaign. We had a great time and enjoyed discussing our common interest, the Civil War. Steve and I engaged in lively conversations about the might-have-beens in the campaign. He also provided me with invaluable insight and references used in this book.

Finally, I must thank my parents, Jack and Edith, and grandparents, Jean and Armando. These people gave me the life tools I would need to be a success. Thanks to all.

Contents

Acknowledgments — vii
Introduction — 1

1. A Lost Opportunity? — 7
2. The Antagonists — 24
3. Pressure in Both Camps — 40
4. "10,000 Damned Gorillas" — 53
5. "The State of Things … Was Very Discouraging" — 68
6. Three Wasted Opportunities — 89
7. "A Protecting Shield" — 109
8. "This Fatal Campaign" — 119

Appendix 1: Campaign Chronology — 129
Appendix 2: Order of Battle — 133
Appendix 3: Maps — 139
Notes — 155
Bibliography — 171
Index — 177

Introduction

The 1864 Red River Campaign is a relatively unknown chapter of the Civil War even to those who profess a keen interest in the war. Most people do not know any battles took place on the west side of the Mississippi River. This is because the campaign took place in a theater that, even at the time, was considered a backwater — the banks of the Red River in Louisiana. Yet a closer look at this relatively unknown campaign reveals that both sides committed major resources to it and fought in complex joint operations that involved naval and ground forces. The campaign's outcome was influenced significantly by the personal conflicts embroiling the high commands of both sides. As I researched the campaign for my master's thesis, a question arose: Could the Confederate army have achieved more decisive results from the Red River Campaign — perhaps even have changed the outcome of the Civil War — if the Confederate command climate had been different? It is a question I attempt to answer in this book.

Because even Civil War buffs have only a passing knowledge of the campaign, I provide a brief overview to set the stage. This introduction gives a glimpse of the strategic situation in 1864, links it to the upcoming national election, and briefly covers the colorful cast of characters who decided the fate of the campaign. Finally, it acquaints the reader with the Louisiana fields where the campaign took place and the results that guaranteed the campaign would fade into obscurity.

Hopes were running high in the North as 1864 began. Federal armies had won hard-fought victories at Gettysburg, Vicksburg, and Chattanooga in 1863. Everywhere it appeared that the blue tide would continue to roll forward in the spring of '64. Additionally, the Union had a new commander in Lieutenant General Ulysses S. Grant. His string of successes in the West seemed to spell doom for the staggering Confederacy.

Mixed with the feelings of optimism in the North was the knowledge that the Confederacy was not yet defeated and, moreover, still maintained a viable army. Every time the Rebels seemed on the ropes, they would quickly recover with an unexpected blow. War weariness had taken deep root in the North, and Southern military successes in 1864 would only deepen the desire among many within the Northern public to end the war. This could spell doom for the Lincoln administration and the Union cause, for 1864 was an election year. Setbacks for the Union armies in 1864 could translate into defeat at the polls for Lincoln in November.

President Abraham Lincoln had summoned General Grant to take command of all Union armies in March of 1864. Prior to Grant's assumption of command, the Union armies had witnessed a long line of failed commanders. With these men came a string of humiliating defeats at the hands of a much weaker Confederacy. After three years of searching, Lincoln thought that in Grant he finally had the commander who could bring the Rebels to defeat. Grant arrived in Washington in March with a plan to bring about the destruction of the rebellion.

In the East the hard-luck Federal Army of the Potomac faced the tough Confederate Army of Northern Virginia, commanded by Robert E. Lee. After three long years of fighting these two armies stood toe to toe in northern Virginia at virtually the same points they started from in 1861. West of the Appalachians the Union armies (recently commanded by Grant) had fared much better. These armies held most of the state of Tennessee and, in July of 1863, cut the Confederacy in two with the fall of Vicksburg. Everything west of the Mississippi River was, for all practical purposes, inaccessible to the Southern nation, including the rich area of the Red River Valley. Furthermore, three Federal armies stood in north Georgia ready to press into the Confederate heartland, making for Atlanta. To stop these armies the Confederates fielded the stout but luckless Army of Tennessee, commanded by General Joseph E. Johnston.

The problem with subjugating the Southern states, as Grant viewed it, was that heretofore the Union armies had never acted in a coordinated manner. As a result, the Rebels always had been able to use their interior lines to shift forces and mass at threatened points. To prevent this, Grant planned to apply unstoppable pressure against all the Confederate armies in a simultaneous offensive. The far superior weight of the Federal forces would eventually crack the thin Confederate lines, exposing the Rebel vitals.

Grant's plan was fundamentally sound — if he could execute it. A problem arose, however, immediately upon his ascension to command. Grant's predecessor, Major General Henry W. Halleck, already had set the wheels in motion for a campaign west of the Mississippi along the line of the Red River. Although the region—called the Trans-Mississippi by the Confederates—lay isolated from the rest of the Southern states and eventually would wither on the vine, Halleck committed vast resources to an expedition. The reasons behind Halleck's penchant for a campaign up the Red ranged from complex political machinations to socio-economic motives. At this juncture in the war, a Union effort in this quarter represented more of a needless diversion away from the main theaters than a serious effort to bring the war to an end.

Although Grant considered stopping the whole operation, he let it continue against his better judgment. This diversion of close to 50,000 Union troops and over 30 naval vessels to a faltering corner of the war presented the Confederacy with a great opportunity. If the Confederates could draw the Federals in, close the trap, and then destroy their army and navy, it could have serious repercussions on the direction of the war. The destruction of an army and naval vessels would deprive the Union war effort of veteran troops and send morale on the home front plummeting. That possibility could produce defeat for the Lincoln administration at the polls and give the Rebels victory at the bargaining table, a victory that had long eluded them on the battlefield.

The men in command on both sides present a colorful series of contrasts and similarities of leadership. The Union commanders, Major General Nathaniel P. Banks and Admiral David D. Porter, tolerated each other at best. Banks was the former Speaker of the United States House of Representatives and had the irritating tendency to run an army as he would have moderated a House proceeding. Porter, commanding the naval contingent, despised all politicians, and Banks' vacillating command style enraged the headstrong admiral. The animosities on the Union command team very nearly spelled disaster for the Federal forces in the Red River Valley.

The Confederate commanders shared a relationship similar to that of their Yankee antagonists. Lieutenant General Edmund Kirby Smith commanded all the Rebel forces west of the Mississippi. Though a conscientious, dedicated man, he struggled to deal with the challenges of defending the large region encompassed by his command. Much like Banks, he tended to waffle in deciding how best to defend the region. Major General Richard Taylor, Smith's primary subordinate, found this trait intolerable. Taylor, the son of a United States president, felt he knew how to utilize Rebel forces and never hesitated to offer his ideas to Smith. His suggestions were never tactfully presented and, in many cases, were no less than verbal attacks on his superior officer. This led to a stressful command climate as the two attempted to stop the vast superiority of the Union invasion force.

While both sides experienced the same challenges of command harmony during the course of the campaign, they diverged in how they dealt with the supreme crisis of the campaign. One command team remained divided and cast verbal barbs in every direction, while the other pulled together for the good of their cause. This determined the outcome of the campaign.

The Federals began the Red River Campaign with an air of confidence that rose steadily as the column progressed deeper into the valley of the Red. The Union army and navy managed to penetrate deep into Louisiana within two weeks of the jump-off date, March 12, 1864. Smart victories at Fort DeRussy, Alexandria, and Henderson's Hill seemed to promise a swift and successful campaign with laurels for all the participants. However, shortly after the Yankees arrived at the hamlet of Grand Ecore, plans for success went awry. A combination of low water in the Red, orders from Washington, and careless leadership conspired to produce defeat and near disaster for the army and navy in April.

The Confederates found themselves presented with an opportunity to "bag" the army away from its naval support and force Porter's gunboats aground. General Taylor, in spite of his badgering of Smith, managed to pull together enough of the scattered Confederate forces to bloody the nose of Banks near Mansfield, Louisiana. Through sheer audacity, Taylor defeated a Federal force twice the size of his own and was in a position to destroy the Union army and isolate the fleet in the river. Yet his vacillating superior decided to pull critical support from him, allowing the Federal army to make a hurried escape.

This turn of events set in motion an explosive period of fighting among the top leaders in the Confederate army, resulting in Taylor's relief and, arguably, the Confederates' missing the biggest opportunity of the war. Taylor launched a string of acerbic dispatches at his chief that alienated Smith more than they persuaded him to see Taylor's point of view. In the end, Confederate infighting only ensured that the teetering Federal force would escape. The flight of the Federal army later added strength to the primary theaters east of the Mississippi. These veteran Union troops would make their weight felt at the main theaters of the war by playing a major role in pivotal battles at critical times. The failure to destroy Banks' army in the Red River Valley helped vindicate Lincoln's war policy and enabled him to carry the 1864 election.

In the final analysis, the Red River Campaign was a remarkable effort by the Rebels—even with its indecisive outcome. The outnumbered and ill-equipped Confederate force managed to frustrate a major thrust into the Trans-Mississippi region while inflicting moderate casualties and enormous losses in equipment on the Union army. The Federals suffered well over 5,000 casualties and lost hundreds of supply wagons loaded with a mountain of provisions as well as dozens of ships in the river. The Rebels accomplished this feat through sheer audacity and the firm leadership of Richard Taylor. Yet they failed to do further damage to the Federals when the opportunity offered itself after the Battle of Mansfield. This is because Kirby Smith defanged Taylor at the decisive point in the campaign. What if he had listened to his irascible subordinate and allowed Taylor to pursue Banks?

Evidence suggests it is possible that Taylor could have destroyed the Union army in the Red River Campaign. The demise of the army would have forced the navy, trapped by a rapidly falling river, to succumb as well. What impact might this have had on the overall outcome of the war? A disaster such as suggested above would have deprived the Union cause of over 30,000 veteran soldiers and a large part of their "brown water" navy— a huge blow to the morale of the Northern public. It could have derailed Grant's plan to win the war until after the November elections. With the Union armies seemingly mired, as they had been for more than three years, Lincoln most certainly would have lost at the polls. The Red River Campaign represented the South's best opportunity for victory in 1864.

The Confederates in Louisiana achieved much in turning back the Union invasion, but could more decisive results have been achieved? In answering this question, this book examines the dynamics of leadership and the working relationship of the command teams on both sides. Additionally, it explores the strategic military and political situations and the influence this campaign could have had on each. I believe this obscure campaign held great promise for the Confederacy at a time when it seemed the fledgling nation would soon die. However, a combination of complex factors watered down the results and sealed Federal victory with the reelection of President Lincoln.

Chapter 1

A Lost Opportunity?

"One cannot afford to neglect opportunity."—Sun Tzu

Contemporary historians such as Ludwell Johnson and William R. Brooksher agree that the Red River Campaign amounted to a "strategic absurdity" for the Union army. From the Union perspective the road to victory lay in the east, where the Confederacy maintained its primary armies.[1] To divert forces from the main objective weakened their power and opened opportunity up to the Confederates. How much of an opportunity was there?

Major General Richard Taylor believed at the time and later that there was a great opportunity open to the Confederacy. He thought that Lieutenant General E. Kirby Smith's decision to disengage from Major General Nathaniel P. Banks after the battle of Pleasant Hill prevented him from achieving greater results. In a dispatch written on April 28, 1864, near the end of the campaign, Taylor laid out for Smith his vision of the dashed prospects. Taylor could not understand why Smith had decided to "abandon the certain destruction of an army of 30,000 men, backed by a huge fleet, to chase after a force of 10,000 in full retreat." This decision prevented the Confederacy from reaping "the moral effect at the North and the shock to public credit [that] would have seriously affected the war." Taylor argued that the destruction of Union forces under Banks and Admiral David D. Porter could have "by midsummer relieved the pressure from our suffering brethren in Virginia and Georgia."[2] Taylor, in other words, was convinced that the Trans-Mississippi army had the rare opportunity to influence the outcome of the war. The disaster he envisioned would have prevented these same troops from reinforcing the more important theaters in the east. This, coupled with the moral effect of defeat, would sway voters toward a peace candidate in the November elections, delivering victory to the Confederacy at the ballot box rather than on the battlefield.[3]

Taylor's ardor rose, if anything, after the war when he described the lost opportunity:

> Far away from the great centers of conflict in Virginia and Georgia, on a remote theatre, the opportunity of striking a blow decisive of the war was afforded. An army that included the strength of every garrison from Memphis to the Gulf had been routed, and, by the incompetency of its commander, was utterly demoralized and ripe for destruction. But this army was permitted to escape, and its 19th corps reached Chesapeake Bay in time to save Washington from General Early's attack, while the 13th, 16th, and 17th corps reenforced Sherman in Georgia. More than all we lost Porter's fleet, which the falling river had delivered into our hands.... With this fleet, or even a portion of it, we would have at once recovered possession of the Mississippi, from Ohio to the sea, and undone all the work of the Federals since the winter of 1861. Instead of Sherman, Johnston would have been reenforced from west of the Mississippi, and thousands of absent men, with fresh hope, would have rejoined Lee. The Southern people might have been spared the humiliation of defeat, and the countless woes and wrongs inflicted on them by their conquerors.[4]

Some of Taylor's assertions are grandiose. For example, in all likelihood Porter would have destroyed his fleet rather than allow it to fall into Confederate hands.[5] But Taylor is quite correct in pointing out that all of Banks' army was used to bring Generals Robert E. Lee and Joseph Johnston to bay in Virginia and Georgia. These units were instrumental in winning the great victories at Mobile, Atlanta, and Cedar Creek before the November elections. Without them could the Union have pulled off these victories before the voters spoke?

Once again contemporary historians agree that the campaign did little more than lengthen the outcome of the Civil War. Johnson states that "even the capture of Banks' entire army could only have the effect of lengthening the war, not of reversing the outcome. Before the fall of Vicksburg such a victory might have exerted a powerful influence on the course of events; now it was too late."[6] Brooksher contends that Taylor would not have been able to destroy the enemy forces, and that even if they had, "the end result of the campaign would have been unchanged."[7]

Johnson and Brooksher discount Taylor's assertions as an emotional outpouring rather than a measured assessment. In some respects they are correct, but Taylor makes enough of a case to cast doubt on the premise that Union victory was the inevitable outcome of the war. Sometimes the difference between victory and defeat is a change in a few decisions and the ability to recognize opportunity. Certainly the capture of Banks' army and the forced destruction of Porter's fleet would have had a huge moral effect in the North.

The Red River Campaign of 1864 was one of the most successful campaigns that any Confederate army fought during the Civil War. The small, under-equipped Confederate forces in the Trans-Mississippi defeated two Union armies — one in Arkansas and the other in Louisiana — maintained the region's territorial integrity, and diverted critical enemy reinforcements from more important theaters for months. The joint effort by E. Kirby Smith and Richard Taylor unquestionably delayed the eventual outcome of the war by a few months. But was there an opportunity in this campaign not simply to postpone defeat, but to actually secure victory for the Confederacy? The record suggests that with changes in a few decisions and a better working relationship between the primary men in the Confederate high command, a Confederate triumph was indeed a possibility.

Major General Richard Taylor, Commander of the Confederate District of West Louisiana, General Smith's primary subordinate commander in Louisiana. Taylor's bold leadership stopped Banks' thrust toward Shreveport at Mansfield, but his lack of tact in dealing with Smith led to a crisis in the Rebel high command during the Red River Campaign. *Courtesy Jack McCormack Irish Collection at the United States Military History Institute.*

The Confederate Trans-Mississippi Department encompassed a huge land area west of the Mississippi River that included the states Texas, Arkansas, and Louisiana, except for the parishes east of the river. The Confederacy also claimed Missouri, although it never seceded, and the Indian (modern-day Oklahoma) and Arizona territories. Altogether the department covered approximately 600,000 square miles stretching from the Mississippi to Southern California. The region was rich in manpower — its population represented a quarter of the South's total population — but lacked other essential war-making resources.[8]

The Union foray into the department in 1864 was a two-pronged attempt at permanently wresting control of the region from the Confederacy. The Union main effort came up from Berwick's Bay via the Red River, while a supporting force moved south from Little Rock, Arkansas. Both aimed at Shreveport, Louisiana, the capital of the department. The Union navy also supported the thrust up the Red, with nineteen gunboats and a host of transports. The Federal troops involved in the offensive numbered nearly 50,000 soldiers, while the South could muster only about half that many to stop them — but stop them they did. Major General Richard Taylor's force in Louisiana never comprised many more than 15,000 men of all arms. The Federal force drove into Louisiana with about twice that number and yet the Union army found itself frustrated at every turn. Deflecting the Union drive was a remarkable achievement, but if the Confederates leaders had made certain decisions differently they could have realized even greater success.

The campaign began on March 10, 1864, and lasted until May 22, 1864, when the Union Army of the Gulf stumbled back into Simmesport. Over the course of those seventy-three days of campaigning the Federal army gained nothing tangible and barely maintained the status quo, suffering significant casualties in the process.

Union Losses in the Red River Campaign

	Wounded	Killed	Missing	Total
Men:				
Soldiers	2191	454	2600	5212[9]
Sailors				320[10] includes 120 from fleet & 200 from the transports
Material:			**Naval:**	
Field Pieces	20		Gunboats	3
Naval Guns	37		Hospital Boat	1
	57[11]		Transports	5
Wagons	175[12]			9[13]
Animals	3507[14]			

These losses disheartened the Union high command and President Abraham Lincoln. Major General William T. Sherman mused that the Union failures in the campaign had cost his army the services of 10,000 veteran troops. At the same time the Confederates on his front witnessed a corresponding increase in their strength with the addition of Polk's Confederate Corps from Mississippi.[15] More important than the Union high command, the Northern public became distraught by yet another disaster for Union arms.[16] With a presidential election set for the fall, a setback such as that in the Red River Valley would inevitably cost Lincoln votes.

For the Confederacy the campaign brought tangible gains in the Trans-Mississippi. For the South as a whole it raised sagging morale and proved that Southern arms were still a dangerous force. John B. Jones, an employee of the Rebel War Department in Richmond, wrote in his diary on April 30, 1864, "Federal papers now admit that Gen. Banks has been defeated in La. [sic].... There is excitement at last ... [and] no one seems to doubt our final success," he noted a few days later. The reports "from the West, in Georgia, and beyond the Miss., all seem bright enough."[17]

In contrast to the large Northern losses, the Confederates lost only an estimated 4,300 men, 50 wagons and 700 horses, and three light steamers in the river.[18] Not only did Southern morale receive a huge boost, but Southern arms frustrated some specific Federal goals for the campaign. The Union objectives for the campaign were to occupy Texas, obtain cheap cotton for New England textile mills, and gain readmittance of Louisiana and Texas to the Union.[19] These Federal objectives were political and economic, but in the end the misdirection of Federal power into the Trans-Mississippi for such purposes gained the North nothing strategically. The failure to occupy Texas enabled the Confederates to maintain access to one of their few remaining trade outlets—Mexico. New England's starved textile industry would continue to suffer slow economic strangulation without the bountiful cotton of the Red River Valley and east Texas. Finally, the Lincoln administration failed to readmit the states of the Trans-Mississippi to the Union. The electoral votes from this region, although few, could prove critical to Lincoln's reelection bid, but the Federal defeat dashed hopes for any electoral boost in the South.[20] Considering the precarious position of Confederate forces at the start of the campaign, their success was a towering achievement. But the campaign could have been even more decisive for the Confederacy; it gave Rebel leaders a chance to inflict a disaster of monumental proportions on the Federal war effort.

The Red River Campaign, while offering the Confederacy an opportunity, ran counter to Union strategy and characterized unsound judgment. Lieutenant General U. S. Grant, upon taking command of all Union armies in March of 1864, came up with a war plan encompassing all Union forces in all theaters. Grant's plan called for the Union to focus all efforts east of the Mississippi River, where the Confederacy had its primary armies.

Already cut off from the rest of the Confederacy by the fall of Vicksburg, the Trans-Mississippi would wither on the vine. In the meantime, thought Grant, the force under Major General Frederick Steele in Arkansas would be sufficient to keep the Confederates west of the Mississippi occupied.[21]

Orders for the campaign had come from Major General Henry W. Halleck, the general-in-chief prior to Grant. Grant let them stand although he seriously considered canceling the expedition. Grant's target for Major General Nathaniel P. Banks and the Army of the Gulf was Mobile, Alabama. This point was critical to the Confederacy's survival, and the Army of Tennessee had detached Polk's Corps to the vicinity of Mobile to protect the city. This seriously weakened Joseph Johnston's Army of Tennessee in Georgia, which found itself badly outnumbered by three Union armies. By throwing Banks against Mobile, Grant would have deprived Johnston of Polk's services, thereby easing Sherman's task of taking Atlanta. The Red River Campaign delayed the thrust to Mobile by several months and allowed the Confederates to shift forces from that sector to areas under pressure, such as north Georgia.

Grant wanted the offensives launched when roads were passable, to support movement of the armies and their supplies. All armies would move at the same time to prevent the Confederacy from shifting forces from one theater to the other using interior lines. Grant's target date was April 25, 1864, road conditions allowing.[22] Since Banks had already embarked upon a sideshow in the Red River Valley, he ordered Banks to cut it short at Shreveport and turn over operations to Steele. Grant wanted Banks ready by the jump-off date to move to Mobile in concert with other Union forces.[23]

Banks' blunders in the Red River Campaign postponed effective implementation of Grant's plan by at least a few months. Banks found himself reeling under hard blows from Richard Taylor's army, and only because of miscues by the Confederate command did he escape entrapment. Banks' Army of the Gulf did not reach safety until May 22, three weeks after the other Union armies had started their moves. Elements of the Army of the Gulf did not actually move toward Mobile until late July, a delay of almost three months. Since Polk felt no pressure in his direction, he moved his corps back to North Georgia to assist Johnston in the defense of the Confederate heartland.[24] At the same time, Major General

Opposite: Major General Nathaniel P. Banks, commander of the Federal Department of the Gulf, commanded the Federal Army in the Red River Campaign. *Courtesy Massachusetts Commandery Military Order of the Loyal Legion and United States Military History Institute.*

1. A Lost Opportunity?

Andrew J. Smith—commanding three divisions of troops from the XVI and XVII Corps detached from Sherman—could not get back across the Mississippi. This took strength away from Sherman when he needed it most. Meanwhile, Nathan Bedford Forrest wreaked havoc in west Tennessee, threatening Sherman's supply line to Georgia and the success of his campaign. The missing XVI Corps divisions could have kept Forrest's hands full in north Mississippi, but their absence allowed the audacious Forrest to take the initiative and cause Sherman fits.[25] Sherman wrote in a dispatch that someone had to stop Forrest even "if it costs 10,000 lives and breaks the Treasury." A. J. Smith's men did not make it back across the Mississippi until June to reinforce Sherman and deal with Forrest. Confederate command policy and friction allowed these forces to make it back to safety. What if General E. Kirby Smith, the overall Confederate commander of the Trans-Mississippi Department, had adopted a more aggressive defense?

Smith adopted a defensive strategy that he styled a Fabian policy. It involved concentration of limited resources and the use of interior lines. With the concentrated force of all Southern troops west of the Mississippi, Smith would pounce on individual enemy thrusts into his theater and push them back. The policy traded space for time and involved minimal risk to Confederate forces. Smith believed that bolder action could lead to the destruction of his thin army and with it the loss of the entire department. Taylor, Smith's primary subordinate, fiercely disagreed with that policy; over the course of the Red River Campaign he sent highly insubordinate dispatches to Smith demanding bolder action. In Taylor's view, the opportunity to destroy Banks' forces was plain and he strongly urged Smith to seize it.[26]

The source of friction between Smith and Taylor dated back to Smith's assumption of command of the Trans-Mississippi in 1863. Smith maintained the bulk of his troops in central Arkansas to protect the interior of his department. Taylor, a Louisianan, thought that his home state should receive the preponderance of manpower resources. In his view, the greatest threat to the department came from the south via New Orleans and the many waterways branching from it. In the summer of 1863 Taylor's nemesis General Banks had launched offensives into the interior of Louisiana up Bayous Teche and Atchafalya. With little guidance from Smith and less real support, Taylor succeeded in driving back Banks' efforts with one quarter of Banks' strength. Taylor's success emboldened him to attempt the recapture of New Orleans, but Smith withheld needed troops. It was at the conclusion of the Teche counteroffensive that Taylor threw his initial veiled barbs at his superior. "The plan I had arranged for an attack [on

1. A Lost Opportunity?

New Orleans] fell through," he pointedly told Smith, "as soon as I was advised that Walker's Division would not join me."[27] These barbs grew steadily more acidic and direct the following year as Smith's plans and Taylor's ideas diverged.

As the Red River Campaign heated up, Taylor became impatient with his superior's indecisiveness and pummeled him with insubordinate correspondence. When Smith, in March 1864, retained reinforcements at Shreveport meant for Taylor's army, Taylor exploded with anger. "Two weeks have elapsed since the fall of Alexandria and I have cherished the hope from day to day that assistance would reach me before I was forced to give up the producing country," he complained.[28] Dispatches such as this only increased the friction and volatility of the working relationship between the two. With receipt of every acerbic dispatch, Smith seems to have hardened in his own opinions, which were opposite Taylor's vision of success. Smith's medical director and close confidant, who held a deep-seated hatred for Taylor, encouraged the department commander's opposition to Taylor's appeals. He advised Smith to do many of the things that so angered Taylor. The "only field for great results in this Department is the District of Arkansas," he remarked to Smith.[29] "The only way to defeat Steele's movement [in Arkansas]," Taylor insisted in frustration, "is to whip the enemy in the heart of the Red River Valley."[30]

Lieutenant General Edmund Kirby Smith, Commander of the Confederate Department of the Trans-Mississippi, found himself in a quandary over how best to defend the vast territory west of the Mississippi against invasion by Federal forces up the Red River and down from Arkansas. *Courtesy Massachusetts Commandery Military Order of the Loyal Legion and United States Military History Institute.*

Taylor's emotion and sentimentality for his own state undoubtedly clouded his thoughts; Smith, charged with the defense of the whole department, had to maintain an objective viewpoint. Therefore, Smith judged both Union thrusts toward Shreveport a serious threat and planned accordingly. When Taylor defeated Banks at Mansfield and the Union army withdrew,

Smith made up his mind to strike in Arkansas in accordance with the Fabian strategy. He stripped Taylor of three infantry divisions in order to pursue Steele in strength. This rekindled the ire of Taylor, who groused that he had planned a vigorous pursuit of Banks so as "to capture or destroy both" the enemy fleet and Banks' army.[31] Friction between the Confederacy's primary commanders thus influenced military decisions and, as a consequence, shaped the outcome of the campaign.

Smith got his opportunity to put the Fabian policy into action when the Union army launched its two-pronged offensive in March 1864. The challenge for Smith, during the course of the campaign, was to identify the effort that posed the main threat to the Department, deflect it, and then turn to meet the other one. Smith, however, could not decide which column posed the greater danger, and as the situation evolved he did not exercise the flexibility needed to meet the changes that took place. This indecision gnawed at Taylor. He expressed his discontent pointedly, time and again, to his superior, which only drove deeper a personal wedge between the two.

After the Battle of Pleasant Hill it was clear that the Union army intended to retreat. It appeared to Smith that his strategy had worked by turning the first column, the one commanded by Banks, away. He now needed to reorient his forces to stop Steele's column coming down from Arkansas. Or did he? Taylor believed that he did not have to turn away from Banks and pursue Steele. "Steele will no doubt commence retreating as soon as he hears the news [of Banks' retreat] from this quarter." Smith disagreed. "To win this campaign," he declared, "his [Steele's] column must be destroyed."[32] As it happened, Taylor was correct. Steele reversed course within four days of Banks' being checked on April 8, and completely abandoned his part of the expedition on April 24. Taylor wanted to keep the force he had at Pleasant Hill intact to pursue Banks, to destroy him and the Union fleet. If Smith had accepted the counsel of his irascible subordinate, the results might have been profound.

First, Smith would have had three opportunities to capture the Army of the Gulf: at Grand Ecore, between the Cane and Red Rivers (Monette's Ferry), and finally at Alexandria. In each case, the Confederates attempted to entrap the hemmed-in Federal force, but inadequate manpower prevented them from making an effective siege. When Smith stripped Taylor of three infantry divisions—those under Churchill, Parsons, and Walker—to pursue Steele, he left Taylor with only 5,000 troops to contend with the Federals, whose strength approached 30,000 backed by the fleet in the Red. Had Smith left Taylor's force intact, Taylor would have had nearly 15,000 men.[33] It is not unreasonable to conjecture that Taylor could have made an effective siege with this force at any of the three points mentioned above.

Smith, furthermore, could have achieved at least the destruction of nineteen gunboats and several transports from the Mississippi River Squadron. During the Red River Campaign there existed the grave danger that the Union would lose its fleet due to the low level of the Red. When entering the campaign, Admiral Porter expected that the Red would undergo a seasonal rise in March, which would make the river navigable from the Mississippi all the way to Shreveport, enabling the navy to support the army. However, due to strange phenomena the river failed to rise. The last time this had occurred had been in 1855 and before that in 1846.[34] At Alexandria there is a falls complete with a double rapids

Rear Admiral David D. Porter, Commander of the Federal Navy's Mississippi Squadron, in cooperation with General Banks commanded the naval forces in the Red River Campaign. *Courtesy Massachusetts Commandery Military Order of the Loyal Legion and United States Military History Institute.*

in the river. The ship channel narrows at the falls and jagged rocks are exposed during periods of low water. The gunboats of Porter's fleet required a minimum of seven feet of draught to negotiate the falls and river. The low state of the river meant that once Porter passed the falls en route to Shreveport, he might be unable to come back down if the water level lowered. This was exactly what happened. Porter aggressively took the squadron over the falls toward Shreveport on March 29. During his subsequent retreat, the level of water at Alexandria fell off to three feet at the falls. This effectively trapped the fleet and, had Taylor had the force he desired, he probably could have prevented the fleet's escape in May. How would the loss of 30 ships and 30,000 soldiers affect the Union war effort in 1864? The Confederate navy never at any time during the war had seriously challenged the Union fleet — with the possible exception of the C.S.S. *Virginia* in 1862. The South simply lacked the ability to manufacture capital ships of the caliber available to the North. If the Confederates had captured at least a portion of the Union fleet on the Red, however, it would have seriously loosened the Union's grip on the Mississippi. The C.S.S. *Arkansas*, one solitary ironclad, wreaked havoc on that river in 1863, temporarily neutralizing Federal naval power. If the Confederates could have captured three or four of Porter's gunboats in 1864, anything might have been possible.

But the Confederates, in all likelihood, could not have captured the Federal fleet. In a letter to Secretary of the Navy Gideon Welles on April 23, 1864, Porter stated that if forced "to surrender or blowup ... I will promise you the latter."[35] What Porter was promising was that he would scuttle the fleet rather that allow it to fall into Confederate hands. Porter knew better than anyone what could happen if the Confederates gained the use of his boats. In another letter to Welles, five days later, he even expressed fear that the Southerners might gain access to the destroyed hulks. "If we have to destroy what we have here," he remarked, "there will be material enough to build half a dozen iron-clads."[36] Porter believed that the industrious Confederates would salvage anything he destroyed and use it against the Union fleet in the future. With a portion of the fleet the Confederates could have loosened the noose the Federals had on the Mississippi, allowing the Trans-Mississippi to offer support to their brethren to the east.

The possible loss of 30,000 Federal troops becomes significant when one takes into account what these same troops did after their escape from the Red River Valley. The XIX Corps made up the heart of the Union Army of the Gulf. It was the victor at Port Hudson in 1863 and participated in all the major actions fought in the region. After the Red River Campaign the Corps redeployed to the Eastern Theater by order of Lieutenant General Grant. The Army of the Potomac had suffered in excess of 50,000 casualties during its overland campaign against the Army of Northern Virginia. The addition of the veteran XIX Corps compensated for some of the Army of the Potomac's losses. There also existed a more pressing need for troops in the East in the summer of 1864. General Robert E. Lee dispatched the Army of Northern Virginia's 2d Corps, under Lieutenant General Jubal Early, to the Shenandoah Valley in June to secure it for the growing season and to relieve pressure on the Army of Northern Virginia penned up around Richmond.[37] Early liberally interpreted his orders and not only swept the valley clean of Federal troops, but marched right on into Maryland. He did not stop here either: On July 12 his small army stood outside the gates of Washington threatening to snatch it from under the government's nose.

The Lincoln administration clamored for assistance from Grant down in Virginia. He responded by dispatching the VI Army Corps from the Potomac army and diverting the XIX Corps from Richmond to Washington before the XIXth could even disembark.[38] This move saved Washington. The XIX Corps became part of Major General Philip Sheridan's army, which chased Early out of Maryland. In October, just prior to the presidential election, the XIXth played an instrumental role in defeating Early at the decisive Battle of Cedar Creek.[39] This battle forever wrested control of Virginia's granary, the Shenandoah, from Confederate control. Without the XIX Corps, Grant would have had to detach two corps from the Army of the Potomac instead of one. This could have cracked the door of opportunity just enough for Robert E. Lee to take the initiative around Richmond, seriously upsetting the Federal design for 1864.

The two divisions of the XVI Corps left the Red River bound for West Tennessee and northern Mississippi. Forces under Nathan Bedford Forrest were causing enormous difficulties for Union troops in the area and threatened to break Sherman's tenuous supply line coming down from Nashville to Chattanooga. Sherman wanted Forrest stopped at all costs to prevent him from cutting Union communications.[40] Smith's return to Mississippi with 10,000 men did the trick. Few adversaries ever got the best of Forrest in a stand-up fight, but Smith actually fought him to a standstill at Tupelo, Mississippi, in July. Smith's offensive against Forrest in the summer of 1864 kept Forrest occupied with fighting Federals rather than allowing him the opportunity to wreak havoc in Sherman's rear area.[41] Had Taylor captured or delayed Smith's corps longer on the Red, Sherman might have had to detach men from his army in Georgia to contend with Forrest. This would have further diminished his numerical advantage over the Army of Tennessee. Although Joseph Johnston probably would not have taken the offensive, any weakening of Sherman's forces would have delayed the taking of Atlanta. For how long is speculation, but if the Confederates could have held off Sherman's spectacular victory in Atlanta for sixty more days, the voters might have voted differently in November.

The XVII Corps division, under Brigadier General T. Kilby Smith, returned to Sherman's army after escaping the Red River Valley. Although the reinforcement numbered only 3,000 men, and thus did not substantially increase Sherman's troop strength, it certainly did not hurt to have them.[42]

The XIII Corps found itself dismembered at the close of the campaign.[43] The XIX Corps absorbed part of it; some units participated in throwing Early back from Washington and the Shenandoah; and the rest took part in the long-anticipated attack on Mobile in August.[44] These men stormed the land face of the forts at Mobile, while Admiral David Glasgow Farragut sailed into the harbor with his famous quote, "Damn the torpedoes, full speed ahead."[45] If Taylor had captured these men, where would the Union have procured soldiers for the thrust on Mobile? This victory in August boosted Northern morale and was the first in the string of Federal successes leading up to the elections. News of the victory at Mobile, said Gideon Welles, "sent a thrill of joy through all true hearts."[46] The absence or further delay of the men who participated in the Red River Campaign could have had a profoundly negative effect on the Union offensives that summer. With morale in the North at a low ebb, any more reverses or delays would have encouraged voters to turn against Lincoln.

After the great victories of 1863 — Vicksburg, Gettysburg, and Chattanooga — the Northern public hoped for an early end to the war. The reverses in the spring and early summer of 1864, however, severely undermined that hope.[47] Lincoln knew that the November election would be a referendum on his war policies, and that his chances for reelection hinged on the progress on the battlefront. With public morale plummeting, his prospects did not seem good. Lincoln's position all along had been that only full reunion without a compromise peace was acceptable. The election of a Democratic candidate would represent a departure from the prior administration's policy and give the Confederacy victory at the ballot box rather than on the battlefield. Newspapers in the North castigated the administration with every reverse. The *New York World* published an editorial in June, 1864, stating that, "the age of statesmen is gone.... The age of rail-splitters [Lincoln] and tailors [Andrew Johnson], of buffoons, boors and fanatics has succeeded.... God save the Republic?"[48] Such inflammatory editorials served to lower reelection prospects, and nobody knew this better than Lincoln. On August 23 he sat down in the privacy of his office and composed a letter. "This morning, as for some days past, it seems exceedingly probable that this administration will not be reelected," he wrote. "Then it will be my duty to so co-operate with the President-elect as to save the Union between the election and the inauguration as he will have secured his election on such ground that he cannot possibly save it afterward." Lincoln sealed the letter in an envelope and had his cabinet sign it with the agreement that they would not open it until after the election.[49]

The failed Red River Campaign had a profoundly negative short-term effect on morale in the North. When added to the reverses in the Shanandoah Valley, the butchering in the Overland Campaign in Virginia, and

Sherman's stalled offensive before Atlanta, the campaign made it appear to many that 1864 would sputter along as the three previous years. The war, it seemed, would never end. But the stain of the Red River Campaign eventually went away because it was less decisive than it appeared on the surface. That was because the army and navy both escaped to fight another day. In the end Lincoln did win reelection to bring the war to its final conclusion. So, why was the Red River Campaign not more decisive?

There are four reasons that the Confederate victory was an empty one. First, the two senior commanders in the Trans-Mississippi Department simply could not get along with one another. This conflict, which was personal as well as professional, paralyzed Confederate operations at critical junctures of the campaign. Taylor, who was defending his home state, fired off frequent acidic dispatches expressing his views on how to fight the campaign while criticizing his superior. Kirby Smith handled the criticism — which stepped over the line of insubordination — and attempted unsuccessfully to placate his subordinate. The constant barrage of criticism from Taylor probably helped push Smith into doing the exact opposite of what Taylor desired. This, more than any other factor, prevented the Confederates from achieving more decisive results from the campaign.

Kirby Smith's indecisiveness also played a key role in diminishing the end result. T. Harry Williams described Smith as a "promising" leader, but one who "seemed to shrink from the responsibility of command."[50] Nowhere was this more true than in the conduct of the Red River Campaign. Smith's Fabian policy did not establish a main effort and therefore the Confederates succeeded only in repulsing the Federals, rather than destroying one of the columns. When Smith did have the opportunity to destroy a column, he turned from one column to focus on the other, depriving Taylor of the opportunity to imperil the Army of the Gulf.

Confederate policymakers in Richmond never believed that the Trans-Mississippi amounted to anything more than a backwater. In 1864, therefore, they didn't fully appreciate the golden opportunity that existed there to influence the war. Richmond believed that the Trans-Mississippi army could either draw Federal troops away from the East or could contribute Confederate troops to the East, but never believed the region could materially influence the war. This "hold your own" policy toward the region heavily influenced Smith's formulation of the Fabian defensive strategy and allowed an unprecedented opportunity to slip away.

The final reason the Confederates failed to make more of the Campaign on the Red had nothing to do with the Southerners. The two Federal partners-in-command, Major General Nathaniel P. Banks and Rear Admiral David D. Porter, overcame their immense differences to save the force from very possible destruction. Banks, a political general, and Porter, a career naval officer, held a deep-seated animosity toward each other. As the admiral put it, "[T]he two commanders had but little personal intercourse — a state of affairs which was not conducive to the perfect understanding which should exist between the Army and Navy."[51] But in the emergency they managed to overcome their personal differences and focus on the higher good — the overall war effort. Porter even stated that this saved 30,000 men and some of the best boats in the "brown water" navy for more important work in the East at a critical juncture of the war.

What success the Confederates did achieve was a result of various factors. For one thing, General Richard Taylor absolutely dominated his opponent in terms of decisiveness and battlefield presence. T. Harry Williams said that a commander must "have in his make-up a mental strength and a moral power that enables him to dominate whatever event or crisis may emerge on the field of battle."[52] Taylor certainly exhibited these qualities, and because of them he won a spectacular victory at Mansfield on April 8, 1864, turning back the Army of the Gulf. Taylor's opposite, Nathaniel P. Banks, had a propensity to command by coalition — as if he were still the Speaker of the House of Representatives. He left too many critical tactical decisions to subordinates and failed to oversee properly the dispositions made by those subordinates until it was too late. Administration of his army got away from him because of his hands-off approach to command. In addition, he exhibited crippling indecisiveness at times that required strong leadership. Taylor, who fought the "cold, timid, easily foiled" Banks in Virginia in 1862 under Stonewall Jackson, knew well his adversary. "My confidence of success ... was inspired by accurate knowledge of the Federal movements," Taylor recalled, "as well as the *character* [italics added] of the commander, General Banks, whose measure had been taken in the Virginia campaigns of 1862 and since."[53] Taylor used this knowledge against his opponent and ably turned his columns back at Mansfield, Louisiana.

Pressure from Grant further diminished the possibility of success on Banks' part. Grant sent him a dispatch in mid-March stating that if he could not take Shreveport "as soon as possible," he should send A. J. Smith's troops back to Sherman by April 15. Grant also insisted on an expeditious conclusion of the campaign, telling Banks that he should return to New Orleans soon in order to "be a part of the plan for the spring campaign to move against Mobile ... even if it leads to the abandonment of the main object of your expedition."[54] These instructions caused Banks to make hasty, uninformed decisions, including the one he made to diverge from the Red and his naval support to take an inland road to Shreveport. That decision enabled Taylor to entrap him in the "pine desert"[55] of West Louisiana.

Friction within the Federal navy and within the Army of the Gulf created an unfavorable command environment and also contributed to Confederate success. Porter the career naval officer despised Banks the politician and this impeded cooperation. Another professional officer, A. J. Smith, also caused Banks tremendous problems. Smith at one point during the campaign proposed that General William B. Franklin depose the commander and install himself to command of the army. Only a harsh rebuke from Franklin himself defused the potentially explosive situation.[56]

Finally, poor tactical decision making doomed Union efforts. Banks failed to order reconnaissance when required, allowed the army to march in unsupportable dispositions, and did not always place himself at the proper location to make decisions. In effect, the Federal army contributed to its own defeat and also placed itself in a situation to be destroyed. The Confederates, however, failed to capitalize on the opportunity and allowed those same Federals to make material contributions toward the eventual defeat of the Confederacy in the Civil War.

Chapter 2

The Antagonists

The men who commanded the opposing armies and the Union navy present a series of contrasts and similarities. Each pair of men formed a team that would decide the fate of the Trans-Mississippi Department. The Confederate commanders, Edmund Kirby Smith and Richard Taylor, came from aristocratic backgrounds, while the Union men, Nathaniel P. Banks and David Dixon Porter, had more humble beginnings. All had distinguished pre-war careers and varying degrees of success during the early days of the war. Curiously, both pairs had troublesome working relationships. While the Confederates were unable to overcome their differences, the Union commanders put theirs aside for the good of the cause. Each man's character and experiences before the Red River Campaign provide a good starting point for understanding why the campaign unfolded the way it did.

Major General Richard Taylor was born on January 27, 1826, near Louisville, Kentucky. He represented the sixth generation of a prominent Virginia family. His father was the venerable Zachary Taylor, hero of the Mexican War and president of the United States. Taylor's family background played a significant role in developing his attitudes about society and politics.[1] As an army brat Taylor lived in far-flung places, from Wisconsin and Minnesota to Fort Jesup, Louisiana. However, his father's land holdings in southwest Mississippi and Louisiana led him to claim Louisiana as his home state. Taylor spent a great deal of time on the lower Mississippi in his late teens while his father pursued his military career.[2]

Because of his separation from his son, the elder Taylor developed a strong sense of guilt and a feeling that he did not know his children. In an effort to compensate for this, he made certain that his children received a thorough education. Richard, therefore, spent much of his adolescence in private schools preparing for college entrance exams. In part because his father was not around to provide male discipline, Richard developed an independent and erratic personality.[3] This independent streak manifested itself during the Red River Campaign, producing spectacular success as well as reprehensible childishness.

Taylor graduated from Yale University in the 1840s. Yale lent itself to Taylor's evolving image of himself as the model Southern aristocrat. His attitudes concerning society hardened in the 1850s as he settled into the life of a Southern planter. He believed there were three classes of people: the planters, peasant farmers, and humble servants. Each of them, he thought, should remain in his place, maintaining the natural order of things for the good of society as a whole. He felt a great disdain for the individualism, greed, and political confrontation associated with American democracy. Yet, in a twist of irony, his pursuit of wealth as a planter made him practice those traits he frowned upon.[4]

Taylor's years at Yale were critical to the development of his character and personality. For one thing, it was here that he was stricken with rheumatoid arthritis. This malady would flare up at intervals for the rest of his life, especially during periods of extreme stress. His disposition during these bouts would sour to the point that associates (and subsequently subordinates and superiors) found him unbearable to deal with. Taylor's health would at times impair his better judgment during the Red River Campaign.[5]

Taylor's social attitudes carried over to politics and he naturally fit a conservative mold. Following in the path of his father, Richard became a Whig.[6] The disintegration of the party in the early 1850s left him without an affiliation. He, like many other Southerners, joined the Democrats as the only alternative to the "black" Republicans. In 1855 he won election to the Louisiana state senate, which he served until the wave of secession fever persuaded him to retire.[7]

Taylor, in keeping with conservative ideals, felt that it was in the best interest of the South to remain in the Union. As a delegate to the 1860 Democratic Convention in Charleston, he continually found his policy on the defensive in the face of such orators as William Yancey, Barnwell Rhett, and Edmund Ruffin. These men stirred up the South into a secession frenzy. "At the time and since," he later wrote, "I marveled at the joyous and careless temper in which men, much my superiors in sagacity and experience, consummated such acts." Taylor gave only tacit support to secession when it came to Louisiana. After the state secession convention in January, 1861, he vowed to remain at his sugar plantation, Fashion, and serve the Confederacy only if called by Louisiana. Taylor was, in other words, a reluctant Confederate at best.[8]

He would not wait long, for Brigadier General Braxton Bragg requested his services in organizing recruits at Pensacola in May, 1861.[9] After serving in Florida a few weeks as a civilian aide-de-camp, he received a telegram from Governor Thomas Moore in Baton Rouge appointing him Colonel of the 9th Louisiana Infantry. Much to Bragg's regret, Taylor quickly returned to Louisiana to organize his regiment.[10]

Although he had no formal military training, he quickly established himself as a solid drillmaster and strict disciplinarian. One observer stated that, despite his lack of military education, "probably no civilian of his time was more deeply versed in the annals of war."[11] By mid-July the 9th had been accepted into the Confederate service and embarked for the seat of war in Virginia.

Taylor's regiment arrived at Bull Run the day after the battle and did not share in the glory. The regiment was brigaded with three other regiments from Louisiana, and Taylor received a promotion to Brigadier General and command of the brigade. The next reorganizational step saw the brigade become a part of the division led by Major General Edmund Kirby Smith, the man who would later become Taylor's nemesis in the Red River Valley.[12]

In the spring of 1862, Taylor's brigade was detached from Smith's division and sent to the Shenandoah Valley. There Taylor met the man who gave him his philosophy of fighting—his new commander, the diminutive Stonewall Jackson. Taylor made an immediate impression on Jackson, who complimented him on his brigade's marching discipline, stating "you seem to have no stragglers.... You must teach my people."[13] For Jackson to give such praise was out of character, but he liked what he saw in Taylor and in his own peculiar way took Taylor under his wing.[14]

Taylor absorbed much from fighting with Jackson in the 1862 Valley Campaign. Taylor adopted Jackson's dictum that "it is better to lose one man in marching than five in fighting." Using this philosophy, Jackson fought and won five battles, marched 450 miles, and relieved pressure on the embattled Southern capital. The same philosophy would shape Taylor's plan for clearing the Red River Valley two years later against the same enemy commander, Major General Nathaniel P. Banks.[15]

Taylor missed the Peninsula Campaign in 1862, fighting off a particularly harsh flare-up of rheumatoid arthritis. The tough campaign, coupled with the heat of the Virginia summer, forced him to relinquish his command at times during the Seven Days.[16] While Taylor convalesced in Richmond, President Jefferson Davis, his former brother-in-law by virtue of marriage to his deceased sister Sarah, came to see him. Davis needed a new commander in Louisiana to try to stabilize a steadily deteriorating situation. Governor Moore had sent Davis a series of letters requesting a competent leader to stem the Union tide on the lower Mississippi.[17] Taylor accepted the command of the District of West Louisiana on July 24, 1862, and took up his new duties on August 20. A herculean task lay before him. Louisiana was in an utter shambles militarily and Davis gave him a threefold mandate to bring order out of the chaos. First, since the main Confederate armies could send no troops to prop up minor theaters, Taylor was to recruit new regiments for defense of the state. Second, he had to bolster sagging civilian and military morale while providing competent, native leadership. Finally, his general mission was to defend the interior of Louisiana and force the Federal troops to protect their footholds on the lower Mississippi. With this challenge before him, Taylor called upon all his determination and previous command experience to defend his home state.[18]

General Edmund Kirby Smith claimed a background similar to that of his subordinate. Born on May 16, 1824, in St. Augustine, Florida, he descended from a distinguished family. The Kirbys and Smiths contributed sons to the struggle during the Revolution and Smith's father, Joseph, served as a lieutenant colonel during the War of 1812. Joseph Smith left the army in 1821 because he grew tired of the long periods of separation from his family. He secured appointment as a federal judge in the new Florida territory and moved the family to St. Augustine.[19]

Smith's older sister Frances, twelve years his senior, assumed a motherly role toward her younger brother and was instrumental in his early educational success. His parents quickly recognized a keen intellect in young Ned and groomed him for West Point. At age twelve he was sent to Ben Hollowell's boarding school in Alexandria, Virginia, to prepare for the academy's tough entrance exams.[20] Young Smith easily met the entrance requirements and accepted appointment to the academy at age seventeen. He quickly established himself as an excellent student, placing fifth in his class in his plebe year. The pettiness of the rules and the monotony of cadet life, however, did not sit well with Smith, who complained to his father that "it is neither remarkably sensible nor philosophical" to charge demerits "for a button off a coat, or because of his clothes, bed, windows, room, mantle, shelves, books, face, hands, or nails out of order."[21] Kirby Smith graduated from West Point in 1845, having dropped to 25th in his class. Shortly after commissioning, he found himself assigned to the 5th Infantry Regiment at Fort Jesup, Louisiana. In a twist of irony his post commander at Fort Jesup was none other than Zachary Taylor. Soon after Smith's arrival in the 5th, the regiment deployed to the Mexican border in response to the impending crisis.[22]

Smith served with distinction in the Mexican War, earning two brevets for bravery in the battles of Resaca de la Palma and Cerro Gordo. At Resaca de la Palma his company captured a Mexican cannon, and his performance at the battle of Cerro Gordo was of such notable character that his regimental commander mentioned him in his official report.[23]

Following the war, Smith transferred to the 7th Infantry posted at Jefferson Barracks, Missouri, and also served as a professor of mathematics at West Point. At this point he decided to make military service his career. "I have chosen the army, or rather the army has been selected for me as a profession, and I see no prospect of its ever being changed," he wrote his mother. "I do not regret it, I am proud of it."[24] It was with that decision that the paths of Smith and Taylor diverged sharply. Taylor summarily rejected a military career as detrimental to intellectual development. As he once stated to a friend, "Take a boy of sixteen from his mother's apron strings, shut him up under constant surveillance for four years at West Point, send him out to a two-company post on the frontier ... [and] he will furnish the most complete illustration of suppressed mental development."[25] This quote may shed some light on the querulous future relationship of Smith and Taylor.

In 1855 Smith was promoted to captain and assigned a company command in the newly formed 2d Cavalry Regiment. This was one of Secretary of War Jefferson Davis' pet projects. The 2d was to protect the ever-expanding frontier as an elite unit. Therefore, Davis filled it with officers of favorable reputation in the regular army. Many of them, such as Lee, A. S. Johnston, Thomas, Hood, and Van Dorn, became general officers in both the Union and Confederate armies. Smith led his company successfully through several skirmishes with Indians and was once shot through the thigh.[26]

The national question of secession affected even the far flung 2d Cavalry serving on the frontier. Smith, as a Southerner, agreed with the grievances of the secessionists. He was fearful, however, that a Civil War was not in the South's best interest. In a letter to his mother he discussed the issue, expressing his hope that the Union would not dissolve but concluding that, "right or wrong I go with the land of my birth."[27] Soon after writing that letter, Smith found himself forced to choose his allegiance. On March 3, 1861, following Florida's secession, he resigned his commission at the request of the now forming Confederate government. In April he accepted a colonel's commission in the Confederate army. He received orders to proceed immediately to Virginia to organize recruits pouring into training camps at Lynchburg.[28]

2. The Antagonists

The following month he reported to General Joseph Johnston at Harper's Ferry and assumed command of a brigade in the Valley army. On the eve of First Bull Run, Smith received promotion to brigadier general. After First Bull Run, he became a household name in the South. On July 21, at a point when the Battle of Bull Run appeared to be a disaster, Smith disembarked his troops from a train. He immediately moved the brigade to the sound of the fighting, throwing his men into the left flank of the Union troops on the Henry House Hill. His quick action tipped the scales of victory to the South and won for himself general admiration across the South and the sobriquet "Blucher of Manassas."[29] President Davis elevated Smith to divisional command and major general in October 1861 for his performance at Manassas. Smith returned to duty in November after recovering from a thigh wound he received in the battle and served out the remainder of the '61-'62 winter at the front.[30]

Smith reluctantly accepted command of the Department of East Tennessee at the behest of President Davis in March 1862. It was an especially troublesome assignment because the East Tennessee and Virginia Railroad was a critical line of communication for the Confederacy and an inviting target for Federal forces. Moreover, the department was a hotbed of disloyal, Unionist activity. But Smith took up his duties with determination and the post turned out to be a good training ground for him, helping to prepare him for future challenges in the Trans-Mississippi.[31] He spent the spring and summer of 1862 protecting the railroad and quelling Unionist activity. Although frustration nearly overcame him, he carried out his tough assignment in admirable fashion. He declared martial law to restrict movement and had East Tennessee Confederate troops of questionable loyalty transferred to other theaters, replacing them with loyal troops from other states.[32]

By mid-summer of 1862, Smith had shifted his thoughts from his own department and looked toward Kentucky. He conceived a plan to make a foray northward into Kentucky in order to clear Tennessee and relieve the state of the ravages of the war. In July he opened correspondence with Braxton Bragg, proposing his plan and encouraging Bragg to cooperate with him on a movement north. Bragg was thinking along the same lines and had already taken steps to transfer the seat of war to the Ohio Valley. The two held a conference in Chattanooga at the end of July 1862 to begin making arrangements for a drive into middle Tennessee and Kentucky.[33]

Smith moved first and enjoyed great success in the closing days of the summer. He won a battle at Richmond, Kentucky, bagging over 4,000 prisoners and nine pieces of artillery. Smith's 18,000 men soon occupied

Lexington and Frankfort and awaited the arrival of Bragg to consolidate forces. Bragg arrived in central Kentucky on September 25 and Smith "cheerfully" placed his troops under Bragg's command. Smith's hopes for a successful invasion were misplaced, as Bragg squandered his opportunities. After an ineffectual battle at Perryville, the Rebel troops began a long and discouraging retrograde movement back to East Tennessee.[34]

Smith was highly critical of Bragg's performance, but would not have time to dwell on the situation. Late in October, Secretary of War G. W. Randolph informed Smith of his promotion to lieutenant general. Soon thereafter the president summoned him to Richmond to discuss command of the Trans-Mississippi Department, which at that time suffered from the uninspired leadership of Theophilus Holmes and needed a change to energize the theater. The challenges awaiting Smith in the Trans-Mississippi dwarfed those of East Tennessee, but none other than Robert E. Lee stated, "I consider [Smith] one of our best officers." Smith accepted the challenge and officially assumed command on March 7, 1863.[35]

The conditions Smith found west of the Mississippi appalled him: there were "no soldiers, no arms or ammunition, and no money, within the limits of the district." He knew that his prospects of receiving help were minimal and that he would be on his own in trying to improve conditions in the department.[36] Confederate policy made the Trans-Mississippi a backwater, and positive contributions to the overall war effort would depend entirely on the ability of Smith and his primary subordinate, Major General Richard Taylor.

The men who commanded the Union army and navy were venerable men in their own right. One had been a Bay State politician, while the other was an old salt career naval officer. Their working relationship, like that of their opponents, was strained, but they would overcome their mutual antagonism in order to save an army and navy to fight another day.

Nathaniel Prentice Banks was born on January 30, 1816, in Waltham, Massachusetts. Banks' father was a mechanic who worked for the Boston Manufacturing Company, a New England textile mill. The company was "the first modern factory in America"[37] and produced bolts of cotton cloth using a power loom and modern machinery. The elder Banks earned twelve dollars a week, but this was not enough to support a large family. Accordingly, young Nat obtained employment in the factory at age eleven to help support the family.[38]

Banks went to work as a bobbin boy in the textile mills. His duty was to replace full bobbins with empty cylinders to keep the looms running. The job was tedious and paid only two dollars a week. It was while performing such menial jobs that Banks developed a determination to rise above his post in life and succeed in a more meaningful occupation. Banks quit his job and found work as a machinist's apprentice at age seventeen. He developed a fondness for reading and attending political speeches by such orators as Daniel Webster and Caleb Cushing. This ignited an interest in politics that would drive him the rest of his life.[39]

His rise in politics was not meteoric, but was nevertheless steady and represented his survivor's attitude. Banks aligned himself with the Democrats, who represented workers' concerns similar to those of his family. The brilliant Bay State Democratic leader Robert Rantoul Jr. befriended young Banks in the late 1830s and was instrumental in propelling him to public office in 1848.[40] In that year he won election to the lower house of the Massachusetts legislature.

Since Banks' financial success and livelihood rested on winning elections, he developed a tendency to change his position abruptly on issues. His talent for accommodation and compromise allowed him to bring together diverse voting blocs and continue winning elections. He even changed political parties no less than five times over the course of his career to maintain his position in politics.[41]

During Banks' initial foray in politics as a legislator, his attitudes toward the sectional crisis took on definitive proportions. He opposed slavery, but feared that the abolitionist rancor would eventually cause a split in the Union. As a result, Banks adopted a moderate stance, supporting the Compromise of 1850 and choosing not to agitate potential Southern allies.[42] This allowed him to build a coalition of Democrats and Free-Soilers and win election to the House of Representatives in 1852. His tone of moderation changed two years later, when he opposed the Kansas-Nebraska Act. This act would allow slavery north of the thirty-sixth parallel and effectively repeal the Compromise of 1850. Since most New Englanders held anti-slavery sentiments, Banks fell in line with the abolitionists to maintain standing with his constituency.[43]

Banks' stand helped propel him to the Speakership of the House of Representatives in 1856. Sectionalism was fast turning bitter in American politics. Although he was anti-slavery, Banks' moderation won over many Southerners who initially balked at voting for him. Some, in fact, later complimented his even-handed oversight of the House. None other than Georgian Alexander H. Stephens, future vice president of the Confederacy, described him as "the best Speaker since Henry Clay."[44]

In 1857 Banks, now a Republican, ran for governor of Massachusetts on a platform that championed the common man and was moderately anti-slavery. His appeal united a cross-section of voters ranging from abolitionists to labor leaders and, of course, he benefitted from the fame he had achieved as Speaker. He won the election after stumping across the state. As governor, Banks continued to straddle issues in order to maintain his viability.[45] At the end of his term as governor, in January 1861, he entered the private sector at the behest of future Union General George B. McClellan, accepting a position as director of the Illinois Central Railroad freight and passenger business.

In April, however, his career as a railroad executive ended abruptly. Following the surrender of Fort Sumter, President Lincoln called for 75,000 volunteers to put down the Rebellion. These volunteers would need leaders, and Lincoln offered Banks a position as major general of volunteers. Popular politicians were instrumental in recruiting and Lincoln recognized that Banks was a key figure in New England.[46] Lincoln's shaky political coalition, moreover, required patronage toward prominent men. Politicians might be useful in rallying men for the cause, but how would a novice perform under combat conditions? In Banks' case, war would provide a negative answer to this question. His penchant for moderation and coalition-building were useful political tools, but spelled disaster for a field commander. Though he was personally courageous, his indecisiveness as a commander led him to grief on many a field, starting in 1862 against a formidable opponent, Stonewall Jackson.

Banks was upset with his assignment to defend the Shenandoah Valley because he feared that he would miss out on the laurels sure to come from capturing Richmond. To his wife he confided his disgruntlement at not being "included in the active operations of the summer."[47] To him, "active operations" translated into press coverage, and that added up to votes after the war.[48] Banks, however, got all the action he could handle. His inexperience was glaringly apparent at every step, from moving his columns to providing adequate security for his troops. The first week of May found his force arrayed in two columns. The first dug in around Strasburg, while the second loosely positioned itself in the vicinity of Front Royal. Jackson, observing that Banks had divided his army, pounced on the weaker of the two columns at Front Royal, capturing most of it. Jackson then raced to cut off the road to Winchester.[49] Banks came quite close to boxing himself in because he believed that a retrograde movement was detrimental to the building of reputation. "We have more to fear from the opinions of our friends," he noted, "than from the bayonets of our enemies."[50] Banks' subordinates eventually prevailed on him to order a retreat back to Winchester to prevent being cut off.

Banks' ragged column arrived in the vicinity of Winchester on the evening of May 24. Rather than taking charge of the defensive preparations, he left the details to subordinates, an unfortunate habit he would continue in the Red River Campaign with disastrous results. The next morning Jackson rolled up both of Banks' flanks in a poorly selected position.[51] None other than Brigadier General Richard Taylor spearheaded Jackson's attack with his Louisiana Brigade.

Banks' army streamed north out of Winchester toward the Potomac with Jackson at his heels. Banks in vain exhorted his men to make a stand. In one humorous exchange he asked a wayward private, "My God, men, don't you love your country?" The young man replied, "Yes and I am trying to get to it as fast as I can." The retreat concluded with the crossing of the Potomac on May 26.[52] The retreat was a huge windfall of supplies and material for the Confederates. So great was the haul that J. E. B. Stuart noted that Banks was the best commissary officer Jackson ever had. This led to Confederate soldiers calling the Union general "Commissary" Banks.[53]

Banks again tangled with Jackson and found defeat at Cedar Mountain. He missed Second Bull Run due to a painful fall from his horse following Cedar Mountain. During his convalescence in Washington, Banks lobbied for reassignment. The timing was perfect. Fellow Bay Stater Benjamin Butler had been ruffling feathers as military governor of New Orleans since its capture. The irascible Butler was a thorn in the side of the Lincoln administration because of his extreme views, insubordination, and failure to implement established policy. Banks, whose moderation was well known, seemed a perfect choice to soothe the agitated residents of New Orleans and systematically institute administration directives. Banks also now had battlefield experience and presumably would perform better as a result. Lincoln, therefore, appointed him commander of the Department of Gulf in November 1862.[54]

Banks faced a series of challenges when he arrived in New Orleans in mid-December 1862. Not only were Louisianans resistant to Union authority, but the state, especially New Orleans, found itself mired in a catastrophic economic depression. Once the leading port of the United States, New Orleans suffered under the stifling effects of the Union blockade and occupation. Thousands of runaway slaves flooded the city from the surrounding plantations, forcing the army to deal with their welfare. Also, Banks had a field command in addition to administrative headaches. It was against this backdrop that he would experience his most exhilarating success and humiliating defeat.[55]

Banks handled his administrative duties with fair success, but his victory at Port Hudson in July 1863 represented the zenith of his military career. The move on Port Hudson was meant to prevent the garrison from reinforcing Vicksburg and to clear the southern flank on the Mississippi.

Although capturing Port Hudson was a major victory for Banks, military mismanagement characterized the operation — in this way it was similar to the Valley Campaign. Banks issued vague orders and failed to supervise operations properly, which resulted in needless casualties and low morale in his army.[56] The worst letdown sprang from the fact that the Federal victories at Vicksburg and Gettysburg far overshadowed Banks' moment of glory at Port Hudson. This would prevent him from capitalizing on the victory politically, ever an aim with Banks. Nevertheless, he did receive formal thanks from Congress and Lincoln, who exclaimed that the "final stroke" — the clearing of the Mississippi — allowed "the Father of the Waters" to flow once again "unvexed to the sea."[57] Banks needed a clearcut success to seal his reputation and enhance his political career. As 1864 approached that opportunity would present itself. It was up to the "Bobbin Boy" from Massachusetts to capitalize on it to insure his future.

Banks' partner in 1864 was Admiral David Dixon Porter. Porter was a man of limitless drive. When given a mission he immersed himself in the task with what Secretary of the Navy Gideon Welles described as more "energy, great activity, and abundant resources."[58] This determination would serve Porter well when the Red River Campaign came close to disaster. Porter had a notorious distaste for politicians and this characteristic put him in direct conflict with Banks.

Porter was born on June 8, 1813 to a distinguished family. His father, Captain David Porter, was the commanding officer of the frigate *U. S. S. Essex* and at the time Evalina Porter gave birth to young Porter, he was cruising at sea. On that cruise, he destroyed two British ships, found himself incarcerated by the enemy, and later escaped, coming home as a national hero.[59] Young Porter's interest in the navy sprung from his father's fame. David Dixon was swept away by the pomp and pageantry of naval service and resolved to take to the sea at age six. Porter's father became his personal hero and he spent his life emulating the elder Captain Porter.[60]

Porter would also spend the rest of his days defending the reputation of his father. In 1825 the elder Porter fell into a dispute with Secretary of the Navy Samuel Southard over accusations by two congressmen that he had sparked an international incident when he seized a city in Puerto Rico where authorities had jailed one of his officers. A man of pride, he demanded a court of inquiry to clear his name. Southard appointed a board that consisted of avowed enemies of Captain Porter, whose own intransigence contributed greatly to an eventual guilty verdict. The verdict disgraced David Dixon's father and the humiliation it caused made a great impression on the young lad.[61] David Dixon developed an intense hatred of politicians; by 1864 this feeling had deepened due to his experiences early in the Civil War with political generals. When he began his association with Banks, Porter thus held a deep bias against politicians.

Captain Porter realized that if his son wanted to follow in his footsteps, David Dixon would need a proper education. He enrolled the younger Porter at Columbia College preparatory school in Washington, D.C., in 1824. When Captain Porter resigned from the navy in 1826, he accepted an offer from the government of Mexico to command its navy. Upon his departure for Mexico, he withdrew his son from prep school and took him to Mexico. David Dixon soon joined the Mexican navy, serving as a midshipman on his father's flagship.[62] After a year at sea, in which David Dixon saw combat against the Spanish in Cuba, Captain Porter sent his son home. Through the influence of his grandfather, retired Congressman William Anderson, David Dixon received an appointment as midshipman in the U.S. Navy. Thus, at age fifteen David Dixon Porter began a naval career that would span more than fifty years.[63]

After his first taste of combat in Cuba, Porter spent the ensuing years before the Civil War chafing for action while earning a paltry income. He would wait for seventeen years before opportunity came, and then it came only because of his incessant lobbying. In 1846 Porter found himself stuck in a scientific post with the Naval Observatory in Washington, D.C. He bombarded the Navy Department with requests for transfer, citing his service with the Mexican navy as a unique qualification for duty in the Gulf. His requests went unheeded until disease decimated the blockading squadron in the Gulf. He reported to the Home Squadron off Veracruz in time to participate in General Winfield Scott's landing in March 1847.[64]

Porter distinguished himself as a determined and steady officer during that operation. The squadron's mission for the assault was to suppress Mexican fortifications near Veracruz while putting troops ashore up the beach. Well-directed fire from Porter's pivot gun contributed to the success of the landing. Scott laid siege to Veracruz on March 12, 1847. Porter, now in command of the gunboat *Spitfire,* took his boat within point-blank range of the Veracruz forts. Here he engaged cannon from the forts, knocking several out of action. This aided Scott's efforts to force the capitulation of Veracruz and prompted the general to send a congratulatory letter to Porter's commander praising the lieutenant's bravery.[65]

Following the Mexican War, Porter worked extensively in the development of steam-powered, ironclad ships, which he believed would comprise the backbone of the fleet of the future. This made him a heretic in naval circles, where many officers still thought in terms of sail-driven ships. Nevertheless, Porter experimented with steam and iron and submitted lengthy reports of his findings to the Navy Department. His reports did little to endear him to senior officers maneuvering in the political arena in Washington; on the eve of the Civil War he found himself assigned to the Coast Survey, mapping and marking the Atlantic Coast.[66]

He had shouldered a heavy debt after the death of his father. The Mexican government never compensated the elder Porter for his service to their navy and he had borrowed excessively to maintain his standard of living.[67] Lieutenant Porter assumed the debt in order to spare his now elderly mother, Evalina, further hardship. The coming crisis offered financial opportunity to Porter in the form of promotion and prize money. The question was which side he would choose.

Porter's family ties were in Maryland, a state torn by the sectionalism of North and South. The forty-seven year old naval officer never expressed a firm stand on the issue of secession. Senior navy officials believed that Porter could choose either side depending upon who offered the best opportunity. Gideon Welles held a deep distrust of Porter in 1861, judging him too "given to intrigues" to be trusted until he had proven his loyalty.[68]

Porter gave such proof in April 1861. Secretary of State William H. Seward cooked up a scheme to save Fort Pickens- off the Florida coast- from Southern capture. Needing a determined and daring naval officer to command the ship that would land the soldiers designated to take the fort, Seward offered command of the *Powhatan* to Porter, who enthusiastically accepted.[69] Porter could not resist this opportunity, which, if successful, would mean advancement and recognition. In concert with Army Captain Montgomery Meigs, he boldly saved Fort Pickens for the Union in defiance of Confederate forces in Pensacola. There was no longer any doubt of Porter's allegiance and he received a long-coveted promotion to commander in October. It had been over twenty years since his promotion to lieutenant.[70]

Promotion would accelerate dramatically over the next two years as Porter distinguished himself at New Orleans and Vicksburg. New Orleans signaled the launch of Porter's meteoric rise. He sailed to New York to have the *Powhatan* repaired and made his way to Washington to present to Welles a plan to capture the Crescent City. The Navy Department had considered just such an operation for some time and Porter's timing was opportune. He proposed an upriver thrust by a combined army-navy force. After reducing the Rebel forts on the lower Mississippi with a strong mortar flotilla, he believed that a strong fleet of ships could pass them and land troops at New Orleans, forcing its capitulation.[71]

Welles liked the plan and had Porter accompany him to present it to Lincoln, who warmly endorsed it. Porter, of course, did not hold the appropriate rank to command the expedition. His foster brother, David Glasgow Farragut, did have the appropriate rank and received command of the expedition.[72] Porter received command of the mortar flotilla that would reduce the forts so the warships and transports could move upriver. The War Department assigned General Benjamin Butler command of the 12,500 army troops that would complete the expedition..[73]

The required mortars (twenty-one of them) did not exist when Porter accepted the command. Part of his mission included procuring the mortars, transporting the mortars, and mounting them on schooners. The vote of confidence received from Lincoln and Welles enhanced the commander's self-esteem. As a result, he threw himself into the project with energetic fury. Within three months he had completed the task and set sail for the Mississippi Delta with his flotilla.[74]

Porter made rendezvous with Farragut's warships on March 11, 1862. After planning conferences and further preparation, the fleet moved into the Mississippi to start the operation. Porter's mortars were to shell Forts Jackson and St. Phillip for forty-eight hours, neutralizing their capability to challenge Farragut's warships. Porter opened the bombardment on April 18 and continued to shell the forts until Farragut ran past them in the early hours of April 24. Although the barrage did not fully meet Porter's expectations, Farragut praised his efforts, saying "you supported us nobly."[75] Farragut took New Orleans that day.

Controversy developed between General Butler and Porter. Porter had the honor of accepting the surrender of Forts Jackson and St. Phillip after Farragut had moved past them. Butler felt snubbed because Porter, a mere commander in the navy, received the surrender, although his troops occupied the forts. Butler retaliated by minimizing Porter's role in the operation in his official report. He wrote to the secretary of war claiming that the forts were "as defensible as before the bombardment ... being quite uninjured."[76] Correspondents traveling with Butler attributed the victory to the general's leadership, slighting Farragut and Porter. Porter was indignant and was soon firing off venomous shots at Butler.[77] How dare a politician usurp the accomplishments of two professional officers?[78] This would not be the last tangle with this Bay State politician, and shortly another Massachusetts man would rankle Porter.

Porter received a welcome surprise following his success on the lower Mississippi. In September 1862 the Navy elevated him to the rank of acting rear admiral and gave him the Mississippi Squadron. He would have to prove himself worthy of the command before the Navy Department removed the "acting" from the title. The navy had selected Porter over the heads of several more senior officers and Welles knew this would anger those old salts, but Porter had "positive qualities, fertile resources, [and] great energy," although he also possessed "excessive and not over-scrupulous ambition."[79] In short, Welles had no other officer better qualified to assume the important Mississippi Squadron. Porter formally assumed his post October 15, when he arrived at his new headquarters in Cairo, Illinois. His first priority upon taking charge was to prepare his command for joint operations at Vicksburg. Porter had learned over the course of the war the importance of well-coordinated joint army-navy operation, even when the army commander was a politician.

Porter discovered quickly what happened to naval ships moving unsupported through hostile territory. The Steele's Bayou expedition in March 1863 was a good example of what happens when one military branch does not properly coordinate its efforts with the other. Steele's Bayou was an attempt by the Union forces to find a water route around Vicksburg's flank. This would bypass the swampy Yazoo Delta and allow the navy to shuttle the army to solid ground west of Vicksburg. The Confederates, however, obstructed Porter's progress through the narrow bayou north of Vicksburg. He did not take the precaution of ensuring troop support on shore as he moved through the bayou and had far outrun Major General William T. Sherman's corps when Confederate infantry began felling trees in front of and behind his gunboats. The pesky Southerners nearly bagged several of the squadron's best boats before Sherman got enough troops forward to quell the threat. "I never knew how helpless a thing an ironclad could be when unsupported by troops," Porter commented in his after-action report.[80] The lesson would stick, to Porter's great benefit a year later in the Red River Valley.

The Vicksburg campaign was a jewel in Porter's crown of achievements. Major General U. S. Grant, after six unsuccessful attempts to flank Vicksburg, finally struck on the plan that would work. He decided with Porter's cooperation to march his army south on the Louisiana side of the Mississippi. Then Porter would run the Vicksburg batteries to shuttle the troops to the Mississippi side of the river. The plan required detailed planning, determination, and daring execution. Porter fulfilled his part of the plan magnificently and Grant, with help from the Mississippi Squadron, took Vicksburg on July 4, 1863. Porter had developed into a naval officer of the first caliber, and Grant later wrote that "the most perfect harmony reigned between the two arms of the service." Without the navy "the campaign could not have been successfully made."[81] For his efforts Porter received the permanent rank of rear admiral and a vote of thanks from Congress.[82] In 1864 an uncooperative associate — Nathaniel Banks — would challenge all of Porter's determination and professionalism, but the admiral had drawn valuable lessons from Vicksburg that would serve him well in the Red River Valley.

No understanding of the Red River Campaign is complete without knowing the colorful characters who took part in the expedition. Each man's pre-campaign experiences, as a commander and otherwise, directly contributed to the successes and failures along the Red. One pair of commanders—the Confederates—failed utterly to overcome their differences. Although their campaign was an overall success, they failed to capitalize on immense opportunities to influence the outcome of the war. The Union men, on the other hand, with disaster confronting them, overcame adversity to save an army and a navy vital to winning the war and reelection of President Lincoln.

Chapter 3
Pressure in Both Camps

The beginning of the year 1864 held ominous tidings for the Confederacy and the Union. In Washington there was guarded optimism based on the twin successes of Gettysburg and Vicksburg. Yet the Northern people were wary of becoming overconfident. Many times in the past two and a half years of war the Union had seemed near victory only to witness some painful reverse. In Richmond there was an air of foreboding. To many citizens of the South it seemed the walls were closing in on the Confederacy. John B. Jones, a clerk in the Confederate War Department, spoke for many Southerners when he wrote that "we have experienced the great agony of 1863 and have become so familiar with horrors that we shall fight [in 1864] with desperation."[1] By 1864 the people of both sections knew that the war had turned a critical corner. While the people speculated about the future, the leaders grappled with developing a strategy to win the war.

The Confederates were reeling in all theaters in 1864. The previous year had been disastrous for Confederate arms. In the Eastern Theater, centered in Virginia, Robert E. Lee's stout Army of Northern Virginia remained a formidable foe. Nevertheless, the disastrous invasion of the North in June and July 1863 took its toll on the army. Lee's army suffered over 28,000 irreplaceable casualties during the campaign. He also sent two full divisions west in September to shore up the collapsing line in north Georgia, which left him with a force of fewer than 50,000 men to face more than 100,000 in the Federal Army of the Potomac. Both armies now faced each other along the Rapidan in northern Virginia, gathering their strength for the next bloodletting.[2]

West of the Appalachians the situation for the Confederacy bordered on desperation. On July 4, 1863 a catastrophe befell the South when Vicksburg fell. When Port Hudson fell three days later the North had opened the Mississippi Valley from Minnesota to the Gulf. This effectively cut off the huge Trans-Mississippi region and its resources from the rest of the Confederacy. In September the Army of Tennessee appeared to have turned the tide in the West, defeating the Army of the Cumberland at Chickamauga. Braxton Bragg, however, squandered an opportunity to annihilate that army by pursuing in a lackluster manner and passing the initiative back to the Federals. In November, Generals U. S. Grant and Sherman relieved the Army of the Cumberland at Chattanooga, chasing Bragg's army pell-mell back into Georgia. The entire state of Tennessee was Union ground. The Confederacy east of the Mississippi amounted to a triangle from Richmond to Savannah to Mobile.[3]

To oppose the Federals between the Appalachians and the Mississippi the Confederacy depended on the hard-luck Army of Tennessee. Following the disaster around Chattanooga, President Jefferson Davis relieved General Bragg, replacing him with General Joseph Johnston on 18 December 1863.[4] Johnston quickly boosted sagging morale in the ranks, prompting one Tennessean in the army to state that "he [Johnston] restored the soldier's pride."[5] The Army of Tennessee consisted of three corps. Two were with Johnston in north Georgia and gave the Army of Tennessee a strength of just over 50,000 men. These corps faced Major General William T. Sherman, whose force numbered more than double that of Johnston's. The third corps was in south central Mississippi guarding the approaches to Selma and Mobile, Alabama.[6] President Davis wanted offensive action, but the situation of the Army of Tennessee prevented this, according to Johnston. Instead the Army of Tennessee would stand ready to absorb the blow Johnston knew would come.[7]

If the situation was desperate east of the Mississippi, conditions were worse in the Trans-Mississippi. J. B. Jones, the Rebel war clerk, writes of his "alarm" at the prospect of losing the region due to its lack of men and material.[8] When Vicksburg fell in July 1863, everything west of the Mississippi found itself cut off from the Confederate heartland. Communication with the Confederate seat of government was prohibitive at best, involving a series of hand-delivered messages across the great river to a Confederate telegraph office. Messengers had to be careful when crossing the Mississippi to avoid Union gunboat patrols that were constantly on the prowl.[9] But the region ranked low on Richmond's list of strategic priorities, so the Trans-Mississippi would have to make do with its own resources—which included an abundant supply of cotton but not the materials required to sustain a war.[10]

President Davis' strategic plan was to defend the Confederacy by retaining the area around Richmond and the vast heartland between the

Appalachians and the Mississippi. Confederate leaders considered the Trans-Mississippi a backwater that could help the war effort in the East, but required little military attention itself.[11] Union war policy paralleled that of the South. Since President Davis had stated officially on several occasions that the Confederacy simply desired "to be left alone," his military strategy took on a defensive character (with some notable exceptions). The Confederacy reacted to Union efforts that took place east of the Mississippi, and its main efforts were in countering the enemy. But was there potential opportunity in the Trans-Mississippi that remained untapped?

The answer to this question is yes. The population of the Trans-Mississippi region exploded in the decade prior to the war while the rest of the South stagnated by comparison.[12] Of the 6.51 million white citizens of the South, 2.17 million of them lived in the Trans-Mississippi — 33 percent of the total population. For Southern armies that were forever deficient in manpower, here west of the Mississippi River was a source to satisfy their demands.[13] The region never reached its potential for providing soldiers for the South, the reasons for which are twofold.

Since the Confederacy considered the main seat of war to exist east of the river, it only made sense that most of the Trans-Mississippi soldiers serve in the East. Also, the Confederate hierarchy believed that no major threat to the region existed militarily. This caused many citizens of the states west of the Mississippi to believe their government had abandoned them. Why then, should they serve in the Confederate armies? Indeed, why support the Confederacy at all? The consequence of that resentment and doubt was extensive pro-Union sentiment throughout the region.[14]

What the planners in Richmond could not see from a thousand miles away was that a serious threat to the region did exist. Throughout 1862 and 1863, Union armies made steady and unrelenting progress in grabbing important territory in the region. Yet the hierarchy in Richmond harangued the commander at the time, Lieutenant General Theophilus Holmes, with requests to send troops east of the river to prop up Vicksburg. Holmes ignored the requests and attempted to defend the evershrinking region. The department also became a point of exile for incompetent officers who had failed in the East, starting with the top man. The combination of stripping soldiers, Union incursions, and poor leadership demoralized the citizens of the department. In spite of the signs that Southern policy (or non-policy) did not work, the leaders in Richmond did little to correct it.[15]

To fix the problems west of the Mississippi, Richmond felt a change in leadership appropriate, but this amounted to placing a Band-Aid over a gaping hole. In the spring of 1863, President Davis appointed Lieutenant General E. Kirby Smith to command of the department in relief of the inadequate Holmes.[16] Davis gave Smith a mandate to boost sagging morale in the West, but not to expect material help from Richmond. What Smith found disheartened him. During an inspection tour made soon after taking command, he reported that "the male population remaining are old men, or have furnished substitutes, are lukewarm, or wrapped up in speculations and money making." Furthermore, "there was no general system, no common head; each district was acting independently."[17]

Smith's experience in east Tennessee helped him cope with the multitude of problems facing the Trans-Mississippi, but he could never turn the ship around. The government wrote off the region early in the war as a reaction to Union policy and because the political center and influence of the Confederacy devolved on the East. With such an attitude Southern policy makers simply expected Smith to hold his own in the West.[18] The thought that events in the Trans-Mississippi might influence the overall outcome of the war did not enter the policy makers' minds. Now in 1864 Union forces planned a major combination of forces in this region that amounted to a diversion of troops needed for more important work east of the river. This represented a major opportunity, which neither the hierarchy in Richmond nor Smith realized because of long-held convictions about the low strategic value of the region.

Kirby Smith made his Trans-Mississippi headquarters at Shreveport, Louisiana. Soon after the fall of Vicksburg, he began speculating about a Federal advance into the region. Major General Richard Taylor also expected an early move.[19] Smith's paltry resources made repelling an invasion a daunting prospect. In the entire region he could muster approximately 30,000 soldiers, and not all of them were combat troops.[20] These men were scattered throughout Texas, Louisiana, and Arkansas, and would take time to mass, since the Trans-Mississippi's transportation network was wholly inadequate. The Union army operating against Smith would have about 50,000 soldiers in two columns.[21] Based on his belief that action was imminent, Smith issued orders in February 1864 to concentrate his scattered forces in the vicinity of Shreveport.[22]

With the situation seemingly collapsing on all fronts, the Confederates had to quickly devise a winning military strategy to support national policy. In order to stop the hemorrhages and win an acceptable peace, President Davis considered three courses of action. Option one involved an attempt at negotiations with the North. Second, the Confederacy could attempt an offensive to force the North to the peace table. Lastly, the

Confederates could finally secure long-sought foreign recognition. But none of those options was really feasible.[23]

Several Southern governors were insisting that Davis get the North to the peace table. What they did not know was that Davis already had attempted this in 1863. The problem was that Lincoln would accept nothing less than full reunion with emancipation. Since the South could not accept that demand without appearing "ready for submission," further attempts were out of the question.[24] Davis, ever ready to take aggressive action, next considered launching a coordinated offensive. But as Shelby Foote pointed out, that idea "amounted to little more than an exercise in the realm of fantasy." The Confederacy, after the attrition of three years of war and failing fortunes, simply could not sustain an offensive. Robert E. Lee cautioned Davis, "we are not in a condition ... to invade the enemy's country." With the Confederacy's arguably most aggressive general counseling a defensive policy, the president had little alternative but to back down.[25]

The option of winning foreign recognition was equally unrealistic. Since the start of the war, the Confederacy, with various devices, had pursued the coveted assistance of the great powers of Europe. The South tried depriving Europe of cotton, invading Northern territory, and aggressive diplomacy, none of which worked. Europe, with its "enlightened" governments, could not recognize the South as long as it maintained its "peculiar institution"—slavery. Lincoln's Emancipation Proclamation made it virtually impossible for Great Britain, the leading anti-slavery nation, to recognize the Confederacy, and after the military disasters of 1863, Confederate hopes of foreign intervention were nothing more than a pipe dream. Davis himself recognized this fact and in an address to the Mississippi legislature exhorted its members to "rest not your hopes on foreign nations. This war is ours; we must fight it out ourselves." This left the Confederates where they began—still trying to devise a winning military strategy—with the situation becoming ever more bleak.[26]

What options were left? There was a window of opportunity left open to the Confederates and it lay in holding out until the 1864 elections. Rather than looking to the capabilities of the South for victory, Davis began to look at capitalizing on the vulnerabilities of the North, where people were suffering from general war weariness.[27] Though the South could no longer muster the resources to win outright on the battlefield, she could give the Union armies a tough challenge. If the Confederate armies could frustrate Union efforts to subdue them, with no visible progress until the November elections, Northern voters might become so disenchanted as to dump Lincoln in favor of a peace Democrat. This became Confederate strategy by default.[28]

3. Pressure in Both Camps   45

There were three elements in the new grand strategy. The Southern armies were to adopt a defensive posture on all fronts, allowing the Federals to batter themselves with bloody offensives. The Confederates would keep their own losses to a minimum while exacting a heavy toll on the enemy. When opportunity offered, they would make limited offensives in order to demonstrate their still potent punch to Northern voters.[29] Finally, the Confederates would foster unrest in the North by sending covert agents to contribute to and incite peace movements, such as the Copperheads in the Midwest. This was a sound strategy and reasonably achievable even at this late stage in the war.[30] The challenge for Davis now was to adhere to the strategy without letting his own aggressiveness push Confederate arms, i.e., Johnston's Army of Tennessee, into an offensive that they could not sustain. Also, Confederate generals in the sideshow theaters like the Trans-Mississippi had to be capable of recognizing opportunity and taking the limited offensives outlined by Davis.[31]

The Union, with all its obvious advantages, had to devise a strategy to overcome the Confederate armies driven by the iron-willed Davis. In the East, the Army of the Potomac, commanded by Major General George Meade, faced Lee's Army of Northern Virginia across the Rapidan. The Army of the Potomac held a comfortable two-to-one advantage over its Southern counterpart. However, throughout the course of the war the smaller enemy had confounded every move the Army of the Potomac undertook.

In the West the Union armies also enjoyed a cushion of nearly two to one. General William T. Sherman commanded everything from Natchez, Mississippi, east to the Alleghenies. He had at his disposal three separate armies to counter the Army of Tennessee. The armies were the stout Army of the Cumberland commanded by Major General George Thomas, the Army of the Tennessee under Major General James McPherson, and the Army of the Ohio under Major General John Schofield. Two of these armies were concentrated in north Georgia facing Johnston. A large proportion of soldiers from all three were garrisoning various points in occupied Confederate territory, taking away from Sherman's effective combat strength.[32]

In the Trans-Mississippi region — referred to by the Federals as the Department of the Gulf — the Union had nearly 50,000 soldiers commanded by Major General Nathaniel P. Banks. Kirby Smith opposed him with fewer than 30,000, but these forces were not in close contact, as were the armies of the other regions. To the east of the Mississippi the Confederates held Polk's Corps in readiness should Banks lunge toward Mobile.[33]

The Union general-in-chief, Henry Halleck, hatched the plan to liberate Texas by way of the Red River. With the closure of the Mississippi to Confederate access, there seemed no reason to undertake such a campaign. What exactly was the motivation for a campaign that on the surface looked like a diversion of forces from more important theaters? The Federal high command undertook the Red River Campaign for political reasons and cotton. The goals of the campaign had little to do with military considerations; they were to obtain cheap cotton, liberate loyal Texans, and make a demonstration to discourage French designs in Mexico. Along with these objectives Republican politicians planned to readmit the liberated states of Louisiana, Texas, and Arkansas to the Union, thereby gaining all important electoral votes in the November 1864 elections.[34] By the time Ulysses Grant took command of all the Union armies in March 1864, the Red River Campaign was already in motion against his better judgment.

Political pressure on the Lincoln administration to do something to help the large anti-slavery German minority in Texas had been building for some time. As early as 1861, abolitionist and emigrant aid advocates clamored for Union occupation of Texas. General George B. McClellan recommended in August 1861 that Union forces move "upon the Red River and Western Texas for the purpose of protecting and developing the latent Union and free-state sentiment well-known to predominate the Western Texas."[35] Many advocates of an expedition believed the German minority, with their anti-slavery principles, would suffer persecution and they wanted to protect them.[36]

By gaining control of a region with pro-Union sentiment these same politicians felt that they would deliver future votes and deny the Confederacy an industrious sector of their population. These votes could help swing the outcome of the looming presidential election. By 1863 the Administration had promulgated a reconstruction plan for Federally occupied states in the South called the Ten-percent Plan. The plan allowed readmittance of a state when ten percent of its citizens reaffirmed loyalty to the Union and adopted a new state constitution recognizing the Union. The state was then allowed to reconstitute its state government and its eligible (Union-sympathizing) citizens could vote in the November elections. Banks, the astute politician, already had the wheels in motion to deliver Louisiana into the fold and Lincoln hoped the same would occur in Texas.[37]

Additional pressure came from the powerful New England textile industry. Production in New England mills fell off to twenty-five percent of capacity by June of 1862.[38] The industry constituted a huge part of the region's economy and New England governors would not allow it to go under without a fight. Textile lobbyists swung into full gear led by Massachusetts Governor John Andrew later in the year. They converged on the

Lincoln Administration with shrill cries for help to jump-start the industry. In addition to the loss of short-term industry share, a real danger existed that foreign competitors, such as England, would cripple New England's ability to compete in the world economy after the war ended. The mills needed quality cotton now to stave off such a threat.[39]

The textile lobby pushed for some different courses of action to alleviate the problem, but the most prominent of them was an expedition to Texas. The New Englanders felt that this plan held the best hope for success in rescuing the industry. The lobby alleged that Texas had the cotton growing capacity of all the rest of the South combined. Obtaining this cotton through the military occupation of Texas would alleviate the strain on the industry. Also, cotton produced by the Free-Soil Germans would demonstrate in no uncertain terms that slavery was not necessary to turn a handsome profit in the production of the commodity.[40] This tempted Lincoln, who always sought to demonstrate the correctness of Republican principles. But he held off because, from a military perspective, the occupation of Texas would not have a major impact on the war effort. The main effort at this time must remain the clearance of the Mississippi River.

The proverbial straw that broke the camel's back, persuading Federal authorities to go forward with the campaign, occurred in mid-1863. The Confederacy's long-standing dream of foreign recognition quite nearly came to fruition. The French emperor, Napoleon III, had designs on Mexico and held out to Confederate diplomats the possibility of a rapprochement. French troops had actually marched into the Mexican capital on June 7, 1863, to seal their influence. Loose talk of annexations in the Southwest set the Lincoln Administration into action. The president's secretary recorded that the president was "very anxious that Texas should be occupied and firmly held in view of French possibilities. He thinks it just now more important than Mobile." Lincoln felt he had to block any possibility of a Franco-Confederate alliance, and he reasoned that the best way to do this was through a show of force in the Trans-Mississippi.[41] Faced with internal political pressure and an external threat from a European power, the Union high command turned its attention to Texas. Lincoln set the wheels in motion that would result in the Red River Campaign.

Grant's predecessor, Halleck, anticipated this and on August 10, 1863, opened a correspondence with Banks urging him to "hoist the flag in Texas with the least possible delay." A few days later Halleck reemphasized the need for action, stating that the reason "was of a diplomatic rather than of a military character" resulting "from some European complications." In the same dispatch of August 10, Halleck added his input as to the best approach. "If it is necessary, as urged by Mr. Seward, that the flag be restored to *some one point* in Texas, that can be best and most safely effected by a combined military and naval movement up the Red river [sic] to Alexandria, Natchitoches, or Shreveport and the military occupation of northern Texas."[42]

The dispatches from Halleck to Banks always suggested courses of action, but, as was Halleck's habit, he never gave a direct order to Banks telling him to use the Red. In this way Halleck could avoid responsibility for any disasters, yet he could take credit for resulting successes. In closing his dispatch of the 10th to Banks, in which he proffered the Red River as a route of invasion, Halleck stated, "I write this simply as a suggestion, not as a military instruction." Banks accepted the advice, but adopted a different course of action because he did not favor a movement up the Red. He wanted to move by sea directly upon the Texas coast. He selected some locations along the coast where he could gain a foothold and then launched small-scale expeditions to occupy them late in 1863. These attempts to "restore the flag" either failed miserably, as at Sabine Pass, or did little to gain positive control of significant or important territory in Texas.[43]

Halleck was not pleased with Banks' ineffectual attempts to occupy Texas by way of the sea and reprimanded him. In a series of letters in December 1863 and January 1864, Halleck admonished Banks for not notifying the War Department of his intent. Halleck pointedly reiterated his view that the Red offered the best route to Texas and he sought support for his view from Sherman and Steele. Both men agreed with Halleck; in the face of these weighty opinions, Banks admitted defeat.[44] By the time Grant took command of all Union armies on March 9, 1864, Banks' army and Porter's fleet were already moving to their assembly areas to start the campaign up the Red three days later.

Halleck sought to strengthen Banks' effort by ordering Major General Frederick Steele in Arkansas to launch a secondary effort overland from Little Rock to link up with Banks in Louisiana.[45] The purpose of Steele's column was to confront Kirby Smith with two Union armies, forcing him to disperse his already meager Trans-Mississippi forces. Steele's VII Army Corps, numbering some 15,000 men, would converge with Banks on the Red in the vicinity of Shreveport. If neither had decisively brought Smith to battle the united force would seek to destroy Smith's troops and press on into Texas. The problem with the plan was that the convergence of two separate forces is among the most difficult of military maneuvers. Halleck, however, disregarded the difficulties and pressed ahead with plans for the expedition.[46] He also had Sherman detach 10,000 men from his army to support the campaign. Commanded by Major General Andrew

Jackson Smith, a hard-bitten man from the "old army," the force would assemble at Vicksburg and move down the Mississippi to Simmesport to link up with Banks, who would then have direct command of these men and his own Army of the Gulf.[47]

Halleck also busied himself enlisting help from the Navy for the expedition. With assurances from Gideon Welles, he sent Banks a series of dispatches urging him to contact Admiral Porter to iron out the details. "I am assured by the Navy Department," he wrote on January 11, 1864, "that Admiral Porter will be prepared to co-operate with you."[48] Porter looked forward to action, but had hoped that Sherman would command the expedition; he did not relish the prospect of working with yet another political general.[49] Porter's attitude and the curious command arrangements would result in noticeably strained relations between the army and navy when the campaign did get underway. Nevertheless, he penned a letter to Banks expressing his goodwill. "I am prepared ... to cooperate with you at any time when the water is high enough," he said.[50]

Halleck, in addition to attempting a difficult convergence of friendly forces in enemy country, failed to establish appropriate command relationships. Banks and Steele ran separate departments and, according to army protocol, were equals. Halleck required that they cooperate with each other, rather than establishing a unified command which would have ensured unity of effort. This would prove a faulty arrangement. The addition of the navy to the equation further complicated matters; indeed, despite Halleck's assurance of naval cooperation, the absence of a joint command stymied the expedition before it started.

In March 1864 the Union witnessed a refreshing change in its high command. There had been several generals-in-chief over the course of the war, including the man who was about to be superseded, Major General Henry Wager Halleck. Nevertheless, the Federal armies suffered throughout the war from a pronounced lack of coordination among the armies. Lincoln recognized this and had long sought the right commander to remedy the problem. He found him in 1864 in the person of Ulysses S. Grant. Cajoling Congress to pass a bill restoring the rank of lieutenant general, the president bestowed the honor on Grant, whose mandate was to coordinate all Union armies with the goal of destroying the Confederacy.[51]

Grant immediately set the wheels in motion. The first part of his plan involved concentrating as much strength as possible against the primary Confederate armies. For far too long Union forces had dispersed troops in extraneous locations, guarding lines of supply and Washington, or garrisoning relatively unimportant posts scattered about the North. This practice kept many potential combat forces away from the main fronts. Grant realized that in order to defeat the Rebels he had to destroy the Armies of Tennessee and Northern Virginia, which he could do only by massing all possible force against them. Within days of taking command he began to strip locations where troops were idle and sent those troops to the North's primary armies.[52]

Grant then turned his attention to the deployment of his strengthened forces, issuing orders to his commanders. In a meeting with Meade he said, "Lee's army will be your objective point. Wherever he goes there you will go also." With troops pulled from various locations, primarily the coastal Carolinas, Grant formed a new Army of the James that would strike at Richmond while the Army of the Potomac kept Lee occupied in northern Virginia. To his friend Sherman he stated that "Joe Johnston's army was his objective and the heart of Georgia his ultimate aim." Last, Grant wanted the Army of the Gulf under Banks to move on Mobile in order to close the port for good and keep Polk from reinforcing Johnston. Lincoln recognized the plan as a departure from past efforts to defeat the Confederacy. He described it as only he, with his Midwestern perspective, could: "any one not skinning can hold a leg."[53] The plan was sound, but one critical element in it would have to wait.

Instead of moving on Mobile the Federal Army of the Gulf had already embarked on the Red River Campaign. This, of course, would upset Grant's master plan for ending the war. Since the start of the war Mobile had harbored blockade runners who brought in materials that were important to the survival of the Confederacy. Taking this vital port would close off one of the South's few remaining arteries to the outside world. In effect, seizing Mobile would place unbearable pressure on the South. To protect Mobile the Army of Tennessee detached Polk's Corps to southwest Mississippi. Launching an assault in the direction of Mobile would force Polk to defend her. But if an attack never materialized, Polk would be free to move back to Georgia, increasing the strength of Johnston's army. This would decrease Sherman's numerical advantage and close the odds for the Confederates.[54] Unfortunately for the Union army, that was exactly what happened. Grant's planned move against Mobile would not materialize — at least for now.

Grant seriously considered calling the Red River Campaign off because it diverted troops from the main effort in the Confederate heartland. As he later put it, "the services of forty thousand troops ... were thus paralyzed." The additional ten thousand men that Sherman's army lost to the venture weakened him in the face of Johnston. Grant feared that any miscue would permanently divert these troops away from the main theater of action. Grant did not cancel the campaign, but "strenuously" opposed it and allowed it to continue only in deference to the previous general-in-chief.⁵⁵ This proved a costly mistake and almost permanently depriving the main Union armies of badly needed combat veterans. Only Confederate miscues allowed them to escape and fight another day.

Lincoln, concerned with his own reelection effort, unwittingly opened the door of opportunity to the Confederates, undermining the campaign. Rather than concentrating Federal power against the Confederacy's main armies, as Grant desired, the Union had two armies numbering 50,000 men prepared to march in the opposite direction. Jefferson Davis could not have planned it any better himself. This gave his armies the chance to use on the strategy the Confederacy developed to frustrate Union efforts in 1864. Furthermore, if the Union leaders, such as Porter and Banks, blundered in their efforts, Davis' desire for a counterstroke might reap far-reaching results. Perhaps if the Confederates could score a decisive victory the election of a peace candidate would become a reality.

Spies in New Orleans kept Kirby Smith well informed of Federal preparations for an ascent up the Red. Armed with this information and knowledge of the hydrography of the Red, Smith could predict with some accuracy just when such an expedition would take place. Early spring in Louisiana usually witnessed a rise in the level of the Red, which permitted heavy boats to navigate the river. Intelligence Smith received convinced him, he told Richard Taylor in January, that Federal forces would move as soon as the water level permitted."⁵⁶ While Smith knew a campaign was imminent, he found it hard to believe that Grant would divert forces away from the primary Confederate armies. Surely, Smith thought, "the enemy cannot be so infatuated as to occupy a large force in this department when every man should be employed east of the [Mississippi] river."⁵⁷ Even the Confederate high command surmised what the Union strategy should have been. However, since the Federal forces prepared to do the opposite, Smith undertook to counter the expected advance.

Smith based his strategy on the capabilities of his paltry force, the vastness of the Trans-Mississippi region, and the converging enemy armies. He described the plan in a dispatch to Taylor: "Our role must be a defensive policy where the enemy is largely our superior," he explained to Taylor, "and where our columns come within a practicable distance of each other, concentrating rapidly upon and crushing one or the other of the enemy's columns."⁵⁸ In essence, Smith advocated trading space for time. Then using interior lines, he would combine all available forces and mass on the most vulnerable Union column. Once he had turned one column back, he would turn and pounce on the other column, again using the advantage of interior lines.

Smith's force consisted of Major General Sterling Price's 12,000 troops in Arkansas, the 10,000 men of Major General John Magruder's District of Texas, and 13,000 in the District of West Louisiana commanded by Taylor. Smith began moving units from the District of Texas to the vicinity of Shreveport in February 1864. Simultaneously, he had Price and Taylor fall back from forward positions toward Shreveport. At the right moment he would concentrate the troops in one of the districts—either Arkansas or west Louisiana—to stop Steele or Banks.[59] Taylor, ever loyal to his home state, thought the primary threat lay in Louisiana and therefore wanted the point of concentration there. Retreating and giving up Louisiana was intolerable to him; he lashed out at Smith's strategy, complaining that "it would have been better to lose the state [Louisiana] after a defeat than surrender it without a fight."[60] Here Taylor sowed the seeds of animosity with his superior that would paralyze conduct of the Confederate campaign.

The year 1864 was the pivotal one for both sides. Each developed a strategy it hoped would finally bring victory. The Union, however, veered from its plan by not applying pressure at the proper location, Mobile, in favor of a sideshow on the Red. This offered the Confederacy the opportunity to capitalize on the Federal army's mistake, in accordance with Southern strategy. On the other hand, would Banks' own potential for indecision and inappropriate command arrangements, and Porter's distaste for politicians, deliver the Confederates a great victory?

Chapter 4
"10,000 Damned Gorillas"

The Red River Campaign began on March 10, 1864, when Brigadier General Andrew J. Smith embarked with Admiral Porter from Vicksburg down the Red River. The expedition started auspiciously, with the Federals capturing some key objectives. Within weeks, though, the tables would turn, as the Federals moved deeper into enemy territory. Personal conflicts, politics, and military necessity would intervene to sour Union fortunes.

Union troops moved to assembly areas the first week of March 1864 in preparation for the campaign. A. J. Smith's men—the XVI and XVII Army Corps—steamed down the Mississippi from Vicksburg supported by Rear Admiral Porter's Mississippi Squadron. They headed for Simmesport, Louisiana, where they would disembark and begin land operations up the Red River Valley. Simmesport was a ramshackle little town situated on the Atchafalaya River a couple of miles from the confluence of the Red and the Mississippi. Simmesport made a good starting point because the road meandering north could support an army on the march and it led to the back door of the first Federal objective, Fort De Russy.

Banks assembled his men in the vicinity of Berwick's Bay, west of New Orleans. The direct supervision of these troops devolved upon Major General William B. Franklin, commander of the XIX Corps, who had led the Left Grand Division at Fredricksburg. He found himself exiled in the West because of his involvement with the failures in the East early in the war. The force assembling at Berwick's Bay consisted of Franklin's own XIX Corps and the XIII Corps under the command of Brigadier General Thomas E. G. Ransom. Brigadier General Albert G. Lee commanded Banks' cavalry division and would lead the Army of the Gulf when it moved out. The route of advance followed the Teche, the same country where Banks

Fort De Russy earthworks at the Red River face.

had come to grief a year earlier at the hands of Richard Taylor. The line of the Teche would lead the Federal Army of the Gulf north from Berwick's Bay through Opelousas to Alexandria on the Red. At Alexandria, Banks' column would link up with Smith and the combined army would then move north to Shreveport.

A. J. Smith arrived at Simmesport on March 12, 1864, and immediately sent forward a reconnaissance force toward Fort De Russy, a stout earthwork named for the Confederate engineer who built her. Mounting twelve guns of varying caliber, it commanded a hairpin turn in the Red about thirty miles upstream from the mouth of the river. The fort effectively blocked the Red to naval traffic and Smith had to take it to allow Porter's gunboats to proceed downstream. Though well situated to contest any naval advance, Fort De Russy was poorly located for fending off an attack from its land face. The fort sat on an island accessible by a bridge and to its rear, or west, was a low range of hills gradually sloping down toward the river. A Federal force occupying this ridge could dominate the fort with field batteries that would have an unobstructed line of fire into the fort.[1]

Taylor commanded the Confederate forces in west Louisiana, which is that portion of the state west of the Mississippi. At the beginning of March, he had his thin force arrayed to provide early warning of an advance by the Union army. The division of Major General John G. Walker manned Taylor's most advanced positions. Commissioned in the 1840s and a veteran of long service in the "old army," Walker had served with distinction in Mexico, earning a brevet for "Gallant and Meritorious conduct" at San Juan de los Llanos. Resigning his commission in 1861, Walker commanded a division in the Army of Northern Virginia at the capture of Harper's Ferry and the battle of Sharpsburg. After these battles the Confederacy promoted him to major general and transferred him west to the Trans-Mississippi — he was one of few officers sent to the department who was not exiled there for incompetence.[2]

Walker's men centered around Marksville with pickets thrown forward to the outskirts of Simmesport. Walker's responsibility included the defense of Fort De Russy, for which he had detached 200 men to assist the gunners in the fort under the command of a Lieutenant Colonel Byrd. Taylor attached Colonel William G. Vincent's 2d Louisiana Cavalry to Walker's division to provide him with reconnaissance and screening capability. Three companies of Vincent's horse had the mission to scout east of the Atchafalaya on the Mississippi to provide early warning of a move from that quarter. The rest of Vincent's men scouted the Teche to provide warning of any Federal moves from Berwick's Bay.[3]

Brigadier General Alfred Mouton's Division posted itself at Alexandria on the Red as the reserve of Taylor's army. This division held itself ready to move either toward the Atchafalaya or the Teche depending on where a threat might develop.[4] Mouton had graduated from West Point and fought at Shiloh, earning recognition as a solid fighter. A native of Louisiana, Mouton was the son of a popular former governor, making him a special favorite of the state troops in his command.[5]

The decision to erect fortifications, such as Fort De Russy, on the Red to stop a naval flotilla had been made by Kirby Smith. During the winter of 1863 to 1864 he had ordered the improvement of defenses along the lower Red over the protests of Taylor. Taylor later recalled that he had "objected to fortifications beyond mere water batteries" because he believed the key to the defense of Louisiana lay in the preservation and mobility of the army. Defending fixed points, he thought, would tie his hands and eventually cost him his army. Events would prove Taylor's assertions correct.[6]

On March 13 A. J. Smith ordered Brigadier General Joseph Mower's division to push forward to Fort De Russy to ascertain Rebel dispositions. Mower, an aggressive officer and a special favorite of Sherman,[7] wasted no time in brushing aside the scratch force picketing between Simmesport and Marksville. He moved so quickly that the Rebels "lost all their cooking utensils" in their haste to get out of Mower's way.⁸ Diarist Felix Pierre Poche, a young staff officer given to criticizing senior officers, recorded that "General Scurry (commanding the troops in the vicinity of Simmesport) in *needless fright* [italics added] foolishly retreated before the enemy ... abandoning their well-constructed camp."⁹ Despite muddy roads and Confederate attempts to slow the advance by burning bridges and obstructing roads, Mower made steady progress. Walker's division attempted to defend Fort De Russy by deploying forward to maintain freedom of maneuver, but Mower flanked him out of successive positions. Walker's final position on the range of hills commanding the island became a decision point. If Mower flanked him from this position Walker could cross the bridge at Fort De Russy and defend it until starved out. This would cost Taylor the services of half his army. On the other hand, Walker could slip away toward Alexandria to prevent encirclement, leaving Fort De Russy to its fate and preserving his division for more important fighting down the road. "It was necessary to either adopt this cruel alternative or," Walker continued, "share the fate of Fort De Russy. After skirmishing for some hours" the division "withdrew and [left] the garrison to it's [sic] fate."¹⁰ This isolated Lieutenant Colonel Byrd and his 300-odd defenders. Mower quickly invested the fort, occupying the low hills vacated by Walker's departure on the evening of March 13. Mower formed his division in line of battle straddling the Marksville–Fort De Russy road in preparation for an assault.

Meanwhile, on the Red, the navy had a rough time going upstream. The Confederates had taken care to obstruct the river eight miles below the fort to slow the passage of the gunboats. Lieutenant Commander S. L. Phelps, in charge of the *Eastport*, reported that "the obstructions consisted of piles [of timber] driven across the river" stacked in the riverbed. The Rebels then cut a "forest of trees" and "floated them down upon the piles" to reinforce the obstruction. Removing the obstruction meant dragging chunks of the obstacle away until the river could break through it, a task that "consumed nearly the entire day." By the time Phelps had cleared and moved through the obstacle Mower had already commenced his attack.¹¹

Before sundown of the 14th, Mower ordered his troops to move forward to the attack. His division had the advantage of commanding the high ground as it moved. Also, the small Confederate force had no artillery support because it had mounted its heavy ordnance to face the river and could not swing the guns around to defend the landward side. In spite of a hot musket barrage from the fort, the attackers had little trouble moving up to it. At about 300 yards Mower's brigades broke—with a yell— into a bayonet charge, and were up and over the parapet within minutes of the order. Colonel William T. Shaw described the events as "a good day's work" and indeed they were. Mower's division had moved twenty-eight miles—much of the way over muddy, obstructed roads—and attacked and taken Fort De Russy, all between sunup on the 13th and sundown on the 14th.[12] Phelps' naval force arrived in time to witness the climax of Mower's assault. The *Eastport* did contribute a lone shot from its 100-pounder rifle, which, Phelps reported, scattered the enemy from the water battery.[13] All in all, Fort De Russy was a neat little fight and kicked off the campaign in admirable fashion. "[T]hus much for our Red River Gibraltar," Taylor would later write, expressing his disgust with Kirby Smith over the affair.[14]

Down at Berwick's Bay, Banks' column spent its time trying to move out of the infernal mud from the recent rains. Banks had planned to rendezvous with Smith's column at Alexandria by the 17th of March.[15] Torrential rains turned the southeast Louisiana roads into quagmires, delaying the column's start by a week. Brigadier General Lee's cavalry finally stepped off on March 7 with Franklin's infantry following him the next day. Franklin had immediate command of Banks' column because Banks was more worried about the upcoming inauguration of the new Unionist governor, Michael Hahn.[16] This agitated Sherman whose 10,000 troops under Smith were already moving toward Alexandria. Sherman steamed down the Mississippi to New Orleans on March 2 to confer with Banks about the coordination of their forces. Sherman found Banks engrossed in the details of the ceremony and unwilling to discuss the campaign until after the inauguration. Sherman left New Orleans in disgust on the 3rd without having coordinated anything. "I regarded all such ceremonies as out of place at a time when it seemed to me every hour and minute were due to the war," he noted in his post-war memoir.[17] While Banks' men struggled northward through the elements, Banks occupied himself with finding a method to fire a one hundred–gun salute using electricity.

A. J. Smith reembarked Mower's Division on transports the day after Fort De Russy's capitulation and steamed up the Red to Alexandria. He appointed Brigadier General Thomas Kilby Smith the task of destroying the works. Kilby Smith's men, veterans of Sherman's Meridian Campaign, took to this work with a vengeance—and in the process precipitated a disaster. Part of the work included destruction of the magazine. Rather than evacuating Fort De Russy to detonate the magazine, someone set the fuze in the middle of the night with troops sleeping in the works. Witnesses report waking up with a start as the fort blew sky high. Kilby Smith reported two men killed and several wounded as a result of the explosion.[18]

The Confederates, with the fall of Fort De Russy, found their position at Alexandria untenable. Diarist Poche best describes the situation on March 14:

> With that victory [Fort De Russy], the enemy was assured free navigation of the Red River, and began to ascend the river with their gunboats and transports full of troops, and Alexandria will fall in consequence into their hands, leaving our army in a very critical position, enemy in front, to the left, and soon to the rear if our generals do not make haste.[19]

Faced with converging Union columns that outnumbered his 5,300 men five to one, Taylor made preparations to evacuate the town. He personally supervised the removal of all government stores in the city. In addition, he had all cotton removed or burned to prevent this precious commodity from falling into the hands of the Federals.[20] Taylor's anger rose as he gave up more territory while awaiting reinforcements from department headquarters at Shreveport. The reinforcements most desired by Taylor were reliable cavalry. His only unit in mid-March was Vincent's solitary 2d Louisiana. Taylor had Vincent's horsemen spread from the lower Red south and west to the Teche, a distance of over thirty miles, and that thin screen could not provide the information Taylor needed to make sound decisions.[21]

Kirby Smith in Shreveport heard Taylor's call and ordered Major General John B. Magruder to send cavalry reinforcements from Texas to make up for Taylor's deficiency in horse soldiers.[22] As these headed toward Louisiana, Taylor slowly moved "back in the pine desert lying between the Red and Sabine," an area described by General Walker as "entirely destitute of subsistence and forage."[23] Having foreseen that the Federals would attempt a campaign up the Red that year, Taylor had taken the precaution of establishing a series of supply depots in that "desert." When he pulled out of Alexandria on March 15, the depots were stocked for his use. Though he knew they were not abundant, they would enable him to keep the field.[24]

A. J. Smith and Porter arrived at Alexandria on March 15, on the heels of the retreating Rebels. Since Franklin had not yet arrived, Smith and Porter busied themselves with foraging and cotton-gathering. Porter, eager to pad his pocketbook, sent out details of sailors in "confiscated" wagons to claim prizes for the navy. Smith's men had a special talent for foraging and went about it with glee, taking everything of value. This was the initial source of friction among Banks, Smith, and Porter.

Franklin's van began arriving at Alexandria on the 20th and did not close the rear of the column until the 24th — a week behind schedule. His men hailed predominantly from the Northeast and regional animosities ran deep through the army. Franklin issued strict orders against foraging to his troops before they moved out from Berwick's Bay, but A. J. Smith's men hailed from the then northwestern United States and they were cut from a rougher cloth than their Eastern counterparts. Instant animosity

4. "10,000 Damned Gorillas"   59

arose when Franklin's men arrived and witnessed the depredations visited by Smith's men upon the citizens along the Red River Valley. Smith's westerners took jabs at Franklin's men, calling them "paper collar" soldiers who were on holiday. To this the men of the XIII and XIX Corps responded that Smith's "uncouth" men were nothing but a set of "10,000 damned gorillas."[25]

Banks himself finally broke away from New Orleans politics; he arrived at Alexandria by steamer on March 25, eight days behind schedule, to assume his military duties. With him was an army of cotton speculators and treasury agents with permits authorizing them to gather cotton and transport it through enemy lines. Much to the speculators' dismay, Porter had already confiscated the available cotton and marked it with the initials "CSA-USN" to denote ownership. Colonel J. G. Wilson, aide-de-camp to Banks, asked Porter jokingly if he knew what the acronym stood for. Porter responded that he did not and Wilson informed him that it meant "Cotton Stealing Association of the United States Navy."[26] Although he spoke in jest, this feeling pervaded the group of speculators and the upper command echelons of the Army of the Gulf.

The agents appealed shrilly to General Banks for help in convincing Porter to stop confiscating cotton and turn it over to the treasury agents for disbursement. Porter later reported that Banks came to him "very indignant" about the state of matters at Alexandria and requested help in curtailing the navy's cotton-gathering activities.[27] The strange command relationship established between the two men by the War Department prevented either one from issuing joint orders. Therefore, neither commander could control the cotton situation. The speculators took matters into their own hands and went into a "cotton gathering"[28] melee of their own to compete with the navy.

While Banks and Porter argued over parochial contrivances, military operations continued. Taylor pulled his force back to a plantation called Carroll Jones. There he had established one of his several depots; he encamped to rest and gather intelligence about the Federals' intentions. Taylor ordered Vincent's cavalry forward to a place called Henderson's Hill—on Bayou Rapides about twenty miles above Alexandria—to monitor Federal activities at Alexandria.[29]

The night of March 21 was miserable for Vincent's horsemen. Gusts of wind blew a cold rain into the faces of the 2d Louisiana that night. Believing the inclement weather would shield them from action, the pickets established by the regiment disregarded prudence and pulled in from their posts to huddle around campfires. Earlier in the day A. J. Smith once again had kicked out Mower's division on a reconnaissance in force.

Vincent had contested Mower's men all day on the 21st before camping at Henderson's Hill. Mower's men, contrary to Confederate hopes, pressed their activities of the day into the night. Obtaining the Confederate countersign from a local citizen, the van of Mower's division relieved Vincent's remaining pickets of their posts without firing a shot. They then moved into Vincent's main camp and bagged the whole crowd before anyone could grab a weapon in defense. Mower scored his second neat victory within a week, making it look as if the campaign would be a cakewalk. Taylor lambasted Vincent for the poor discipline of his command.[30] The rank and file felt as if "a thunderbolt" had hit when the news of Henderson's Hill reached them.[31]

Smith, meanwhile, was in Shreveport wrestling with the decision of where to apply his Fabian policy with a reasonable chance of success. As more information slowly came in, Kirby Smith began to formulate his plan of defense. Since Banks' army was larger and closer to Shreveport than Frederick Steele's column moving down from Arkansas, Smith designated it as the primary threat. He made dispositions, therefore, to strike Banks with all his available strength, while slowing Steele. On March 18 he ordered Sterling Price to rush his infantry — Churchill's and Parsons' divisions — to Shreveport to mass on Banks, leaving Price with about 5,000 cavalry to spar with Steele. Once he had turned Banks back, he planned to shift forces back in the direction of Arkansas to confront Steele. He outlined his strategy to Taylor in a dispatch instructing him to retreat slowly toward Shreveport and admonishing him that "a general engagement should not be risked without hopes of success." He told Taylor to be patient and avoid a major clash unless he was certain of victory. If they lost either of their "little armies," he reminded Taylor, it would be fatal to the department and the Confederacy.

But Taylor could not bear retreating all the way back to Shreveport.[32] Prior to receipt of Smith's dispatch, he became incensed by the fact that reinforcements arriving in Louisiana were halted by Smith's staff at Shreveport. Confederate Congressman Duncan Kenner from Louisiana informed Taylor that Smith believed that he did not want the reinforcements. It appears that Smith's erstwhile medical director — an old friend of Kirby Smith's who revered him and despised Taylor — convinced Smith to retain the troops at Shreveport. Sol Smith, the medical director, apparently believed that this would force Taylor to fall back to meet the reinforcements rather than waiting for them to move up. If that occurred Kirby Smith could take command of the whole and grab credit for turning Banks' column back in the decisive battle.[33]

Upon hearing these revelations, Taylor became incensed and sent a letter to Kirby Smith's chief of staff on March 23 discussing the information

Kenner had provided. In it he expressed his indignance and promised that "when Green joins me [from Texas] I shall fight a battle for Louisiana, be the forces of the enemy what they may." A few days later, Taylor fired off two letters to Smith arguing that "the only possible way to defeat Steele's movement is to whip the enemy now in the heart of the Red River Valley." Taylor also demanded that the reinforcements then at Shreveport move to his aid before the Confederates lost Louisiana without a fight. He ended the second letter by saying he would stop Banks regardless of his numerical disadvantages and he "would never cease to regret the error" of not having already engaged Banks.[34] This outburst began a series of exchanges between the two principal Confederate commanders that would cast a cloud over the campaign, and rekindle the old animosities that began during the Teche Campaign of 1863.

While the Confederates squabbled over strategy, pressure and friction also built up at Alexandria. On March 26 Banks received the dispatch from Lieutenant General Grant written eleven days earlier telling him to take Shreveport "as soon as possible." Then Banks was to "send Brigadier General A. J. Smith's command back to Memphis as soon as possible." Smith's troops were headed "for movements east of the Mississippi." Sherman wanted Smith's men back by April 15, Grant told Banks, "even if it leads to the abandonment of the main object of your expedition."[35] The calendar now read March 26, which gave Banks nineteen days to take Shreveport and return A. J. Smith's troops to Memphis. Banks knew he had to move fast and went to Porter to discuss the next step of the expedition.

Listening to Banks urge an immediate advance, Porter expressed concern that his boats would not make it over the falls due to the low level of the river at Alexandria. Even if he could get his boats over, he might have trouble getting them back down. Banks, however, insisted that naval support was critical and the "success of the expedition would depend upon the cooperation of the navy," and Porter finally agreed. With considerable bravado he now vowed to "go [over the falls] if I should lose all my boats." Porter's pride and stubbornness could not allow Banks the opportunity to say that the expedition failed for want of support from the navy. He promised, therefore, to take his boats "wherever the sand is damp."[36]

Banks, now assured of naval support, issued orders to continue the march up the Red. Banks designated Grand Ecore, a small hamlet four miles north of Natchitoches, as the next objective. Lee's cavalry took the lead on 26 March followed the next day by A. J. Smith's command. On the 28th the XIII and XIX Corps moved out, minus Grover's XIX Corps division. Banks left this division at Alexandria to guard the city, now designated the army's rear supply base. This division also became a workforce of deckhands. Since the Red prevented the passage of ships, all supplies required transloading below and above the falls. A supply ship would dock at Alexandria and then soldiers would load the contents on wagons and transport them to docks above the falls for reloading onto another transport. At a place called Cotile Landing on the Red, A. J. Smith's men boarded transports for the rest of the trip to Grand Ecore.[37]

Porter now engrossed himself with the task of getting his gunboats over the falls. To prove that he could accomplish the feat, Porter decided to throw in his heaviest and most prized gunboat, the *Eastport*. When ordered to take her over, Pilot Wellington W. Withenbury immediately objected. He told Porter that "it was bad policy to put the largest boat into the chute first, as she might get aground, and if she did it would hinder the passage of the other vessels." Porter—whose pride was in control of his mental faculties—refused the advice and curtly ordered Withenbury "to go on aboard and take her over the falls." Withenbury did as ordered and quickly proved the correctness of his judgment. The *Eastport* ran aground right in the middle of the rapids. She stood there for three days, stopping all traffic, while the sailors struggled to pull her off. They finally succeeded, and pushed thirteen more gunboats and several transports over the falls before proceeding on to Grand Ecore.[38]

Banks did not accompany the army or navy on the march to Grand Ecore. Soon after issuing the orders to move, he took off his military hat and put on his politician's cap.[39] Louisiana now had a Union governor, but it also required a new constitution to validate the government for readmittance to the Union. Banks, therefore, remained in Alexandria to hold an election for delegates to convene a constitutional convention. He set the election for April 1, 1864 and supervised the details of its execution.[40] The politician in Banks knew that Lincoln would have to reciprocate for his delivering a state that could supply electoral votes in November. Now if General Banks could deliver a military victory he would ensure the ascendancy of his own star.

The van of the Union army arrived in Natchitoches on 31 March, with Porter's fleet pulling into Grand Ecore the same day. Lee's cavalry had small scrapes with some Confederates along the route, but had little trouble driving them away. The area in the vicinity of the line of march felt the hard hand of war. The retreating Confederates supplemented the supplies from the depots by foraging, much to the dismay of the civilian population. In addition, they burned or took all the cotton they found to prevent its falling into the hands of the Federals. This outraged the local farmers, whose entire income derived from bales of the product.[41] To make matters worse the Federals took or burned whatever the Confederates had failed to make off with, terrorizing the population. "The inhabitants ... were hurriedly quitting their homes, and flying before the approach of the invader," Joseph Blessington of Walker's division recalled.[42] With the Federal's arrival at Natchitoches, Taylor pulled back to Pleasant Hill, which diverged from the line of the river.

Banks boarded a steamer on April 2 following the election and headed for the rendezvous at Grand Ecore. Having met little resistance, and with the knowledge that the Confederates continued to pull back precipitously, his confidence soared. Upon his arrival at Grand Ecore, he took the time to pen a letter to General Halleck, telling him that he expected to reach Shreveport by the 10th and that he could whip the Rebels if they would stand and fight.[43] Halleck briefed the President on the contents of the letter, but Lincoln felt uneasy with this expression of bravado. Lincoln had heard such bombast before from other generals, such as Pope and Hooker, and took it as a sign of pending disaster. "I am sorry to see this tone of confidence; the next news we shall hear from there will be of a defeat," he told Halleck prophetically.[44]

At Grand Ecore Banks had to make a decision that would play a major role in deciding the fate of the expedition. From the start of the expedition up to Grand Ecore, the army had enjoyed the cooperation of the navy for fire support, transportation, and supplies; up to Grand Ecore a river road paralleled the channel, allowing the army and navy to move simultaneously and support each other. At Grand Ecore the river road veered off into the "pine desert." Its path meandered northwesterly from Grand Ecore to the village of Pleasant Hill. From there it lead to Mansfield, where the single-lane road split into three parallel routes that all reconverged at Shreveport and the Red River. The road through the pine forest lay an average of about twenty miles inland from the river. Moving up this road would require Banks to depend solely on his own firepower and transportation until he again reached the Red at Shreveport. Also, this would strip Porter of his army support — which he knew was dangerous based on his experience a year earlier on Steele's Bayou.[45] The challenge for Banks, then, was to find out if there existed an alternative to the Mansfield route to Shreveport.

On April 3 General Charles P. Stone, Banks' chief of staff and scapegoat of the Ball's Bluff debacle in '61, set about learning the local topography by questioning some men familiar with the area. One of the men he spoke to was Pilot Withenbury, the same man who had advised Porter against sending the *Eastport* above the falls. Stone, spreading a map before the pilot, inquired where the village of Pleasant Hill was located. Stone's map did not depict Pleasant Hill, but Withenbury produced a map that did show the location and readily pointed it out to Stone. Stone did not believe him, but Withenbury was adamant and offered Stone the use of his personal maps.[46]

Later in the same day Stone came to see Withenbury again, this time bringing along General Banks. On this occasion he asked about alternative routes to the road to Mansfield. Withenbury described two possibilities, both of which involved crossing the Red to other bank. One of the routes followed the river road on the opposite bank, but this alternative involved traversing some difficult swamps. The other would oblige them to go around the swamps on an old military road to Fort Towson and then down to Shreveport from the northeast. Both of these alternatives were unsatisfactory because Banks did not have the two extra days that Withenbury said the marches would require.[47] Franklin suggested that Banks allow him to conduct reconnaissance to see if there was a river road on the south bank of the river. Banks rejected the idea on the grounds that he did not have time.[48] Grant's dispatch of March 15, which gave Banks a deadline of April 15 to accomplish the mission or abandon "the main object," pushed him into ignoring prudence and taking the inland route to Shreveport through the barrens of the "pine desert." The calendar now read 4 April, meaning Banks now had eleven days to take Shreveport, with nearly ninety miles to cover and an enemy army to brush aside.

If Banks had crossed over the river to take one of the alternative routes he would have flanked the Confederates from their position protecting Shreveport while securing his own line of communications. Additionally, he would have been closer to Steele's army coming down from Arkansas than the Confederates. Had he at least made a proper reconnaissance he would have discovered the river road that followed the *south* bank. This could have secured his line of communication and support from the navy, while forcing Taylor to do something that he did not want to do, namely, fight on ground of his enemy's choosing. But Banks and Stone disregarded all advice and chose the inland route. There is evidence to suggest that the overconfidence Banks expressed to Halleck in the April 2 dispatch also influenced his decision. He wrote his wife on 4 April that the enemy "will not fight … this side of Shreveport[,] if then."[49] This fatal decision led to the forthcoming disaster.

Banks left the details of the march column to Franklin as he had throughout the course of the campaign.[50] Banks remained at Grand Ecore, ostensibly to superintend the arrangements for supplies and the embarkation of the troops going up the river.[51] General Franklin now committed a fatal blunder in composing the march dispositions. He assigned Lee's cavalry to take the advance as horse soldiers should. However, he ordered Lee to have his enormous wagon train, full of forage for the horses and rations and ammunition for the men, follow directly behind in closed column. Behind Lee's train filed the XIII and the XIX Corps followed by their even larger corps trains. A. J. Smith's XVI Corps divisions acted as the rear, while T. Kilby Smith's XVII Corps division boarded transports to provide some army support to the vulnerable gunboats as they moved up the river to Shreveport.[52]

The single-lane road through the pine forest caused the column to string out for a number of miles when it moved out on April 6. The cavalry train of about 200 wagons following the horsemen in the thick pine forest would prevent the rapid passage of infantry to the front if the cavalry made heavy contact. General Lee was uneasy about the march dispositions and made a request that Franklin either allow his wagons to march in the rear of the army or reinforce him with a brigade of infantry. Franklin replied that it was Lee's responsibility to look after his own trains and that infantry would move to his support when required.[53] Lee's apprehension would prove prophetic; the poor dispositions would contribute to the disaster awaiting them down the road. Yet Banks, still in the rear of the column at Grand Ecore, had no control over the unfolding situation, despite his position as commanding officer.

Meanwhile, Taylor's advanced elements, now including Brigadier General Thomas Green's cavalry, reported Banks' divergence from the river road toward Pleasant Hill. Taylor saw an opportunity and began to develop a plan to upset Federal campaign designs. Kirby Smith, however, hesitated. During the last exchange of dispatches, a week earlier, Smith seemed set on attacking Banks first and then turning on Steele. By April he began to doubt the logic of his own strategy. His indecisiveness grated on Taylor and the irascible subordinate fired off yet another condescending letter to Smith, saying:

> Like a man who has admitted the robber into his bedchamber instead of resisting him at the door, our defense will be embarrassed by the cries of wives and children. Action, prompt vigorous action is required. While we are deliberating, the enemy is marching. King James lost three kingdoms for a mass. We may lose three states without a battle.... Unless I receive instructions to the contrary I shall move on Natchitoches.[54]

Smith now believed Taylor would make a rash move and he immediately counseled patience and the avoidance of unnecessary risk. "The whole fate of this department will be staked on the issue...." he told Taylor. "Defeat not only loses the department but releases the armies employed against us for operations beyond the Mississippi." Taylor's response was to request a council of war.[55]

The two men met on April 5 at Mansfield. At this meeting Taylor, of course, expressed his intent to fight it out in Louisiana at the first opportunity. Kirby Smith suggested instead either withstanding a siege at Shreveport or retreating into Texas. Taylor indignantly insisted that Smith's plan would lead to the loss of the army. Smith attempted to smooth things over with Taylor by agreeing to move Churchill's Arkansas division, now at Shreveport, down to Keatchie, a hamlet a few miles north of Mansfield. Smith placed Churchill under Taylor's operational control should Taylor need the division in an emergency. Smith left the meeting under the impression that Taylor had agreed with him, but Taylor later denied it.[56] Taylor had other ideas; as he wrote later, "General Kirby Smith did not insist on the adoption of either of his own suggestions, nor express approval of mine, but when Mansfield was reached, a decision became necessary."[57] General Walker also recalled that "beyond Mansfield the enemy's advance could not be disputed with prudence."[58]

Taylor began to implement his own plans to deal with Banks, explaining, "Three roads lead from this place [Mansfield] to Shreveport, the Kingston, Middle, and Keachi…. Past Mansfield, then, the enemy would have three roads, one of which would be near his fleet on the river, and could avail himself of his great superiority in numbers. This was pointed out to the "Aulic Council" [i.e., Kirby Smith and his staff] at Shreveport," he continued sarcastically, "but failed to elicit any definite response."[59] Taylor's logic made sound military sense. He could hit a portion of the army strung out in the pine woods south of Mansfield where it would be difficult for the Federals to bring their mass to bear. Or, he could allow the Federals to get north of Mansfield into more open country, where they could maneuver and use their great numerical strength to advantage. Taylor, in a manner reminiscent of his mentor Stonewall Jackson, chose the former course of action and immediately issued orders to mass his small army.

Taylor chose to make his stand about four miles south of Mansfield, in an open field about 1,200 yards long and 800 yards wide where he could mount an ambush. He would post his men on the northern edge of the woods to conceal them from the unsuspecting Federals, who would move in from the southern edge, with Taylor's slowly withdrawing cavalry drawing them into the trap. After forcing them to deploy, Taylor would wrap his flanks around the Union force and spring the trap.[60]

Taylor had on hand about 9,000 troops[61] of all arms plus Churchill's 4,400 under his control at Keatchie. Taylor ordered Churchill's division to march to Mansfield at dawn on April 7. The rest of his force fell back from Pleasant Hill toward Mansfield. These troops consisted of Walker and Mouton's infantry divisions; they would deliver the decisive blow of the ambush. He left Green forward to skirmish with the enemy, slowly falling back as the bait for the trap.[62]

There was only one problem with the plan. It ran counter to the departmental commander's guidance. Taylor had to find a way to engage Banks without appearing to disobey his superior. Taylor dispatched a message to Smith saying that he wanted to "hazard a general engagement" and requesting a reply "before daylight tomorrow." Taylor sent the message at 9:00 on the evening of the 7th by a courier he knew could not reach Smith in time to issue a reply. By the time the courier reached Shreveport, Taylor would have already fought an engagement[63] would — but he not have violated his orders from Smith.

The men in the ranks were certainly ready to stop running and anxious for a fight. Poche wrote in his diary that "our reinforcements have all arrived ... and we are filled with the hope that we will repulse the enemy." Another officer, upon learning of Taylor's plans, stated that "every officer present was enthusiastic in his approval." Blessington, of Walker's division, could not wait to recover ground lost in the long retreat from Simmesport.[64]

Kirby Smith believed that he had his irascible subordinate under control. Taylor, however, aggressively sought to frustrate Union designs. Everyone, it seems, was at cross purposes with each other. The force of Taylor's will would dominate Banks on the battlefield, but it would push his boss — Smith — away from him when he needed his support most. Meanwhile, two opposing armies were preparing to clash in the largest engagements ever fought on Louisiana soil.

Chapter 5

"The State of Things ... Was Very Discouraging"

The march from Grand Ecore to Mansfield represented the zenith of Union fortunes during the Red River Campaign. Up to this time Federal forces had enjoyed nothing but success, but this was about to change. Taylor had prepared a reception for the men in blue that would send them reeling back from whence they came. Kirby Smith would dampen Taylor's elation by taking most of his army to pursue Steele in Arkansas. Though the Union army would receive a stinging repulse, Taylor would know that he had not finished the job started at Mansfield and that his reduced force could do little to complete the destruction of Banks.

Franklin moved out smartly on April 6 with the Union commander still confident that the Confederates would show little resistance. Lee's cavalry division took the lead of the army followed by its immense wagon train. The infantry of the XIII and XIX Corps fell in behind Lee's train, bringing along their own massive, 700-wagon train. A. J. Smith's men, minus T. Kilby Smith's division — which had accompanied Porter's fleet up to Loggy Bayou — had the rear. The advance of the 6th proceeded in relative peace. However, the further the Union army moved, the more strung out the march column became on that narrow road in the "pine desert." By the evening of the 6th Lee's advance was approaching a place called Crump's Corners. Here Lee camped for the night, while the tail of the column had not yet cleared Grand Ecore. The column, with its huge and necessary train, now extended over twenty miles in length, but Franklin showed no concern for closing the column within supporting distance of all units.[1] Perhaps Banks' overconfidence had infected Franklin's prudence in terms of security.

5. "The State of Things ... Was Very Discouraging"   69

The same day the Federals made their move from Grand Ecore, Taylor received his first significant reinforcements. Thomas Green's cavalry arrived from Texas, providing Taylor not only with additional striking power but with a reliable intelligence-gathering unit as well. Green reported to Taylor near Pleasant Hill and received orders to delay the advance of the enemy while slowly moving back toward Mansfield. South of Mansfield, Taylor would deploy his infantry for battle and await the Federal advance, using Green to draw them in. Green's cavalry, in three brigades commanded by Arthur Bagby, Hamilton Bee, and James Major, deployed forward to Pleasant Hill to meet the Union advance.[2]

On the morning of the 7th, Lee broke camp at Crump's and pressed on toward Pleasant Hill. This forward movement finally gave A. J. Smith's men at the rear of the column the opportunity to leave Grand Ecore. Smith's westerners took great delight in jeering at Franklin's "dandies" because of their heavily laden trains. Smith's men were accustomed to traveling light and they accused their counterparts of packing in extra paper collars for the trip to Shreveport. The jeers at the rear aside, the day would provide hot work for Lee's cavalry at the front.[3]

As the Union cavalrymen moved toward Pleasant Hill, Lee began to see ominous signs that the Confederates intended to contest the march. Small groups of Rebels stepped up the harassment of the column steadily until it reached Wilson's Farm, a small clearing three miles north of Pleasant Hill. There, Brigadier General James P. Major had prepared a reception for Lee that would convince him that the nature of the march had indeed changed. As Lee recalled,

> I found the country densely wooded. We were then going along a single road, in which it was difficult for wagons to meet and pass each other. Our way led through ... a sparsely settled country, where we found no people. We met the enemy on a little hill. They were mostly cavalry and mounted infantry, but they had dismounted. We went into action, putting in a brigade at first. The enemy drove that brigade back about a hundred yards. I then put in the other two brigades dismounted and drove the enemy.[4]

At 2:00 Lee sent General William B. Franklin a message informing him of the skirmish at Wilson's Farm. "I shall advance a little cautiously," he commented with a note of alarm. He closed requesting an infantry brigade to support his movements. Unperturbed, Franklin informed Lee that since the firing had ceased he would not send infantry support. "The general directs that you proceed tonight as far as possible with your whole train in order to give the infantry room to advance tomorrow," Franklin added.[5]

Lee did as ordered and continued another seven miles to Carroll's Mill, where he found elements of Green's cavalry drawn up in line of battle again — this time with a four-gun battery in support. Lee again sent for reinforcements, but Franklin, by this time irate, admonished Lee that he "must fight them alone — that was what he was there for." Franklin suspected that Lee simply had the jitters, a conclusion that gave rise to what one staffer called "a general tone of censure at headquarters regarding the cavalry." Franklin believed that Lee had blown the affair out of proportion and refused to believe that the Rebels intended anything more that harassment. Lee, still concerned, arrayed his division in line of battle and had his men lie on their arms for the night.[6]

Green's handling of his men delighted Richard Taylor, who observed some of the fighting around Wilson's Farm. He wrote in his memoirs that he "enjoyed his method of managing his wild horsemen: and he certainly accomplished more with them than anyone else could have done." Green, a veteran of the Texas Revolution and the Mexican War, had a reputation for hard fighting. One officer described him as "a general of no mean ability and his courage, dash and bulldog hang-on-a-tiveness was [sic] unsurpassed during the whole war."[7] Taylor, now confident the cavalry could perform its task, issued final orders to his infantry to form at the prescribed location ready to fight on the morning of the 8th.[8] He then sent his late dispatch to Kirby Smith.

Smith, in accordance with a proclamation from the Confederate government, had declared April 8 a day of fasting and prayer and suspension of all military operations.[9] He received Taylor's dispatch on the morning of the 8th and drafted a rather ambiguous reply around noon.

> A general engagement now could not be given with our full force. Reenforcements are moving up — not very large, it is true. If we fall back without a battle you will be thrown out of the best country for supplies. I would compel the enemy to develop his intentions, selecting a position in rear where we can give him battle before he can march on and occupy Shreveport. I will order down ... every available man before a battle is fought. Let me know as soon as you are convinced that a general advance is being made and I will come to the front.[10]

Smith then sent it to Taylor by courier. By now, however, the reply did not matter, for Taylor had already engaged the enemy in the battle that would represent the turning point of the campaign.

General Banks arrived at Franklin's Pleasant Hill headquarters at 9:00 on April 7. One of his aides, a Colonel Clark, briefed him on the situation. Learning of Franklin's refusal to send Lee the reinforcements he had requested, Banks pointedly ordered Franklin to send a brigade of infantry to Lee "by daylight to-morrow morning." Franklin complied, instructing General Ransom of the 4th Division, XIII Corps, to provide a brigade (Landram's) to Lee.[11]

The next morning dawned bright and clear, promising a pleasant march. Lee's cavalry, now closely supported by Colonel Landram's infantry brigade, filed into the narrow road. Lee immediately made contact with Taylor's lead elements, General Hamilton Bee's cavalry brigade. Bee had relieved Major's brigade the night before with orders to continue the delaying action. Bee executed his mission in fine fashion, allowing Taylor's infantry divisions to solidify their dispositions.[12]

Taylor had the ambush set by mid-morning of the 8th. Taylor's force straddled the Mansfield road south of the town in an arc on the north side of the open field. Walker's three brigades went in line of battle about 500 yards on either side of the road. Walker's force — the anvil — would absorb the initial blows from the Union force as they walked into the trap. Mouton fell in on Walker's left with his two brigades and would act as the hammer against the anvil. Green's cavalry filed in on each flank as they drew the unsuspecting Federals into the trap. Bee's men fell in on Walker's right. Taylor pulled together a small reserve, consisting of De Bray's cavalry brigade with a battery, to exploit success realized by the main body and pursue the enemy. Churchill's men moved as rapidly as they could down from Keatchie to provide some extra punch.[13]

With everything now set, Taylor's determination to strike and dominate Banks reached its zenith. While inspecting the line Taylor flagged down Brigadier General Camille J. de Polignac, commanding one of Mouton's brigades, and told him that he would "fight Banks here if he has a million men." Further down the line Taylor told the men of the Louisiana Brigade of Mouton's division that they would "draw the first blood." This attitude permeated from Taylor throughout the ranks and steeled the men for the pending action.[14]

The men in the ranks were anxious to finally come to grips with the enemy. One young Rebel wrote in his diary, "our boys are very anxious to have a 'Hand' in the game."[15] Blessington in Walker's Division reported that even though they were outnumbered, knowledge that he was fighting for his home made him feel "thrice armed."[16] Poche stated in his diary that the preparations "showed clearly that some action was contemplated ... and we are filled with hope."[17] One Rebel perhaps summed it up best saying, "we are ready and eager to meet the damned rascals."

At 11:45, Lee's men, pressing Bee's cavalry back, reached the south end of the clearing. The Rebels kept up a desultory fire, encouraging the

Federals to continue after them — thus baiting the trap. Lee later testified that they moved into "a large open field of perhaps a mile in extent in each direction. The road ran over a hill [Honeycutt Hill] which has an admirable position, and I was surprised, as we came out of the woods, to find that the enemy had abandoned it." Lee stopped here and wrote a message to Franklin describing the nature of the resistance thus far. Landram also sent a note to his corps commander requesting relief of his brigade. Landram's men (they were actually of Emerson's brigade and Landram was the division commander personally accompanying them on the march) had skirmished all day through thickets for eight miles and were nearing exhaustion. Brigadier General Thomas Ransom, upon receiving this note, personally led forward the 2d Brigade of the 4th Division so he could have a look around for himself. Ransom stated that there was something "in the air" that made him feel uneasy.[18]

Ransom, after struggling past the ponderous cavalry train, found Lee had arrayed his forces in a "fine position" on Honeycutt Hill. Landram's troops straddled the Mansfield road on the crest of the hill. Just off the road Captain Ormand Nims' artillery battery shelled the woods on the far side of the field, where the Rebels were posted. On each flank Lee had posted a brigade of cavalry to protect the infantry. Lee had stopped on Honeycutt Hill for two reasons. First, he wanted to give Landram's worn troops a rest, and second, Lee knew he had run into something solid. Lee and Ransom surveyed the woods opposite them and perceived that they could not proceed farther with the force they had on hand. The two commanders reported observing a strong line of infantry supported by artillery and cavalry that moved laterally to get around Lee's flanks.[19]

At about 3:00 General Banks and his staff rode to the front to find out why the column had halted. Upon arrival Banks ordered Lee "to move immediately on Mansfield" without even surveying the situation. Lee, dumbfounded, vigorously protested that "we should be most gloriously flogged" if he advanced. Banks, taken aback by this demonstration, countermanded his own order and sent a staff officer to bring up more infantry.[20] While Banks wallowed in indecision, Taylor itched to whip the enemy.

Bee's cavalrymen had passed through Taylor's lines around noon and taken up their post to the right of Walker's Division. Contrary to plan, the Federals had not blindly pursued the bait. The Union force had stopped short of springing the trap by occupying Honeycutt Hill to the Confederate front. Taylor now feared that the Federals were bringing up additional troops to break his line; he knew that if the Federals brought up their entire army it would outnumber his by more than two to one. Since

5. "The State of Things ... Was Very Discouraging" 73

Mansfield — This is the view from Nim's battery looking northwest toward the point where Walker's division emerged from the woods.

waiting any longer would defeat his strategy of hitting pieces of the Union army, Taylor now attempted to provoke the Federals into attacking him by throwing some infantry forward and opening up with a battery. The attempt backfired when the Federal infantry simply threw the Confederates back and Nim's battery silenced the Rebel guns. The clock now approached 4:00 in the afternoon and Taylor's patience reached its end. He turned to Mouton and issued him orders to lead the advance of the whole line.[21]

Mouton, in theatrical fashion, mounted his horse, drew his sword, and with a yell led them forward. Lieutenant Poche of Gray's brigade remembered receiving orders to "leap over the fence" to the front. Then, "with resounding yells we began running and stormed the enemy." Mouton's division immediately ran into trouble as the Federal line unleashed a volley. "At a distance of one hundred fifty feet the enemy opened fire and we were severely battered.... The balls and grape shot crashing about us ... beat our soldiers down."[22] This volley delivered by the men of the 77th and 130th Illinois staggered the assault momentarily. Mouton, seemingly ubiquitous on this day, placed himself here and rallied his Louisianans. Three minié balls passed through Mouton's chest and he fell mortally wounded, but his leadership maintained the pressure against the Federals.[23]

Mansfield — This snake rail fence stands in the approximate location where the 77th Illinois made its defense. Fences like this one dotted the field in 1864 and made readily accessible breastworks for the troops.

While Mouton's division kept the Union center occupied, Walker's division charged up the road and around the Federal left. Blessington recorded that his company received orders to "Fix Bayonets" and march forward at the "double quick." Then:

> We immediately commenced advancing in the direction of the enemy, who were posted behind a rail-fence. They greeted our coming with a perfect shower of leaden hail. The men shouted at the top of their voices ... many indulging in jokes and witticisms, such as, "This kind of ball-music is fine for dancing." "Here comes another iron pill!" The fire of the enemy increases; it is terrible. He is gathering all his strength for one final struggle. Shells, canister, and bullets are falling around like a hailstorm ... still there is no faltering, but wild cheers, and on they press.[24]

Walker's division fared better than Mouton's, sweeping everything before it. Within minutes of launching their assault, the Texans had fatally broken Lee's flank, forcing the blue soldiers to fall back.

Now the cavalry joined the fray with Green's men curling around the vulnerable Union flanks. Ransom described the Confederate formation as

5. "The State of Things ... Was Very Discouraging"   75

"the wings of a V.... Every time he [Lee] attempted to form a line of battle the wings of the V enveloped his flanks and closed down on them like a nut cracker." While stubbornly attempting to assist Lee's defense, Ransom fell with a severe knee wound that required his evacuation. Banks, also on hand, seemed oblivious to the situation and did nothing while the Union line collapsed around him.[25]

As the Federal left collapsed, the entire line fell away. One by one the blue regiments peeled out of the line from left to right. They conducted an orderly withdrawal until suddenly Green's cavalrymen appeared in the rear of Lee's line. This precipitated a rout. Nim's battery, now exposed, tried to limber the guns and leave the field. The Confederates, however, shot most of the horses, forcing the battery commander to abandon three of his pieces.[26]

While Lee attempted to rally how fractured line, Banks suddenly realized how precarious his situation was, and ordered up reinforcements. Brigadier General Robert A. Cameron responded to the call by double quicking his 3rd Division of the XIII Army Corps up the road to stem the Confederate tide. Cameron had not gone far when he became entangled

Mansfield — This is the location from which Walker's Texans stepped out of the woods for their attack. At approximately the center of the photograph is the location of Nim's battery.

with the cavalry train. He reported finding "the road so full of teams and stragglers on foot" that it was "impossible to move." Finally making it through the morass jamming the road, Cameron formed a line of battle in the woods about a mile south of the Moss Plantation. That line quickly suffered the same fate as Lee's with the Confederates curling around his flanks and rolling right over the blue line.[27] The Confederates scooped up more guns and many prisoners with this attack, including the famous Chicago Merchantile Battery. Franklin admitted on arriving at the front that "the state of things ... was very discouraging," and soon after he fell, painfully wounded.[28]

Taylor now had his blood up. He had scored a spectacular victory by massing his force against individual pieces of the Union army, but he knew the victory was not complete. In Jacksonian style, he intended to relentlessly pursue his enemy to achieve a decisive defeat. The problem now was the onset of darkness and all those wagons loaded down with luxuries unknown to Taylor's scarecrows, who became as disorganized by the victory as the Federals had by the defeat. In spite of the challenges, Taylor pushed the divisions under Walker, Polignac — now commanding Mouton's division — and Green forward to complete the victory.[29]

While Lee and Cameron's men struggled to get out of the path of the vicious mob of Rebels, the XIX Corps was moving into a stout position along a creek called Chatman Bayou. Brigadier General William H. Emory had heard the sounds of battle rise to a crescendo that afternoon and without orders had quickened the pace of his march toward the sound of the guns. Emory commanded the 1st Division of the XIX Corps, and held the respect of his peers in the Union army. During the Mexican War he won two brevets for bravery and early in this war he had earned distinction. On the late evening of April 8 he would finally stem the rout streaming down from Mansfield.[30]

As Emory moved along that afternoon he ran into the unmistakable signs of a headlong retreat. Among the stream of stragglers was an ambulance bearing the wounded General Ransom. Ransom briefed Emory on the situation and the need to stem the tide. Around the same time an order arrived from Franklin calling for Emory to hasten to the front. Emory now moved forward to select a defensible position to stop the victorious Rebels. The position he chose was a small hill fronted by the creek with a small orchard, known locally as Pleasant Grove, beyond that. Emory put his troops in line straddling the Mansfield road, altogether about 5,000 men. Banks, who had tried in vain to rally the remnants of Lee's and Cameron's commands, now happened upon Emory's troops. He encouraged these men to rally on the XIX Corps soldiers.[31]

5. "The State of Things ... Was Very Discouraging" 77

The van of the Confederates now came into view in the lengthening shadows of the day. Rebel commanders threw their soldiers in a headlong charge against this solid blue line. A sheet of flame from the Union line easily broke the charge. The Confederates, however, were not yet ready to call it quits. Confederate units began to work their way around Emory's flanks in an effort to roll up the division. Emory, in the right place at the right time, ordered his flank units to refuse the line, forming right angles to meet the attackers. The assailants now ran into the re-formed Union line and again into a volley from Emory's units. With darkness almost complete the Rebel tide receded, putting an end to "the evil day."[32]

Taylor, frustrated by not completing his victory, had still scored a major success. The Confederate army at the battle of Mansfield numbered about 10,000 men while the Federal force numbered slightly over 15,000.[33] Taylor, in each of the three engagements of the battle, brought the full mass of his troops to bear, while hitting individual fragments of the Federal force. This allowed him to fight each with an advantage of numbers while actually outnumbered overall. Taylor's generalship had proven superior to that of Banks, with the battle representing the turning point of the campaign.

Taylor lost about 1,000 soldiers in the battle while the Federals lost over 2,800.[34] He captured over 200 wagons, 1,000 horses, twenty artillery pieces, and thousands of small arms, while losing no appreciable equipment himself. Taylor now began to make plans to follow up his victory the next day and to compose a dispatch to Smith.[35]

Smith's ambiguous dispatch of April 8 denying authorization for a general engagement had reached Taylor late that afternoon as the Confederates swept down the Mansfield road in pursuit of the Federals. "Too late sir," he replied, "The battle is already won."[36] Taylor had disobeyed his orders, but his success more than made up for the miscue. An irritated Smith, however, would soon reach the battlefield and squelch Taylor's future plans.

Before Smith could get there, Taylor would fight another engagement in an attempt to finish off the reeling Federals. Churchill's and Parsons' divisions now arrived at the front and Taylor planned to use them as his main effort the following day. "Arkansas and Missouri have the fight in the morning," he wrote to Walker. "They must do what Texas and Louisiana did today."[37] Taylor ordered Green's cavalry to pursue the Federals at dawn to maintain contact with and pressure on the enemy. He then ordered Churchill and Parsons to the front of the column to serve as the spearhead for the next day's fight. Walker and Polignac would follow the Arkansans and Missourians and act as the secondary effort for Taylor's attack since they had fought hard on the 8th.[38]

The reverse of April 8 had jeopardized Banks' visions of stardom and shaken him to the core. However, Emory's successful defense in the evening at Pleasant Grove gave Banks reason to hope. If he could now rally his army here, he might yet be able to take Shreveport. Banks summoned his subordinates to a council of war at Pleasant Grove in the late evening following the battle. He argued that the army could resume the march the next day, but the others disagreed. The troops assembled at Pleasant Grove, they contended, were exhausted and Smith's command, still seventeen miles distant, could not close with the column because of the poor condition of the road. Furthermore, the surrounding countryside was destitute of water, with the nearest source located at Pleasant Hill. Their recommendation was that the army fall back to Pleasant Hill where it could concentrate with A. J. Smith's men and also obtain water.[39] Faced with the protests of a group of professional officers, Banks conceded defeat and consented to withdraw to Pleasant Hill instead of advancing. Richard B. Irwin, his assistant adjutant general, would write an appropriate epitaph for the events of April 8:

> So great a change had these few hours wrought that the same sun rose upon an army marching full of confidence that within two days Shreveport would be in its grasp, and set upon the same army defeated, brought to bay, its campaign ruined....[40]

The retirement began at 10:00 on the 8th, "as dark a night as I ever knew," General William Dwight would testify. Banks and his bedraggled army arrived at Pleasant Hill in the early morning hours of April 9. Upon their arrival, Banks made dispositions for defense. Before positioning the troops, Banks first sent the enormous trains on the road back to Grand Ecore with Lee's cavalry as a guard. The deployment, when completed, looked like the work of a blind man rather than of military professionals. Each subordinate commander placed his men in his own way without reference to an overall plan for the army. Banks, in turn, did not check the line when completed and this nearly led to disaster.

Before Banks' men arrived at Pleasant Hill, A. J. Smith had arrived there and pushed forward a brigade—Shaw's—from his command. As Banks pulled in, Emory's Division split to cover Shaw's flanks. Dwight's brigade went to Shaw's right to cover a deep wooded ravine, while Shaw's brigade straddled the Mansfield–Pleasant Hill road. Benedict's brigade went to Shaw's left, but he did not tie in his right with Shaw's flank, leaving a 500-yard gap between the two commands. In the village of Pleasant Hill proper, A. J. Smith formed the rest of his command about a half mile in rear of the rest of the army. This left Benedict's left in the air as well. Banks failed

5. "The State of Things ... Was Very Discouraging"   79

to properly supervise and then inspect unit defensive preparations, leading to the porous Union line. The Confederates had a magnificent opportunity to finish off the unsuspecting Federals.

Taylor set out at dawn with Green so he could assess the situation and hastily determine a plan of attack. Taylor reported running across "many stragglers, scattered arms, and burning wagons, showing the haste of the enemy's retreat." About a mile from Pleasant Hill, Green found the enemy and deployed to learn the enemy's dispositions and strength. Following the reconnaissance Taylor formulated the details for an attack to finish the previous day's work.[41]

The village of Pleasant Hill sat atop a low hill surrounded by several farm clearings. Three roads radiated from the village, starting with the road from Grand Ecore leading through Pleasant Hill to Mansfield. The Sabine River Road led due west to the crossings into Texas, while the Fort Jesup Road ran south to the old military post. Beyond the clearings surrounding the village were pine woods with thick underbrush cut by deep ravines.

Taylor planned to execute a wide flanking movement to the right in order to come up behind Pleasant Hill and cut off the bluecoats' route to Grand Ecore. Churchill and Parsons' combined force would make the flank

Pleasant Hill — This photograph was taken at the location of the old village looking down the Mansfield Road, facing the direction of the Confederate attack.

march around the village through the thick woods until they struck the Fort Jesup Road. At that point, Churchill would make a left wheel, handrailing the road until reaching the road to Grand Ecore. This would cut off the Federals from communication with their rear and effectively surround the Army of the Gulf. Green's cavalry would form the extreme left, prepared to turn the Federal right. Walker's Division would form the center and make an assault when he heard Churchill's attack commence. Polignac's depleted division gave Taylor a small reserve that he would use to exploit any success. Taylor issued his orders and waited for the infantry to arrive.[42]

Churchill and Parsons arrived in the vicinity Pleasant Hill at about 1:00 P.M. When they arrived, Taylor noted with "a glance ... that his men were too much exhausted to attack." Therefore, Taylor accorded them two hours' rest before beginning the attack. In the meantime, he became acquainted with a Mr. T. J. Williams, a former sheriff of De Soto Parish. This man was intimately familiar with every road and path in the area and volunteered to guide the flanking force down to the Fort Jesup Road. Taylor accepted the offer and assigned Mr. Williams to Churchill as a guide. As the clock approached 3:00 Taylor ordered the commencement of the attack.[43]

Banks' men had completed their defensive preparations by mid-morning on the 9th. The pleasant spring day passed quietly for these men until late afternoon, giving them a false sense of security. Banks made frequent visits to the front line to encourage the troops with "kind words." About midday Banks had lunch with his staff and commanders. The absence of the enemy convinced the commander that the army would not fight that day and his hopes for regaining the initiative again rose. His aspirations were crushed around 5:00 when Churchill's command came crashing in on the Union left.[44]

Churchill and Parsons moved through the pine woods around the Union left guided by Mr. Williams. It took these divisions about an hour and a half to work their way down to the Sabine Road. Here, in spite of the presence of their erstwhile guide, the Confederates made their left wheel to move in rear of the Union force. This failure in navigation proved a costly mistake. At about 5:00, after forming into attack columns, Churchill commenced the attack.[45]

Churchill and Parsons' assault landed squarely on the left flank of Benedict's exposed brigade. The Confederates, with two divisions, quickly overlapped the blue brigade and found the gap between Shaw's left and Benedict's right. With the graybacks now heading for their rear, Benedict's unit disintegrated. In the melee, Colonel Benedict fell dead and his brigade's retreat turned into a rout. Colonel Francis Fessenden of the 30th Maine took command and attempted to restore some semblance of order with little success. The Confederates moved into the village of Pleasant Hill itself "like an avalanche," successfully driving a wedge between Emory's and Smith's commands.[46]

When Walker heard the sounds of battle from Churchill's front he immediately launched his assault, which landed on Shaw's brigade of A. J. Smith's command. Major Joseph L. Brent, Taylor's chief of artillery, fired the initial volleys on the left in support of Walker's advance, driving away a Union battery on the attack route. Walker's division found Shaw's left flank exposed and quickly exploited its vulnerability. Shaw's brigade collapsed and fell back toward Pleasant Hill, but during the course of the assault Walker suffered a painful wound to the groin, forcing him by order of Taylor from the field. Green's cavalry on the Confederate left believed that Walker's men had precipitated a rout of the entire line and the aggressive cavalryman launched a headlong assault.[47]

General Emory, witnessing a second disaster in the making in as many days, took steps to plug the holes. He ordered Brigadier General James McMillan, in reserve, to come to the aid of Dwight's brigade, which Shaw left unsupported when his brigade retreated. Emory's action stemmed Walker's advance, emptied many of Green's saddles and stabilized the Union right. With the right holding, A. J. Smith — positioned on the Fort Jesup Road — opportunely threw his divisions in on the unsuspecting right flank of Parsons' division.[48]

The elated Confederates of Churchill's and Parsons' divisions were sure the day was won as the sun began casting long evening shadows. A. J. Smith had other ideas and bided his time on their flank until the right moment. When disorganization from the assault reached its height, Smith ordered Mower to advance with both XVI Corps divisions to roll up the Confederates' right. Taylor stated that "finding themselves assaulted on all sides, the Missourians retreated hastily, and ... fell into much confusion." As Mower's force moved forward, the commands of Shaw and Benedict regrouped and joined the assault.[49] The Confederates now found themselves retreating in confusion — in contrast to the euphoria of victory they had felt to this point.

Walker's reserve brigade, Scurry's, entered the fray to try to stabilize Taylor's line. Blessington said, "General Scurry expected to be assisted by the troops he went to reinforce, but the panic-stricken troops were too slow in rallying to do any good." With Taylor now facing the prospect of having his fine victory of Mansfield squandered, he put his last reserves into the fight. Polignac's division had borne the brunt of the fighting at

Pleasant Hill — The "Dog Trot" House is the only original building still at the battlefield. The Confederates used it as a hospital after the battle.

Mansfield, but now prepared to sacrifice themselves again, to prevent a rout. Brent's artillery performed great service, firing grapeshot and canister into the oncoming bluecoats to slow their advance. Polignac's men, while not stopping Smith's advance, slowed them enough to allow Churchill to disengage.[50]

The Federals, humiliated on the 8th, now tasted victory. They drove the Rebels all the way beyond the Sabine Road northward to the Mansfield Road. The counterattack, however, came to a halt as complete darkness prevented further movements through the thick and smoky underbrush. General Banks, flushed alternately with relief and elation, found A. J. Smith to offer his gratitude. Smith in his official report stated that Banks clasped his hand firmly — as if on the political stump — and exclaimed, "God bless you, General; you have saved the army."[51]

Banks had reason to feel good about the day's events. At Mansfield, he had suffered a serious tactical reverse that had threatened to derail the entire campaign. Pleasant Hill seemed to have changed the fortunes of the campaign, offering Banks the opportunity to get back on track. Pleasant Hill was a complete tactical victory for the Union army. Banks' army held the field after the engagement and had suffered fewer losses in terms of percentages.[52] Strategically, though, sustaining further advance in a country destitute of supplies could prove impossible. Furthermore, up until this point Banks had failed to exhibit the strong will and leadership required to win the campaign. Would Banks, now armed with a tactical victory, have the force of will to turn back toward Shreveport and take the prize?

General Banks held another council of war to decide what to do. He came to the meeting having decided to turn about and follow up the victory of Pleasant Hill. Banks proffered his opinion at the meeting and asked for those of the generals in attendance. Most of the generals objected to Banks' views for several reasons. First, the army could get no support from the naval force on their current route. Second, nobody knew the current status of the fleet or if it could even navigate to Shreveport given the low stage of the river. Third, Frederick Steele's situation was unknown due to prohibitive communications. Next, the calendar read the 10th of April, giving Banks only five days to capture Shreveport and return A. J. Smith's men to Sherman. Finally, the howling wilderness of west Louisiana exacerbated the tough supply situation — especially the scarcity of water. As the council enumerated these reasons, Banks's resolve to press forward evaporated. "[T]herefore, after consulting with my officers, I concluded, against

Pleasant Hill — This is the approximate position where Polignac's division hit the Federal line in their attack. In the distance is where the old village once stood.

my own judgment, to fall back to Grand Ecore and reorganize," he wrote.[53] Banks then issued orders to begin the retreat. Politician Banks' propensity to command by coalition prevented him from enforcing his own will. This flaw helped doom the campaign and ensured it would not recover. Thus, Banks turned a tactical victory into a strategic defeat. Conversely, Taylor's aggressiveness and knowledge of Banks' shortcomings enabled him to cow Banks into retreat, achieving a strategic victory.[54]

The fractious nature of the Union command during the campaign also contributed to its failure. A. J. Smith did not attend the meeting because he was not a part of the army's inner circle. He learned of the outcome of the meeting only when he received orders to withdraw in the early-morning hours of the 10th. Smith became livid and went to confront the commanding general. He asked Banks to reconsider on the grounds that the army could follow up its victory of the previous evening. Also, Smith found the prospect of leaving his wounded on the field distasteful. He could not move Banks, and now considered a drastic and mutinous measure.[55]

Smith went to Franklin, still second in command, to persuade him to weigh in with Banks to continue the advance. Franklin said that he could not do this. Smith then proposed that Franklin arrest Banks and take over command of the expedition. Franklin, in disbelief that Smith even considered such a proposal, asked, "Smith, don't you know this is mutiny?" Without saying another word, Smith left to execute his orders.[56] That Smith — a career professional officer of impeccable credentials — could even think of such a move demonstrates the strained command climate that paralyzed the Federal side during the campaign.

The soldiers in the Union army could not believe a retreat had been ordered. The men believed they had won a great victory. More than one Union soldier would turn to a buddy in the ranks and ask, "Did we lose?" The soldiers of the army began to hurl comments filled with bitterness and derision at the commanding general. During the retreat from Pleasant Hill the troops sarcastically dubbed their commander "Napoleon" P. Banks. When Banks moved along the column it became a common occurrence for catcalls to greet him as he passed. Some soldiers even serenaded him by singing:

> In 1861, we all skedaddled to Washington,
> In 1864, we all skedaddled to Grand Ecore.

The army had in effect given Banks a vote of no confidence in his leadership.[57]

5. "The State of Things ... Was Very Discouraging"   85

While dissension and mutiny threatened Union cooperation, fireworks were bursting over in the Confederate camp on the evening of April 9. Smith had received a series of dispatches from Taylor on the 8th and in the early morning of the 9th announcing the results of the fighting at Mansfield.[58] Smith, thoroughly disturbed, decided to ride down from Shreveport to confer with Taylor. While Taylor might have gained a victory, Smith worried that Taylor had only hit the advanced guard of Banks' army. Smith felt that once massed, Banks' forces would pounce on Taylor, brushing him aside and making Shreveport wide open to capture.[59] Leaving Shreveport at 4:00 in the morning, Smith did not arrive at Pleasant Hill until 10:00 at night on the 9th. Upon arrival he immediately sought out his district commander.

General Taylor made his repose that night with Colonel Henry Gray of the Louisiana Brigade of Polignac's division. Taylor felt depressed over the reverse at Pleasant Hill coming on the heels of the victory at Mansfield. Taylor knew his men had suffered a costly defeat and also knew that the weight of responsibility rested with himself. He wrote after the war, "[T]hese were creditable results [the results of the combined battles of Mansfield and Pleasant Hill], yet of much less importance than those that would have been accomplished but for my blunder at Pleasant Hill. Instead of intrusting the important attack by my right to a subordinate I should have conducted it myself and taken Polignac's division to sustain it." This conclusion did not change his opinion of Banks, however. Even though Banks had stopped his attack, Taylor wrote: "I was confident that the enemy had no intention of resuming the offensive." Based on this conviction Taylor planned to continue to push Banks back to Grand Ecore.[60]

The exertions of the previous week had taken their toll on Taylor, and when he lay down he immediately fell off into a deep sleep. Smith found Taylor sleeping in the road with Gray's brigade. Approaching the field at Pleasant Hill, Smith had witnessed the carnage of the battle. He would write, "Our repulse at Pleasant Hill was so complete and our command was so disorganized that had Banks followed up his success vigorously he would have met but feeble opposition to his advance on Shreveport."[61] Smith woke Taylor and immediately expressed his misgivings about the state of things. A witness reported his saying, "Bad business, bad business General." Taylor disagreed, replying, "I don't know, General. What is the trouble." Smith said anxiously, "Banks will be upon you at daylight tomorrow with his whole army." To this Taylor confidently retorted, "Well, General, if you will listen, you will hear Banks' artillery moving out now on their retreat." Taylor then began to express his wish to follow Banks and to attempt to destroy him at Grand Ecore.[62] Smith disagreed. After a discussion around a campfire, the meeting adjourned with the commanders agreeing to reconvene at Mansfield to discuss future plans.

The two met at Mansfield on April 10. Smith stated up front his intent to turn on Steele rather than pursuing Banks further. Smith still believed that Steele presented the greatest threat to the Trans-Mississippi Department. With Banks now in retreat Smith wanted to take Churchill's and Parsons' infantry divisions back to Arkansas to contend with Steele. This logic was in line with his Fabian defensive policy, and now seemed the perfect time to implement the second phase of the defense. Smith later wrote, "I deemed it imprudent to follow Banks below Grand Ecore with my whole force and leave Steele so near Shreveport." He then "ordered all the Arkansas and Texas [Walker's] troops to Arkansas."[63]

Taylor argued that continuing to harry Banks was the true opportunity. "It was pointed out that the water in Red River was falling, and navigation becoming more and more difficult." "We had but to strike vigorously to capture or destroy both [the fleet and Banks],"[64] he wrote. Further, Steele would retire to Little Rock when he heard of Banks' demise. Smith still disagreed, writing, "To win this campaign his [Steele's] column must be destroyed."[65] He reiterated the order to send the infantry to Shreveport. Walker noted after the war:

> Doubtless it was to have been expected that the whole Confederate force would have thrown itself upon the track of [Banks'] army, but unfortunately for the Confederates, General E. K. Smith was not the leader to comprehend the true line of action.[66]

Taylor considered the taking of any of his infantry a serious blow to his plans, but the taking of Walker's Texans defanged him and angered him. This would leave Taylor with little more than 5,000 men to pursue Banks' 25,000. He did, however, relent in his insistence on pursuing Banks and offered to accompany Smith to Arkansas.[67] The rift between the two commanders was widening, and over the next couple weeks it would rip wide open.

In the meantime, Taylor had already issued orders to pursue Banks with whatever force he still had available. Taylor had his cavalry under Green move by a country road toward the Red River to try to cut Porter's fleet off from Grand Ecore. Intelligence reports had kept Taylor informed of the fleet's progress and he intended to have them feel his wrath as well. With Bee's brigade and the rest of the infantry — Polignac's — Taylor set out on the 10th to harass Banks on his line of retreat. Taylor ordered Brigadier General St. John R. Liddell to impede the fleet on his side of the river. He was determined not to let Banks and Porter escape and stated that "He deserved to wear a fool's cap for a helmet" if they did.[68] Taylor then went to Shreveport to push needed supplies forward to sustain the pursuit and confer with Smith.

On April 10, following the reverse at Mansfield and Pleasant Hill, Banks sent out a covey of couriers with cryptic messages to Admiral Porter. A Captain Andres of the 14th New York Cavalry found Kilby Smith on the evening of the 10th as he pressed inland to Springfield, where he was to rendezvous with Banks. Andres told Kilby Smith of the reverses and delivered a verbal message stating that Smith should immediately reverse course and move back downriver. Smith refused to believe the verbal order and went to consult with Porter.[69]

Porter's confidence in the success of the expedition dropped in proportion to the water of the Red. Water levels sank a couple of inches a day, and as the fleet moved upriver his heavy gunboats frequently grounded. Upon reaching the Loggy Bayou, Porter found his further progress upriver blocked. Enterprising Confederates had sunk a huge steamer, the *New Falls City*, in the channel, effectively stopping navigation. When Kilby Smith's news reached Porter's ears he immediately recommended Smith heed the warning, fearing that the low water and aggressive Rebels would cut him off. Smith agreed, and they turned about to retreat back to Grand Ecore. When Smith arrived at Coushatta Chute on the 11th he found a courier waiting for him with a written message: "The commanding general directs you return immediately to Grand Ecore with supply steamers and your entire command." Now with written proof confirming the defeat of Banks' army, Smith and Porter made haste to reach Grand Ecore.[70]

The falling river gave Porter fits. He stated, "as long as our army could advance triumphantly it was not so bad; but we had every reason to suppose our return would be interrupted ... and we were not disappointed." Porter received a personal letter from Banks at Coushatta Chute in which Banks tried to put a positive light on the defeats. But Porter could read between the lines and knew that this was serious, saying to Gideon Welles, "two or three such victories would cost our existence." Porter's opinion of Banks — never high — plummeted. He now believed that Banks might just retreat without stopping and in the process abandon him. Porter's experience at Steele's Bayou told him that the navy would not survive long unsupported on the river. In the same letter to Welles he said, "if we are left here aground, our communications will be cut off and we will have to destroy the vessels."[71]

On both sides the command climate became more strained. In victory, Taylor and Kirby Smith irritated each other to the point where they could not even work together in a polite manner. Smith preferred to leave his self-professed most competent district commander behind in Louisiana rather than take him to Arkansas because he grew tired of Taylor's discontent. This poor command climate would prevent the realization of greater results for the campaign than Smith could fathom. In the Union camp Banks' abysmal leadership caused a near mutiny. His naval partner had so little confidence in him as to think that Banks would abandon him. The atmosphere in the Federal command had the potential to sink this army in the quagmire of the Red. But the Federals, unlike the Rebels, would begin to focus on salvaging the army instead of their petty differences.

Chapter 6
Three Wasted Opportunities

Following Mansfield and Pleasant Hill, the Confederate army had three distinct opportunities to capture or inflict another disastrous defeat on the Federal army. The Federal army and navy had their collective back against the wall after Banks pulled back from Pleasant Hill. His route of retreat would follow the line of the Red all the way back to Simmesport on the Atchafalaya, a distance of over 150 miles. The entire distance was still more or less enemy country, and every inch of the way the troublesome Confederates were sure to contest. On the river, the situation was bad even without enemy action, as the water fell at an alarming rate and threatened to ground Porter's boats. With an inadequate force, Taylor could certainly make things interesting. With his whole army intact, only his imagination would have limited Confederate possibilities for success. Fortunately for the Federal army and navy, Taylor would find little but frustration in his attempt to bag the enemy.

On April 10 elements of the Confederate cavalry moved in accordance with Taylor's plans. Bee moved into Pleasant Hill and found hundreds of Federal wounded, sure evidence of the precipitous nature of the Federal retreat. On the road leading to Grand Ecore the Confederates found thousands of small arms, abandoned accouterments, burning wagons, and supplies marking the way. Since the Federals had the jump the two armies made little contact until late in the day, when the Rebel horsemen caught up with the enemy rear guard about twenty miles from Pleasant Hill. There a sharp skirmish flared, but nothing that could slow the progress of Banks' army.[1]

Taylor's effort to cut off Porter's fleet widened the gulf between him and Kirby Smith. When scouts informed him that Banks had told the fleet to turn back, Taylor ordered Green to push Bagby and Major to the river to block it. They moved out at dawn on April 11 bound for Grand Bayou Landing, where Green intended to contest passage of the fleet. But before he could reach Grand Bayou Landing, he would have to cross the 330-foot-wide Bayou Pierre. Taylor requested a pontoon bridge from Kirby Smith to assist in getting his cavalry across. Smith failed to act, however, seriously delaying Green's crossing and forcing the cavalry to cross on a small flat. By the time the cavalry reached the opposite bank, Porter's boats had already passed Grand Bayou Landing. The next feasible place to stop the fleet's passage was Blair's Landing, further downstream — so Bagby had no choice but to press on to that location. Taylor bitterly blamed Smith's failure to send down the pontoons for the delay of his cavalry and the mix-up over the bridge served to expand the chasm between the two men.[2] Did Smith merely fail to send the pontoons or was this a subtle way for him to demonstrate who was in command? For Taylor, it represented a personal slap in the face. But for now the Confederates pushed on down the river to stop Porter.

The fleet bumped along slowly in the river with the naval officers full of anxiety concerning the safety of their boats. The gunboats husbanded the army transports to protect them from enemy action as they floated downriver. In a post-war article, Captain Thomas O. Selfridge stated that "the return of the fleet was fraught with peril." In his testimony before the Joint Congressional Committee on the Conduct of the War, Selfridge said that the vessels had run aground frequently as they made their way back to Grand Ecore. To compound the delays caused by the sandbars, Brigadier General Liddell began to make his presence felt on the north side of the river near Campti. With his small cavalry force Liddell was able to hold up the progress of the fleet for half a day, which enabled Green's cavalry to get into position at Blair's Landing.[3]

Green had driven his men hard after getting across the Bayou Pierre. By mid-afternoon of the 12th, they had pulled up on the bluffs overlooking the Red at Blair's Plantation. Simultaneously with his arrival, the Union fleet rounded a bend above the plantation. Green had made it just in time to contest the fleet's passage and the opportunity to fight elated him. Green had with him about 1,000 horsemen and three guns. Hoping to spring an ambush, he immediately formed for battle, ordering his men to hug a ditch close to the river. If he could ground one enemy boat and halt the others long enough Green felt he just might be able to destroy all of them and deal a staggering blow to the Union fleet.[4]

6. Three Wasted Opportunities

While Green formed for combat, Selfridge on the *Osage* busied himself with pulling along the cumbersome transports. As the *Osage* neared Blair's Landing, the pilot noticed the movement of some cavalry ashore dressed in blue overcoats. The pilot believed they were Union men, but Selfridge noted that horse holders were leading the horses away from the river. These men were the enemy and forming up for a fight. Selfridge gave orders to the *Osage* to take up battle stations and signaled the other boats to do the same. Before the Rebels could spring the ambush, Selfridge got off the first shots, preempting the would-be attackers.[5]

The Confederates now opened up on the shore with everything they had. The "armor"—some of it cotton bales—of the ships and the protection of the ditch kept casualties low on both sides despite the high volume of iron and lead flying back and forth. A couple of the boats drifted toward the shore and grounded in shallow water. Green, thinking he could board them, led some of his men in a wild charge into the water. Selfridge observed "an officer on a white horse" directing the troops closest to the shore and quickly ordered the *Osage*'s guns trained on this lucrative target. The *Osage* fired. "When the smoke cleared away [I] saw him no longer," Selfridge later recalled. "I learned after, that the officer killed was their General Green." The shot blew Green's head "clear from his shoulders." The Confederates suffered a crushing blow with Green's death. He had faithfully provided valuable intelligence and hard fighting, and Taylor judged his loss to be "an irreparable one."

Though the graybacks continued to fire away at the Federal fleet, for all intents and purposes the affair at Blair's Landing had ended.[6] The Confederates had done little damage to the fleet and neither side had suffered more than minimal casualties. Porter, however, "knew that he was in for it."[7] While the Confederates mourned, the Federals saw in Green's demise a reprieve of sorts. Porter himself stated that Green's presence was worth 5,000 armed Confederates.[8]

The Federal army arrived at Grand Ecore on the evening of April 11 and the troops began entrenching the place without any orders from the officers. The next day A. J. Smith, hearing of the fleet's plight, pushed out a couple of brigades to provide some additional support. This helped silence Liddell, who had again taken to harassing the fleet from the opposite bank of the Red. A. J. Smith's initiative made the rest of the trip down to Grand Ecore uneventful as far as the enemy was concerned. The fleet finally pulled in at Grand Ecore on 16 April, successfully reuniting the army and navy.[9]

As Taylor pursued Banks and Porter, he also turned up the pressure on Kirby Smith. Taylor reluctantly had agreed to give up most of his infantry to chase Steele in Arkansas, and even offered to accompany Smith to Arkansas, but he requested that Smith countermarch them in the event that Steele withdrew. Taylor believed that Steele would turn back when he heard of Banks' defeat.[10] He hoped that his early request for his troops back would make Smith turn around the infantry columns out of deference to Taylor.

On the 13th Smith rode down to Mansfield to confer with Taylor before departing for Arkansas. Taylor one last time went to great pains to convince Smith that the true way to maximum results lay in defeating Banks on the Red, but it was futile: Smith stuck to his plan to take Churchill, Parsons, and Walker. On April 14 Taylor reported to Smith, now back in Shreveport, that the three divisions were on their way to that city. Taylor followed them the next day, intent on going north with them to pursue Steele.[11]

Upon reaching Shreveport on the 15th, Taylor learned from Smith that Steele had begun a retreat, just as Taylor had predicted. His hopes skyrocketed and he pressed to have the divisions returned to Grand Ecore to complete an investment of the Union army. Taylor had Polignac's small division and the late General Green's cavalry in a loose cordon about the place, but he knew he could not hold it without the three infantry divisions. Smith, to Taylor's chagrin, refused to let the divisions go, believing that Steele presented the greatest threat and that Banks would continue to retreat. Taylor pointed out that there existed an opportunity to do more that just force Banks to retreat, but Smith would not listen.[12]

Smith delivered the ultimate slap in the face when he informed Taylor that his services were not required for the march into Arkansas. He was to remain at Shreveport in nominal command of the department to conduct affairs in Smith's absence. Smith told him that he could move forward to Grand Ecore if he believed the situation required his presence. Taylor bitterly wrote in his memoirs that Smith informed him of "all this with the curt manner of a superior to a subordinate, as if fearing remonstrance."[13]

Smith probably did fear remonstrance, knowing Taylor had an unrestrained tongue. He also likely did exactly the opposite of Taylor's wishes in an air of spite. In addition, Smith rejected Taylor's request to accompany him because he had, in all likelihood, had enough of Taylor's acidic comments and unsolicited advice. Leaving Taylor behind would free him of the close personal criticism Taylor was sure to mete out if the two had daily contact. Kirby Smith departed for Arkansas on the 16th with the divisions of Churchill, Parsons, and Walker on what Taylor referred to as a "wild goose chase."[14] In taking off on his "wild goose chase" Smith had allowed one of the great opportunities of the war to slip through his fingers. He did so in great part because his and Taylor's personalities clashed to a point at which they could not work together. Banks would break out of Grand Ecore within days.

In his post-war memoirs, Smith's chief of staff: Brigadier William Boggs, wrote:

> He [Smith] knew that he ought not to fight [Steele] except under the most favorable circumstances.... He also ought to have known that his army should have been pushed across country toward Alexandria.[15]

Smith's senior staff officer perceived what he could not. He had allowed a personality conflict to cloud his thinking and caused one of the Confederacy's few remaining opportunities to evaporate.

Taylor, for his part, would not allow their separation to prevent him from venting his frustrations. He engaged in conflicts with his close subordinates and wrote Smith frequently of his objections to Smith's conduct of the campaign. Taylor's health would decline over the coming weeks, adding to the venomous nature of his criticisms. A comparison of his personal writings shows that his rheumatism flared considerably after Pleasant Hill, about the time of his greatest irritation.[16]

At Grand Ecore, Banks had to contend with what to do next. After arriving Banks seems to have regained his nerve, planning to once again take up the march to Shreveport. Porter came to see Banks one evening at the general's headquarters to confer with him about the next move. Porter found Banks "looking as placid and as handsome as ever; he wore a handsome dressing gown, a velvet cap on his head, and comfortable slippers on his feet." Banks was reading a copy of *Scott's Tactics*, as he claimed to do every night. Upon seeing the admiral Banks inquired, "How did you get back here?" Porter replied, "I got back ... more by good luck than good management; we floundered along day and night."[17]

Porter then asked about the defeat at Mansfield, and was astonished by Banks' answer. The general exclaimed indignantly, "Defeated me? ... why, sir, I defeated them all to pieces." He further stated that he intended to advance up the river route in a couple of days. Porter disagreed on the grounds that the river could not now support the movement of the gunboats and transports back upstream. Banks persisted and with that Porter left.[18]

Porter wrote a series of confidential letters to Gideon Welles concerning the state of affairs at Grand Ecore. He obviously wanted to paint a sad picture of Banks, the political general, while absolving the navy of any failures of the expedition. Porter described the "demoralization" of the army and Banks' attempt to depict the setbacks as victories. Porter did take some liberty with the truth, but he was essentially accurate.

"There is a faint attempt to make a victory out of this [Mansfield and Pleasant Hill]," he said, "but two or three such victories would cost us our existence." Porter believed that Banks had convinced himself he had won and would now turn about. Porter knew that if Banks moved forward or retreated he simply could no longer support him because the river would prevent it.[19] Therefore Porter had to disassociate himself from the failures and bring down Banks as the responsible man.

Gideon Welles received these letters about ten days later and expressed his anxieties in his diary. He recorded:

> It is plain from Admiral Porter's account that Banks is no general, has no military capacity, is wholly unfit.... [further] The President thinks he has Presidential pretensions and friends to back him, but it is a great mistake. Banks is not only no general, but he is not much of a statesman. He is something of a politician, a party man of his own stamp, and for his own advancement.... There is an attempt to convert the reverse into a victory, but the truth will disclose itself. The President should, if Porter's statements are reliable [Welles knew Porter sometimes exaggerated], dismiss Banks or deprive him of military command.[20]

Porter's machinations behind Banks' back were working, demonstrating the complete lack of trust and real cooperation in the Union camp. Porter would change his tune — at least to Banks' face — when he realized that Banks held the fate of not only his army but also the navy in his hands. Porter's aversion to anything that would reflect negatively on his reputation would push him toward a more cooperative mood.

Banks' resolve to continue the campaign once again evaporated. Banks received dispatches from both Sherman and Grant requesting A. J. Smith's troops quick return and the beginning of preparations for the move on Mobile. The general realized that support from the navy daily became more of an impossibility. Finally, he was in enemy country with a pesky enemy loosely surrounding him in his present position. To stay longer would appear as disobedience to Grant's orders and could lead to an even bigger reverse than that of Mansfield. Therefore, Banks issued orders to Franklin to take charge of the march column (once again passing the mantle of responsibility to a subordinate) and prepare to retreat back to Alexandria.[21]

Porter had made a trip back downriver to retrieve two pump boats he needed to keep the boats afloat. Upon his return with the boats to Grand

Ecore, Franklin informed him of Banks' orders to leave. Banks' decisions seemed to Porter to bounce around like a rubber ball. Porter inquired of Franklin what Banks intended to do with all the troop transports, which were property of the army. Franklin gave Porter the impression that the army would abandon them. Porter already suspected that Banks would abandon the gunboats to save his skin, and this intimation that the general would leave his own transports served to deepen Porters suspicions. Porter took the initiative and prepared all the transports and gunboats to move as soon as possible. On the evening of April 21 the army brushed aside the small force Taylor had ringing Grand Ecore and started for Alexandria.[22] The Confederates had missed their first opportunity to destroy the Union army and fleet.

Before Banks moved from Grand Ecore he made some adjustments to his staff and subordinate commands. Knowing the campaign was a complete bust, Banks, like Porter, sought to deflect some of the blame for his failures. A couple of easy targets were his chief of staff, Charles P. Stone, and cavalry division commander, Albert Lee. Relations between Banks and Stone had been strained for some time and Banks had complained to his wife of Stone on occasion.[23] Banks knew Stone had the mark of the Ball's Bluff affair staining his reputation, and Banks believed he would make an easy scapegoat. Therefore, on April 16 Banks relieved Stone from his duties and sent him packing. Though Banks couldn't care less for Stone, he had kind words to speak of Lee in relieving him. Banks described Lee as "active, willing, and brave," but said the general "condition of the cavalry" necessitated a change in command.[24] Try as Banks would, though, nothing could dissuade the high command in Washington of their "unanimous" opinion of the "incapacity of General Banks."[25]

On April 19 Taylor departed Shreveport to rejoin his tiny army, arriving in the vicinity of Grand Ecore on the evening of the 21st. He brought with him Major General John A. Wharton, formerly of the Army of Tennessee, to command the late Green's cavalry. Taylor described Wharton as "a trump and a splendid fighter"; he would certainly fill the void left by Green very neatly.[26] Taylor's scouts informed him of Federal activity indicating the bluecoats were preparing a retrograde movement. Taylor lamented that he could not hold Banks at Grand Ecore. But at a five-to-one disadvantage he knew trying to stop Banks from retreating was nothing more than a pipe dream.[27] He blamed Kirby Smith for defanging him and began to stew in his anger.

Taylor did have a couple of options that had some promise even with the paltry force at hand. Brigadier General Liddell—a man who rivaled Taylor in terms of ego and stubbornness—offered up the first option to

Taylor. Liddell suggested that he should by rapid marching occupy Alexandria before Banks' army could reach the place. As Liddell stated it "would give us all of Banks' supplies at Alexandria. It would cut off all Banks' reinforcements coming up the river. All must end in our capturing or destroying the fleet and disintegrating Banks' army." Taylor never even responded to Liddell's suggestion, instead opting for his own plan.[28] Perhaps Taylor rejected the plan because he was too "self-important," as Liddell put it. Or maybe he could not deal with a subordinate who resembled himself. Liddell and Taylor's working relationship would sour very soon after Liddell offered his course of action.

Taylor adopted a plan that he thought could achieve decisive results. When the Union army began its retrograde movement from Grand Ecore, they took the road that led to Natchitoches and crossed the Cane River at that point. The Cane is the old channel of the Red and frequently changes its course. The Red and Cane Rivers run parallel to each other for several miles before coming back together about twenty miles above Alexandria. They form a long island whose terrain is characterized by marshy swampland and growths of impenetrable canebrakes. The road ran the length of the island and recrossed the Cane at a place called Monette's Ferry. The ferry was the only place the Federals could cross the Cane going south to Alexandria. Taylor believed that here existed a second opportunity to bag the Federal army.

Taylor had Brigadier General Hamilton Bee move to Monette's Ferry and take up a strong position to prevent the Union army from crossing. South of Monette's Ferry is a ridge that rises abruptly and overlooks the Cane. This was a superior position from which to contest a river crossing and Taylor wanted it occupied by Bee. With the rest of his force — Polignac's infantry and the remaining cavalry — Taylor would closely crowd the Federal rear guard. This would move the enemy along quickly and force them headlong and unexpectedly into Bee's blocking position. Finally, Taylor ordered Liddell to the confluence of the Cane and Red to ensure the Federals did not throw a pontoon over the Red to escape in that quarter. Taylor hoped that Bee would stand firm so that he could "make Banks unhappy on the morrow." With an adequate force this plan had merit; the terrain was well suited to hemming in an enemy force.[29] Taylor, however, did not have enough troops and chose the wrong man to command the force barring the way at Monette's Ferry.

One brigade of Union cavalry — now led by Brigadier General Arnold — led the retreat from Grand Ecore. The other brigades protected the right flank of the army and formed the rear guard. The XIXth Corps led the infantry units, followed by the XIIIth Corps and A. J. Smith's combined XVI and XVII Corps bringing up the rear. Major General Franklin once again took charge of the march dispositions as Banks, true to form, abdicated responsibility.[30]

The van of the Union army set a blistering pace for the march. "Orders inspired by urgency" pushed the bluecoats forward. Within twenty-six hours the Federals had covered "38, perhaps 40" miles. They moved all night with the help of fires lit by the advance to guide the way for troops following.[31]

Soon after A. J. Smith's "gorillas" started their march they began to add to the fires marking the way by firing property along the route. The Federal troops, especially Smith's men, were in a foul mood over being ordered to retreat. As a result, they vented their anger on the people living between the Cane and the Red. Blessington, whose division found the destruction a couple of weeks after the fact, observed:

> Their entire route could be traced by the melancholy monuments of their devastating march.... Every fine residence, every corn-crib, smokehouse, cotton-gin — all that could give comfort to men — were committed to the flames.[32]

Though the Confederates found Smith's destructiveness discouraging Poche felt confident, for "news from above [General Taylor] ... is certain to capture all of the enemy's naval forces and transports."[33]

Taylor inspired this confidence in spite of his own anger at not having the strength he wanted to challenge Banks' retreat. Soon after Banks abandoned Grand Ecore, Taylor had his Confederates biting at A. J. Smith's heels. At times Taylor's pressure forced A. J. Smith to deploy in line of battle to beat off the persistent graybacks. As Richard B. Irwin chronicled, this skirmishing remained "almost continuous" all the way to Alexandria, but "without material result." The advance of the Army of the Gulf finally halted in the vicinity of Cloutierville in the late evening of the 22d.[34]

At dawn on the 23rd the XIXth Corps again took up the march led by Henry Birge's brigade. The wound General Franklin had received at Mansfield caused him a great deal of discomfort, forcing him to relinquish command to General Emory. Scouts had informed Franklin on the 22d that the Confederates occupied the hills opposite Monette's ferry. Their strength was unknown, but it seemed certain that the Confederates intended to challenge a crossing at the Ferry. Banks wanted to keep the torrid pace of the march going and ordered Franklin to attack the graybacks in the morning. With Franklin now down, responsibility for executing the attack fell on Emory.[35]

The Federals conducted a reconnaissance that morning to ascertain if there existed an alternate crossing site. Banks sent forward an engineer named Lieutenant Colonel Joseph Bailey — who will soon figure prominently in the campaign — to assist in the effort. Bailey failed to find a suitable crossing site,[36] but this did not stop Emory. General Birge found a local Negro who said he would show the Federals a little-known ford they could use. This waist-deep ford was about two miles upstream from Monette's Ferry and hidden from Confederate observation. Armed with this information, Emory now formulated a plan to dislodge the Confederates on the other side of the Cane.[37]

Emory's plan called for an ad hoc division under General Birge to make the crossing at the hidden ford. Birge's force would consist of his own brigade; the 3rd Brigade of the 1st Division, XIXth Corps; and the survivors of Cameron's XIIIth Corps division. While Birge secretly crossed upstream, Emory planned to make a demonstration at Monette's Ferry itself, using the 1st and 2nd Brigades of his own division to draw attention away from Birge's flanking force. To augment this force Emory ordered his corps artillery commander to keep "a steady and well judged fire against the Confederate position on the hill" opposite the Ferry. Further downstream Emory sent a cavalry brigade to feint a crossing in order to draw away Confederate troops in that direction. Birge stepped off at about 9:00, setting the attack in motion.[38]

Hamilton Bee had four brigades with him at Monette's Ferry organized into a new division. This division consisted of Debray's, Major's, Bagby's, and Baylor's brigades augmented with four batteries for fire support at the ferry. Four brigades sounds like an impressive array, but in actuality Bee counted about 2,000 men in his command with which to contest the march of the Union army. Taylor told Bee in no uncertain terms that he must hold the crossing in order to tighten the trap around the Union army between the rivers. He also told Bee exactly where he wanted Bee to contest the crossing. In accordance with his orders Bee disposed his brigades on the hills overlooking the ferry. On the left he placed Baylor's brigade on a prominent wooded hill that offered flanking fire on the ferry while giving Bee's own force flank protection. In the center directly overlooking the ferry, Bee emplaced Debray's and Major's brigades while Bagby covered the right flank. Bee gave Baylor a battery while the rest of the artillery overlooking the ferry.[39] Since, Bee assumed, the Cane was too deep to ford, Monette's Ferry then was the only suitable crossing site, and his force would be adequate to contest a challenge there. Bee would soon have a surprise.

The Confederates overlooking Monette's Ferry knew that today they would have some action. The Federals had camped at Cloutierville the night before and the day's march promised to carry them straight into the sights of the Confederate muskets. A light rain had left a mist in the morning air on April 23, which would make for steamy conditions in the lowlands around the river. As the mist lifted the Confederates peered out from their positions and eyed the entire Federal XIX Army Corps, 15,000 strong, in the valley below them. The sight of this massive force arrayed to his front gave General Bee pause.

In the early afternoon events occurred that further shook Bee's resolve to hold his position. Birge's command appeared out of nowhere on Bee's left flank. The Confederate believed that the only way the Federals could get at him was by the front, which he had fully covered. Now a sizable enemy contingent appeared on his left rear, forcing Bee to order Baylor to change front to meet the Union challenge. Shortly after this the cavalry feint appeared downstream. Bee now believed the Federals would effect a crossing in this quarter and roll up his right flank. Almost simultaneously, the Federals in front, including Captain Closson's XIXth Corps Artillery, opened up on Bee, preventing him from reinforcing his flanks. Threatened in front and on both flanks—so he believed—Bee's resolve evaporated and he ordered the position abandoned.[40]

Birge's men had struggled through the thickets by the Cane that morning. The crossing also went slowly because of the waist-deep water and underbrush on the other side. By the time Birge got his command across the clock had already struck noon. Handrailing the Cane to his left Birge brought his command down to the wooded hill occupied by Baylor's brigade of Confederates. Upon reaching the hill, Birge deployed his men in two lines of battle. The duty of taking the hill rested with Colonel Frances Fessenden—the same Colonel who had taken command of Benedict's brigade when that officer died at Pleasant Hill.[41]

Fessenden made a quick reconnaissance of the area to size up the situation before attacking. He found the Confederates posted on the hill facing the ferry with the river on the left and "a thick impenetrable swamp which opened into a lake" on the right. The nature of the ground forced Fessenden to make his attack straight up the hill. Once Fessenden had made his dispositions he ordered his brigade to charge. They knocked down two fences and charged straight up and over the hill with the whole attack "not lasting more than five minutes." Baylor's men took to their heels and occupied a second hill to their rear.[42]

Emory, upon hearing Birge engaged on the other side of the Cane, ordered the cavalry and his own division to make their demonstration. Closson's artillery quickly silenced the Confederate batteries on the bluffs south of the ferry. Some of Emory's cavalrymen took advantage of the

Monette's Ferry — This wooded hill is where Emory's flanking column, led by Brigadier General Henry Birge, pushed Bee away from the ferry allowing the Federals to continue to retreat to Alexandria.

cover fire from the Union artillery and moved forward to capture Monette's Ferry. Meanwhile, Fessenden's men, without stopping, continued their attack as if by inertia and carried the second hill. Bee, with his left collapsed, the Ferry captured, and a threat on his right, pulled back. Instead of retreating south to stay between Banks and Alexandria, Bee sidestepped the Federals, retreating west toward Beasley's Depot.[43] The road to Alexandria now stood wide open for the Federals and Taylor had missed a second opportunity.

Taylor flew into a rage at the failure of his latest plan. He immediately lashed out at Hamilton Bee for what he deemed a dereliction of duty.

> You were in a position to annihilate the enemy. You accomplished nothing. After you gave up your position at Monette's Ferry you retreated at once thirty miles to Beasleys.... Had you done your duty I would have sung your praises.... That you are not a commander is not your fault, but were I to leave you in a position to ruin my plans again, I would be responsible.

Taylor relieved Bee of his command.[44] Taylor was now quarreling with his subordinates as well as his superiors, and in the process lessening the cooperation and effectiveness of his small army.

Though Taylor blamed Bee for the failure at Monette's Ferry, he believed the real blame rested with Kirby Smith. Smith had taken all of Taylor's infantry north to pursue Steele in Arkansas, an endeavor that Taylor termed "a wild goose chase." Taylor believed that this was the root cause of his failure to capture Banks and Porter at Grand Ecore and Monette's Ferry. On April 20 Smith had once again changed his mind and ordered Walker to halt, turn back, and rejoin Taylor on the Red. Taylor's heart leaped for joy at the prospect of doubling his force. The addition of Walker's division could probably give Taylor just enough strength to realize the success of his plans. But only three days later Smith recanted and ordered Walker back to Arkansas.[45]

Smith's indecision drove Taylor into melancholy and rage. In a private letter to General Walker, written on April 26 — three days after Monette's Ferry — Taylor lamented Walker's absence. "I wish to God your division had been with us," he said in frustration, "and Banks' army would never have reached Alexandria — *certain*."[46] Taylor may have been right. The addition of 5,000 veteran infantry certainly would have made it infinitely tougher for Banks to break out of Grand Ecore or Monette's Ferry. A defending force can hold against three-to-one odds, and Taylor's force ratio at both places was five to one against him. The presence of Walker's division would have narrowed it to two and a half to one.[47]

Two days after this letter to Walker, Taylor vented his rage on Kirby Smith. First, he castigated Smith about the disposition of Walker's division. Then he questioned the rationale of conducting the campaign against Steele when the field for decisive results, he maintained, rested in the Red River Valley. He also wrote of what he could have done.

> General, had you then left the conduct of operations in my hands Banks' army would have been destroyed before this; the fleet would have been in our hands or blown up by the enemy. The moral effect at the North and the shock to public credit would have seriously affected the war.

This is an allusion to the November elections, which depended on the public credit of the administration. But Taylor did not stop there. He went on:

> I would have been on the way with the bulk of my army to join Price at Camden, enriched with captured spoils of a great army and fleet; Steele would have been brushed from our path as a cobweb before a broom ...

> [B]y midsummer [we would have] relieved the pressure from our suffering brethren in Virginia and Georgia.... You might have had all the glory; I would have been contented to do the work either under you or General Price.

The last sentence was a barb cast because Smith had engaged lately in self-aggrandizement. Finally, Taylor concluded:

> I have supported you, even when your policy was fatally wrong, for I believed it my duty to give my commander a warm and earnest co-operation. The events of the past few weeks have so filled me with discouragement that I much fear I cannot do my whole duty under your command, and I ask that you take steps to relieve me as soon as it can be done without injury to the service.[48]

This letter thoroughly irritated Smith and ensured that no further cooperation would occur between commander and subordinate. A disgusted Smith returned the letter with a curt note that read:

> Respectfully returned to General Taylor. This communication is not only improper but unjust. I cannot believe but that it was written in a moment of irritation or sickness.[49]

Smith knew of Taylor's maladies and the gentleman in him gave Taylor the benefit of the doubt before he relieved Taylor. However, Taylor would not let the matter rest and in a few days launched more venomous assaults. Walker agreed that Smith had prevented Taylor from exploiting an excellent opportunity, but he also laid some blame at Taylor's door for the failure at Monette's Ferry. "General Bee's force was entirely insufficient to bar the passage of a retreating army," he lamented, "but the position itself was so advantageous that with a more skilful [sic] handling of his troops and a more vigorous resistance, the Federal army would have found it extremely difficult ... to force a passage."[50] Walker thought Taylor had given Bee too small a force to deal with a full army. He also faulted Taylor for assigning such an important post to Bee, a commander inexperienced in independent command. Nevertheless, the second opportunity had evaporated and there would only be one more — at Alexandria.

While Banks struggled to get back to Alexandria, Porter experienced a nightmare. He did not wait until Banks left Grand Ecore before starting the fleet downstream. The fall of the river convinced the admiral that he had to get the fleet downstream before the low water levels made it impossible. The pride of the Mississippi River Squadron, the *Eastport*, would lead the boats down the river. They departed Grand Ecore on April 17 and it did not take long to run into trouble.

6. Three Wasted Opportunities 103

The *Eastport* bumped along downriver at a painfully slow pace. About eight miles out of Grand Ecore the huge ironclad hit a torpedo and went to the bottom in a few feet of water. Porter made his way to the site, bringing along the two pump boats in an attempt to raise the most prized of his squadron. The *Eastport* had been built by the Confederates on the Tennessee River and bore the name of the town where the keel had been laid. The navy had captured her after the fall of Fort Henry when the Confederates abandoned her at the Federal approach. Not only did Porter want to save her out of pride, he also did not want the Confederates to capture and raise her. The thrifty Rebels would then be able to use this powerful boat to challenge Union supremacy of the Western rivers. Because of this Porter and the skipper of the *Eastport*, Lieutenant Commander S. L. Phelps, went at the task of raising the boat with a vengeance.[51]

The pump boats successfully drained out the water as Phelps' crew plugged the huge hole. The crew also lightened the boat by throwing any unnecessary equipment overboard. After this "epic struggle," the skipper got his boat refloated and underway downriver on the 21st. For the next four days the *Eastport* scraped the bottom, snagging at least eight times, but kept going largely because of Phelps' efforts and the two boats assigned to pull her off of the snags. Finally on the 25th, the *Eastport* ran aground for good in a bed of logs.[52]

Porter of course wanted the ship saved, but his pilots told him that they could do nothing more. The ship was stuck. Now enemy snipers began to appear on the banks of the river to harass the work crews trying to pull her off. The admiral painfully concluded that the time had come to destroy the *Eastport*. In his *Naval History* Porter wrote, "The Admiral had stayed by the vessel as long as there was the slightest possibility of getting her down." But when it looked like raising the boat "would risk the capture of the little squadron ... he acceded to the proposition to destroy her."[53] Commander Phelps and Porter personally oversaw the setting of charges on the boat. Sailors placed fifty barrels of powder in her hull and then lit the fuze. By tradition Phelps and Porter were the last to leave the ship. They nearly came to grief as their launches were too close to the boat when she blew. Porter reported that "great pieces of hull fell all around us."[54]

Porter blamed his troubles on Banks and mused that he feared the army would abandon him. He wrote in a letter to Gideon Welles, "Had the army held Grand Ecore a fortnight, we could have saved the vessel." Further, Porter stated that he could not "blame himself" for the problems. He believed they had come about because of Banks' poor leadership. He now thought that Banks intended to sacrifice the fleet "without an effort to save them [the boats]."[55]

The end of the *Eastport* did not mean the end of Porter's troubles. The enemy began to compound the navy's trials by stepping up the effort to stop the fleet. For the next two days Confederates on both sides of the river fired incessantly at the fleet. Near the mouth of the Cane the Confederates got a battery and 200 infantrymen in position and gave Porter's boats all they could handle. Over the next few hours the fleet struggled to get past the ambush. Admiral Porter found himself piloting a boat when the pilot of the *Cricket* suffered a disabling wound. The losses in this engagement totaled two tinclads, the two pump boats, and over 100 runaway slaves, who were tragically scalded to death. Porter and company finally pulled into Alexandria on the 27th much worse for the wear. His fleet was not out of the woods yet, for now they would have to pass back over the falls, whose water level now stood at only three feet. Porter, after the ordeal of coming back down the Red, believed more than ever that "we were a secondary consideration of the army."[56]

The fleet and army had once again reunited, this time at Alexandria. Though Taylor had already missed two opportunities, he made plans to try one last time to bag the Union army and navy. Across the river Taylor ordered Liddell to step up harassment of the fleet and prevent a Union lodgment on that side of the river. He ordered two brigades of cavalry, William Steele's and Arthur Bagby's, to block the roads north and west of Alexandria. He ordered the third brigade, Major's, to move well south of Alexandria to a place called David's Ferry. Here Major, with a battery of artillery, was to block all traffic on the Red from moving upstream or downstream. This would effectively cut off the Union army from outside communication. Finally, Taylor had Polignac's infantry division block the Beouf road, which led south. This road most likely would serve as Banks' final escape route back to Simmesport and the Mississippi.[57] Taylor had nothing more than a thin cordon around Alexandria, but if he could hold Banks there long enough to receive reinforcements he could possibly realize his goal. This, however, was his last chance and he knew it.

Taylor could not allow Banks to escape after the Army of the Gulf had destroyed so much of his beloved Louisiana. The Confederate governor of Louisiana recalled that "From Mansfield to the Mississippi River the track of the spoiler was one scene of desolation. The fine estates on Cane and Red rivers, on bayous Rapides, Robert, and De Glaize, were all devastated. Houses, gins, mills, barns, and fences, were burned; negroes all carried off, horses, cattle, hogs, every living thing driven away or killed."[58] General Walker agreed, recalling that "nothing was spared from Grand Ecore to Alexandria, and clouds of smoke by day and pillars of fire by night marked the progress of the retreating army."[59] Given Taylor's attachment to his state, the desolation most certainly drove him to do all he could to keep up the impression that he would capture Banks.

"We have run the Yankees to earth in Alexandria," Taylor stated in a letter to Walker. "Our cavalry now surrounds on all sides, and keeps the devils in a constant panic by shooting into their pickets every night at various points."[60] Indeed, Taylor's cavalry stayed active not only in picket firing, but also in creating deception. "Taylor adopted all kinds of feints and subterfuges to deceive the enemy as to the number of his men," one observer recorded. "He used to have fires built up around at great distances, to stimulate camp-fires; he put drummers and buglers on horseback, and made them sound the calls in every direction for miles around."[61] His confidence in capturing Banks and Porter was based on intelligence that informed him of difficulties in cooperation between the Union commanders. In the same letter to Walker, Taylor wrote:

> The army and navy have split. Banks "wishes every gunboat was in hell and he [Porter] with them," (he made this remark to a citizen in Natchitoches) Porter dams [sic] Banks and swears he'll stay if Banks runs. In fact, *his boats* have to stay not one that is above the falls can get out.[62]

Taylor believed that dissension between the Union commanders and deception would buy him the time he needed to receive reinforcements from Arkansas. Kirby Smith met Steele at Jenkin's Ferry in Arkansas on April 29. Though Smith got the worst of it, Steele continued retreating back to Little Rock. Taylor hoped Walker would soon rejoin him to finish off Banks at Alexandria.[63] Porter and Banks, however, came together to prevent disaster.

Porter continued to send letters to Welles describing the deplorable condition of the army and his belief that Banks would abandon him. He wrote:

> Blind carelessness on the part of our military leader, and our retreat back to Alexandria from place to place has so demoralized General Banks's army that the troops have no confidence in anybody or anything.... I have no confidence in his [Banks'] promises.... I do not think that General Banks will make the least effort to save the navy blockaded here.... There is no foreseeing what other calamities may arise from the errors of one man, who, absorbed in his own interests and diseased with political aspirations, cares little or nothing for the lives of those he has sacrificed, or thinks of anything but the effect this may have upon his future career.[64]

Whatever Porter may have believed, evidence suggests that Banks intended to see things through to the bitter end. On April 27, Major General David

Hunter arrived in Alexandria. He carried orders from General Grant advising Banks of his relief from command and ordering him immediately to New Orleans. Banks, however, stayed on as commander, determined to not only see the army back safely, but also get the navy back over the falls to safety.[65]

The water level had fallen continuously in the Red since the start of the campaign. Before Porter took the fleet above the falls in March many of the navymen worried that without a rise the boats would not make it back. Now their fears had come to fruition. The water, about seven feet at the falls in March, stood at three feet at the end of April. All of the naval officers made plans to do the unthinkable — destroy the fleet. In all, ten gunboats and several transports were crowded above the falls. One man, instead of preparing to blow up the boats, came up with a plan to save the fleet with a little bit of "Yankee ingenuity."[66]

Lieutenant Colonel Joseph Bailey was a staff engineer for the XIX Army Corps. He had won distinction at Port Hudson by building a dam that enabled the navy to refloat a couple of grounded steamboats. Before the war Bailey had worked as an engineer on the northern rivers, constructing dams, mills, and bridges. The challenge of the Red was certainly daunting, but Bailey's pre-war expertise told him that he could get the boats over. Bailey came up with a plan to build a series of dams that would compress the width of the river, forcing it to flow through a narrower channel. This, Bailey knew, would raise the water to a level that could get them over the falls. Bailey just had to get someone in the high command to accept the idea so he could start building.[67]

Officers of the army and navy universally scoffed at the idea, but Bailey persisted and won the approval of Porter. Bailey briefed Franklin on his idea and, though skeptical, he sent Bailey to see Porter. Porter was impressed with the plan and seized on it as the only way to get the boats over. Before this could happen, Porter had to get Banks to approve the plan so that soldiers could start the project. If Porter could get Banks on board with the plan, the army would be committed to stay at Alexandria until the boats passed the falls. This would ensure survival of the fleet, so Porter wrote to Banks in a forceful but complimentary manner that convinced the general to try the project.[68]

Banks approved the plan and issued orders on April 29 that would set in motion the massive dam project. Banks placed about 3,000 troops at Bailey's disposal and work began on the 30th. Lumbermen from Maine cut down trees for the dam on the Pineville side of the river while midwesterners set to work ripping down buildings and quarrying to build crib foundations for it. Troops from the all-black Corps D'Afrique worked in

6. Three Wasted Opportunities

the river itself—sometimes in water up to their necks—placing the cribs and timbers. Amidst all the activity Porter still despaired of success and worried that the army might yet abandon him.

Porter wrote to Banks in a very friendly tone—in contrast to his critical letters to Welles—encouraging Banks' efforts. He wrote, "I really see nothing that should make us despond.... I hope sir, you will not let anything divert you from the attempt to get these vessels through safely even if we have to stay here and eat mule meat."[69] Banks did exactly that, attentively seeing to all details of the construction. The Federal commanders had come together—although reluctantly—and were steadily working their way toward salvaging something from the failed campaign.

Bailey built two dams, one each at the upper and lower rapids. At the lower rapids the river was about 758 feet wide with a ten-mile-per-hour current. Here, Bailey constructed a wing dam protruding from each bank using sections of stone cribs and tree dams. Just below this point and beyond the rocks of the rapids, Bailey had a bracket dam built to prevent the boats from crashing into the rocks as they passed. Additionally, Bailey had barges sunk loaded with stones, brick, and iron to help raise the level of the river. The two wings left about a 150-foot gap in the center of the river to pass the boats through. Bailey originally thought that he could use this dam to get the boats between the two rapids. Then at an appointed time Bailey would blow up this dam and the water pressure that had built up behind it would force the boats over the upper rapids. This proved impractical so Bailey had the builders build the second dam at the upper rapids to raise the water levels here as well. As work began many of the army and naval officers snickered at the project. However, as the river rose, the naysayers' voices began to fade.[70]

On May 6 the water had risen four feet. Two days later it rose an additional foot. As the river rose the builders' excitement rose proportionally. Three light draft vessels passed the dam on the 8th as the soldiers redoubled their efforts. On the 9th, though, a near disaster occurred as the pressure from the water burst part of the dam. Banks had feared this would happen for some days and had encouraged the navy to do everything possible to be ready to make a run at a moment's notice. On the morning the dam broke, Banks jumped from his bed, the crashing having startled him in his sleep. Porter, witnessing the accident, "jumped on a horse and rode up to where the vessels were anchored and ordered" an immediate "attempt to go through the dam."[71]

The *Lexington* got up steam and passed through the gap with "several spasmodic rolls; hung for a moment, with a harsh, grating sound, on the rocks below." Then suddenly the *Lexington* "swept into deep water, and rounded to by the bank of the river." The nearby soldiers and sailors raised a cheer. The success of the *Lexington* inspired the troops to immediately begin rebuilding the broken section of dam. Bailey also constructed the dam at the upper rapids at this time. This dam would not only get the ships over the upper rapids, but it would reduce pressure on the lower dam as well.[72]

Many of the army officers felt that while the army had gone to great lengths to save the fleet, the navy itself had done nothing. One officer accused the navy of loading their holds with cotton and contraband when they should have been lightening the boats. Banks' aide-de-camp told Banks that he did not think the army "should be working like beavers, night and day, to construct a dam ... when they were loaded down with cotton." As a result of this clamoring, and to keep good faith with the army, the navy took steps to lighten the vessels.[73]

On the 12th of May the work crews completed the dams and the navy prepared to pass over the falls. Thousands of soldiers, sailors, and local citizens lined the banks in anticipation of the run. Bands played national airs as the boats got up steam. The *Mound City* went through the chute first, successfully passing the gap in much the same fashion as the *Lexington*. On May 13 Porter sent the rest of the fleet, including the *Carondelet* and the *Pittsburg*, over the falls. By early afternoon the entire fleet was safe below the Alexandria rapids ready to steam down to the Mississippi.[74] Banks had faithfully discharged his duty, helping to save the fleet, and would now bring out the army. Lieutenant Colonel Joseph Bailey, for his part in saving the fleet, received a formal resolution of thanks from Congress, which he richly deserved. Taylor had missed his third and last real opportunity to bag Banks and Porter.

Chapter 7
"A Protecting Shield"

While the Federals worked feverishly on the dam, the Confederates continued the harassment of the Union army and fleet. Liddell's small force attempted to apply pressure at the dam itself without much success. Major's cavalry at David's Ferry up the Red had much better luck. By cutting off Union communication upriver and impeding dam construction, Taylor felt he would force the Federals to finally succumb if not to force then to starvation. Taylor hoped that his efforts would pay off, but he knew that he needed more men. Reinforcement would elude Taylor and he would use it as an excuse to lash out in all directions.

Major's cavalry went into position to block the river on April 30. At David's Ferry Major put his battery into action overlooking the river and spread his cavalry out to provide small arms fire. Major's men did not have long to wait, for soon after Major completed his dispositions the next morning the transport *Emma* happened into view. The cavalry attacked the unprotected transport with everything they had, chasing her for some distance. Finally, after a two-mile run, the whooping Confederates forced *Emma* aground and burned her.[1]

Three days later Major had a more lucrative target come into his sight. Based on the previous disasters the Federals had begun convoying down river instead of sending vulnerable single boats. On May 4 the gunboats *Covington* and *Signal* came in sight at David's Ferry escorting the *Warner*, a quartermaster boat. The *Warner* was loaded down with cotton taken from Alexandria and 400 infantrymen. Major placed his artillery across from Dunn's Bayou and waited. As soon as the boats came in range, the Confederates opened a "furious fire" on the *Warner*. The *Warner* had her boiler pierced in this volley and the pilot lost control, causing her to drift into the opposite bank.[2]

The gunboats, seeing what had happened, quickly came to the aid of the disabled boat to protect her. Soon the gunboats were suffering under a relentless pounding from Major's artillery and cavalry. After a battle lasting several hours by accounts, both gunboats had their boilers perforated and steering cables cut. The *Covington* had expended all her ammunition and was unable to continue fighting; Lieutenant George Lord ordered her abandoned and set afire. Lord and his men escaped by the far shore away from the Confederates. The *Signal*'s commander, Lieutenant Edward Morgan, continued to fight for another half hour, but soon discovered that further resistance was useless. Morgan had many wounded on his decks and refused to abandon his ship. He ran up the white flag to offer surrender rather than have his wounded sacrificed.[3]

The Confederates accepted the surrender, capturing valuable cannon from the gunboats and scores of prisoners from all three vessels. The Confederates then moved the *Signal* out into the channel and sunk her to obstruct further traffic up or down the river. There would be no more traffic on the Red for the next couple of weeks. Major's small force had successfully cut off the Union army and navy from communication with the outside world.[4] Now if Taylor could prevent completion of the dam he might possibly force Federal capitulation. This would not happen because Taylor's force amounted to nothing more than a thin veneer that the Union army could easily brush aside.

Liddell attempted to stop work at the falls, but his force was simply too small to have much effect. Liddell's command numbered about 700 men of all arms and included a four-gun battery. Liddell organized his force into a small brigade though it numbered less than a full-strength regiment. His command consisted of "raw levies" and deserters from Confederate commands in the East. This made for a brigade of questionable reliability, but even Taylor acknowledged — at least early in the campaign — that Liddell handled them well. He would have to handle them in an extraordinary manner to stop construction of Bailey's dam.[5]

Liddell had earlier suggested to Taylor that he occupy Alexandria before the Federals did to deny them a base of operations. Taylor had not accepted the advice, instead adopting the present course of action. Liddell felt that his suggestion offended the touchy Taylor and wrote, "[F]rom this time, he never ceased to find fault with everything I did." On top of Taylor's "enmity" Liddell now began receiving contradictory orders. Originally, Taylor had ordered Liddell to do everything he could to disrupt "their works on the falls." Then he received an order to move a portion of command down to help Major on the opposite side of the river. In response, Liddell left a company at Pineville and moved the rest of his force to assist Major.[6]

The Federal force on the Pineville side of the Red consisted not only of the work parties, but also a force to protect them. With only a company available to the Rebels to disrupt progress on the dam it did not take much for the Federals to stop them. While Liddell attempted to challenge the Federals, Kirby Smith sent an order taking Liddell's battery from him. Even if Liddell had been able to break through to the work site, there is little he could have done with small arms only. Nevertheless, Taylor accused Liddell of failing to discharge his duty and said that if this continued it "would necessitate a change in command." Liddell told Taylor, in effect, not to make empty threats and requested relief. This request Taylor obliged, losing a hard-nosed fighter in Liddell.[7]

Liddell believed that Taylor had a better position and greater force to affect work on the dam. One officer felt that the terrain at Pineville better supported operations against the dam than the Alexandria side. But, as Liddell pointed out, he couldn't affect this with fewer than 700 men and no artillery. Taylor not only had "six thousand infantry," but also "at least fifty pieces of artillery" at his disposal. He had failed by not using the force on his side to the fullest while lethargically awaiting Walker's return from Arkansas.[8] Taylor stated in his post-war memoirs that "like 'Sister Ann' from her watch tower, day after day we strained our eyes to see the dust of our approaching comrades arise…. Not a camp follower among us but knew that the arrival … would give us the great prize." During the campaign Taylor wrote to Smith that "troops from above [Walker's in Arkansas] cannot reach me in time…. His presence [Walker's] here at the right time would have insured the most brilliant results."[9] Perhaps Liddell was correct when he intimated that Taylor sat back and waited instead of doing more himself on his side of the river.

Confederate commanders were now embroiled in near constant bickering, but the Federals achieved at least a bit of toleration between the commanders. Porter now admitted that Banks had loyally done a great deed in standing by the navy to save them from destruction. He wrote the following in a letter to Gideon Welles on May 16 following the escape.

> To General Banks personally I am much indebted for the happy manner in which he has forwarded this enterprise, giving it his whole attention night and day, scarcely sleeping while the work was going on, attending personally to see that all the requirements of Colonel Bailey were complied with on the instant.[10]

Indeed, Banks did devote all of his energy to the project. Daily he could be found down at the riverbank checking on progress and ensuring the builders had everything they needed. It is unclear whether Banks did this out of conscience or political motivations. Most likely both guided his energies. Whatever the case, Banks came through with decisive determination at the most critical point of the campaign. Had he wavered at Alexandria, as he had so many times before, it is highly likely a disaster would have befallen the Union army and navy.

On May 13 the Union army marched out of Alexandria. As they departed a tragedy befell the citizens and city. On that morning Banks' army stepped off with the cavalry once again leading the advance. Emory's XIXth Corps followed with A. J. Smith's westerners acting as the army's rear guard. Smith's men took advantage of the fact that they were last to leave as only they could. These men were already responsible for the path of destruction on the retreat from Grand Ecore. Now they would leave one final reminder of their presence in Louisiana by giving Alexandria over to the flames.[11]

Prior to the departure of the Union army, rumors raced through the camps and town of the pending destruction of the town. Banks, upon hearing this, instructed General Grover — whose troops garrisoned the place — to organize a guard sufficient to protect Alexandria. Whatever force Grover organized did not or could not prevent what happened. Local citizens witness Federal soldiers moving through the town with mops and buckets of turpentine wetting down the buildings in the town. When asked what they were doing, the soldiers replied that they "were preparing the place for Hell."[12]

Soon after the lead troops pulled out of town, smoke began to rise over the town. The recent dry spell and wood frame building materials caused a conflagration. The blaze became so intense that Admiral Porter feared the fire would ignite the boats still tied up at the Alexandria wharves. Citizens came running down to the levee begging the navy to take them on, but they were refused on grounds that the boats had no room. The guard left behind could do nothing to prevent or fight the blaze. Soldiers from the XVIth and XVIIth Corps allegedly whooped in the streets as the town went up. Even A. J. Smith got into the act. He reportedly was seen riding through the city exclaiming, "Hurrah, boys, this looks like war!" The disaster left hundreds homeless, including citizens who had recently taken the oath of allegiance and voted in Banks' elections.[13]

It did not take long for the Confederates to start nipping at the retreating Federals' heels. Taylor directed General Wharton and Polignac to maintain constant pressure on the retreating Federals rear and right flanks. He ordered Major and Bagby to do everything they could to obstruct the retreat at the head of the column. From May 13 to May 16 the Federals kept in constant contact with the pesky Rebels. Although the action became hot at times, the Confederates could never seriously challenge the Federal army, which still outnumbered Taylor five to one. Walker's division had arrived back in Louisiana after suffering horribly in Kirby Smith's attack on Steele at Jenkin's Ferry. The pace of the Federals, however, would make it impossible for Walker's jaded troops to assist Taylor in halting Banks' retreat.[14]

Taylor's missing a third opportunity and the burning of Alexandria caused him deep agony. He reported that the "enemy left Alexandria after midday today, burning the place…. Two houses only reported left between the ice-house and railroad."[15] Deep in his soul Taylor blamed Smith for the inferno at Alexandria; as soon as the Federals made their escape good, he would sit down to write a scathing critique of Smith. In his memoirs, Taylor also blames indirectly General Sherman for the conduct of Smith's troops. Taylor knew that A. J. Smith's men had been trained by and came from Sherman's army east of the Mississippi. Taylor concluded that he "could hardly expect that troops trained by this commander would respect *the humanities*."[16] Anger aside, Taylor still intended to try to stop the Yankees before they could reach Simmesport and safety.

The Federal army approached the small hamlet of Mansura on May 16. About five miles south of Fort DeRussy and twenty miles north of Simmesport, Mansura lies on a wide prairie called the Avoyelles. Here, Taylor managed to get the bulk of his "army" across the path of the retreating Federals. The Confederate line of battle centered on the village itself. To the left Taylor had Polignac's infantry division with a small detachment of cavalry. On the right Bagby and Major — just pulled back from David's Ferry — held the line.

The openness of the prairie made the engagement an event that common soldiers on both sides could witness much as a fan would view a baseball game. Taylor described the terrain as "smooth as a billiard table … an admirable field for artillery practice." This is about what the engagement amounted to. For around four hours each side engaged in an artillery duel that one observer claimed "as the finest military spectacle they ever witnessed." Neither side was willing to risk a frontal assault across the perfect field of fire provided by the prairie. A. J. Smith finally broke the stalemate late in the morning. Emory's Corps made the initial contact and shook out a line of battle to front the Confederate line. As A. J. Smith's men closed the column, he directed them to the right, flanking the Confederate line. Taylor, greatly outnumbered as always, pulled his forces back rather than risk a disaster.[17]

The soldiers in particular enjoyed this battle. The long battle lines spread out before them on this late spring day sparked romantic visions of war. The din of artillery thundering across the green prairie only served to add to the pageantry. Probably the most important factor contributing to the soldiers' actually enjoying the spectacle was the absence of casualties on both sides. In fact, casualties were so light that neither side bothered to make up returns for the action.[18] By mid-afternoon, Banks' army had moved out on the road again, now only twenty miles from safety. This left only one last act for the two sides to play out before the campaign ended.

The retreat continued on the 17th with the Confederates constantly nipping at the heels of the Federals. Though these forays never seriously challenged Union progress, the Confederates did make a complete nuisance of themselves. Near Yellow Bayou a part of Wharton's cavalry broke through to the bluecoat wagon train. The raiders ran the guard off and burned many of the wagons before the Federals could drive them away. The Federals camped for the night around Yellow Bayou, only eight miles from Simmesport.[19]

On May 18 the Army of the Gulf moved out on the final leg of this disheartening campaign. The Union army began arriving at Simmesport around midday. A. J. Smith's command, however, had to hold back one last dash at them from the ever-present graybacks. General Wharton's cavalry pressed hard against the Federal rear guard division, commanded by General Joseph Mower. Mower deployed a force to drive back the Rebel skirmishers and pushed them over two miles across the Yellow Bayou. Here Mower's men ran into a solid line of battle deployed by Wharton.[20]

The Confederate force consisted of Wharton's own cavalry and a brigade of Polignac's division. It appeared that Wharton intended to draw Mower's men into an ambush reminiscent of Mansfield. Just as at Mansfield, the Federals halted before stumbling into the trap. Wharton soon lost his patience—as Taylor had—and ordered a charge. This time the Federal line held firm; their flanks were covered by a swamp to the right and heavy woods to the left. The charge by Wharton proved a disaster, as his men were easily cut down in their frontal assault. Much of the underbrush caught fire during the engagement, adding a stifling pall of smoke to the thick air of the dank swampland. Wharton's heavy losses convinced him to break contact. This engagement cost the Confederates over 600 casualties while the Federals suffered about 300. The Battle of Yellow Bayou marked the last engagement of the two forces, and although the Confederates held the field Taylor admitted that it was not worth the cost.[21]

While the Confederates would no longer harry the bluecoats, the Federals still had one more obstacle with which to contend. The Red had failed to provide the seasonal rise that might have prevented the whole misadventure, but the Atchafalaya had risen. The Mississippi had drained excess water into the Atchafalaya, causing the river to swell to a width of six to seven hundred yards. The Federal army did not have a pontoon large enough to bridge this unexpected obstacle, but one man had a solution. Lieutenant Colonel Joseph Bailey once again came through with a brilliant plan to conquer the obstacle and bring out a trapped Union force.[22]

Bailey came up with a scheme to assemble a "floating bridge" similar to a pontoon. First, he had twenty-two army transports lined up side by side across the stream. Then, using locally available materials, he assembled gangplanks to connect the boats. These local materials consisted of timbers and planks ripped off the buildings of the village of Simmesport, which now existed in name only. The bridge—rough as it was—worked like a charm. On May 19 most of the soldiers, trains, and artillery had crossed the river. On the 20th the remainder crossed, taking up the bridge and bringing "the disastrous campaign of the Red River to an end."[23] Though this campaign undoubtedly ended as a disaster for the Federals, it was a hollow victory for the Rebels and Richard Taylor knew it. In a letter to Smith a couple of days before the campaign concluded, Taylor states with an air of defeatism, "There can be no doubt that this is the last campaign of the war."[24] Though the Yankees had been driven out of west Louisiana, these same Yankees would go to other theaters and play decisive roles in defeating the Confederacy.

Taylor watched in disgust as the final bluecoats left west Louisiana. His anger with Kirby Smith reached its zenith and he launched the most venomous diatribe against his commander to date. On May 18 Taylor began by denigrating Smith's Fabian policy. He described in his after-action report how this policy prevented the great results he desired.

> Nothing but the withdrawal of Walker's Division from me has prevented the capture of Banks' army and the destruction of Porter's fleet. I feel bitterly about this because my army has been robbed of the just measure of glory and the country of the most brilliant and complete success of the war.[25]

A few days later Taylor attacked Smith's staff in their conduct of administrative affairs in the department, while again requesting relief from command.

> The condition of my health precludes the hope that I will be able to participate in a Missouri campaign. I scarcely believe I will be able for some time to conduct affairs of my present command.... The Clothing Bureau is liberal in promise and utterly barren in performance. A radical change is imperatively required.

Taylor then launched into a long tirade about the inefficiencies of the departments of transportation and subsistence. He also took occasion to attack another subordinate, Thomas Churchill, saying that "he is no soldier and will never succeed in the field." He concluded this rambling and insulting letter by saying:

> I should respectfully but frankly express my opinion. No campaign dependent on the present system of bureauocracy [sic] will succeed.... The number of bureaus now existing in this department, and the army of employes [sic] attached to them, would do honor to St. Petersburg or Paris. Instead of making the general staff a mere adjunct to promote the efficiency of the little army in the field, the very reverse is the case.... I repeat, my health precludes the hope that I can share in the Missouri campaign, and I have the honor to repeat the request previously made that I may speedily be relieved from duty in this department.[26]

Smith had taken a vast amount of unsolicited criticism from Taylor over the course of the campaign, but now his patience started to wear thin. He responded to Taylor's latest salvo by writing:

> In your letter of the 18th ... you complain bitterly of the withdrawal of Walker's division, and say it has robbed your army of the just measure of glory and the country.... This most unjust complaint, though repeated, remained unnoticed. It was attributed to your ill-health, and that irritability of disposition which at Mansfield, on April 10, you regretted and begged me to bear with. I have again today received a communication from you, written in the same tone and spirit, which is objectionable. Walker's division was detached from your command ... [with] your approval.... The fruits of your victory at Mansfield were secured by the march of that column [Walker's]. The complete success of the campaign was determined by the overthrow of Steele's at Jenkin's Ferry.[27]

Taylor received Smith's letter on June 5, two weeks after the campaign ended. Smith's rebuttal of Taylor's earlier dispatches hit a raw nerve in Taylor. He sat down and wrote a long letter, painful to read, in which he dressed down his commander. He wrote:

> You are mistaken in supposing that my communications are intended as complaints. I have no complaints to make. My communications were statements of facts, necessary, in my judgment, to the proper understanding of the campaign.... I am at a loss to conceive what connection the fruits of Mansfield have with the fight at Jenkin's Ferry.... How was the "complete success of the campaign determined by Steele's overthrow at Jenkin's Ferry?" In truth, the campaign as a whole was a hideous

failure. The fruits of Mansfield have been turned to dust and ashes.... The remains of Banks' army have already gone to join Grant or Sherman and may turn the scale against our overmatched brethren in Virginia and Georgia.

Taylor also took occasion to air his indignation at being told his services were not required in Arkansas.

> You replied that Steele "was bold to rashness" and that he would not hear of Banks' defeat, and insisted that the movement [to Arkansas] be made, proposing to select troops from my command. It was then that I desired to accompany the troops ... expressing my entire willingness to serve under General Price and give him all the assistance in my power.... My offer to serve under General Price drew from you many compliments; yet at that very time ... [you] had determined I was not to make [the move to Arkansas].

In closing Taylor stepped so far over the line of insubordination that Smith had to act. Taylor concluded:

> The same regard for duty which led me to throw myself between you and popular indignation and quietly take the blame of your errors compels me to tell you the truth, however objectionable to you. The grave errors you have committed in the recent campaign may be repeated if the unhappy consequences are not kept before you. After the desire to serve my country, I have none more ardent than to be relieved from longer serving under your command.[28]

Smith could take no more of Taylor's barbs. He relieved Taylor of duty on June 10 and sent him to Natchitoches to await further orders from the Confederate president. The following day Smith composed a letter to President Davis apprising him of how Taylor's relief came about. Smith attached all Taylor's dispatches as evidence to support his decision for relief. Smith was obviously irritated by Taylor, yet throughout the letter to Davis he was respectful of Taylor's acknowledged abilities. He told Davis:

> The tone of [these] letters, the feeling exhibited, and the untruthfulness which characterized it throughout surprised and astonished me. I attributed it to sickness and irritation, with the interests of the service at heart and desirous of conciliating General Taylor, I returned it with the accompanying endorsement and without further official action.... I would have arrested Taylor on receipt of the first letter, but acknowledging his merits as a soldier and feeling kindly disposed toward him, I passed it by. I

have since borne and foreborne [sic] him with self-control ... by love of country and a desire of promoting her best interests. [But] I have relieved General Taylor until the pleasure of Your Excellency can be known.... I shall attempt no refutation of General Taylor's statements.... [Finally if Davis disagreed] I will willingly with no feeling of envy or abatement of interest in the service of my country, turn over my arduous duties and responsibilities to a successor.[29]

Davis sustained Smith's decision to relieve Taylor and this concluded both the Red River Campaign and one of the ugliest command partnerships of the Civil War.

Many of the men's contemporaries were critical of Smith's handling of the Red River Campaign and supportive of Taylor's ideas for defeating the Union foray. Liddell — who was no fan of Taylor's — recorded in his *Record* that Smith "should have kept his [Taylor's] forces together and pushed these successes at Mansfield and Pleasant Hill." General Walker said, "To this fatal blunder [breaking Taylor's army apart] Banks was indebted for his safety." Yet another veteran, a junior officer, wrote that "All generals make mistakes; he [Smith] may have made one" here.[30] All these observations were made in hindsight, when the "fog of war" had cleared from the Red River Valley. Though they are probably right, these assessments do not take into account the human factors of command.

Taylor's attacks, ego, and self-righteous attitude irritated Smith to no end. Smith's indecisiveness and seeming lack of concern for Louisiana angered Taylor as well. The two men, individually completely dedicated to the cause, simply could not get along together. Though each was militarily competent they could not come to an agreement on a course of action. Taylor's continual harsh criticism of Smith probably caused Smith to choose a course of action opposite that favored by his subordinate and then deny him a part in executing the move to Arkansas. The more Smith clung to his Fabian policy, the angrier Taylor became, much to the detriment of their counter-campaign against the Federals. Imagine if these two could have submerged their personalities long enough to focus on the job at hand. It is highly probable that Taylor's assertions that he could capture Banks and Porter would have come to fruition. But, this did not happen, and Taylor would write in his post-war account that Smith seemed "determined to throw a protecting shield around the Federal Army and fleet."[31] Smith and Taylor could not come together and the result was a hollow victory for the Confederates instead of a complete disaster for the Federals.

Chapter 8
"This Fatal Campaign…"

The Red River Campaign stands as one of the most successful campaigns conducted by any Confederate army during the Civil War. A Union army over twice the strength of the widely dispersed Rebels invaded west Louisiana in March 1864. The Federals managed to penetrate over 150 miles into the interior of the Trans-Mississippi, taking several cannon at Fort De Russy, capturing thousands of dollars in cotton, and taking several hundred enemy troops prisoner. Yet, through sheer audacity and superior leadership, General Taylor turned back the invaders, driving them all the way to the Mississippi River. In the process, the Confederates made good all their losses by capturing a huge supply train, dozens of field guns, thousands of stands of small arms, and over a thousand prisoners. In the river, the Union navy lost several boats, including the pride of the fleet, the *Eastport*. By any standard, this is an impressive haul for the small, undersupplied Confederate army. But what was the impact of the campaign on the outcome of the war?

First, the campaign prevented dismemberment and occupation of the Trans-Mississippi by Federal forces. The Confederate defense enabled the Rebel government to maintain territorial integrity of the region west of the Mississippi until the very last days of the war. Although the Trans-Mississippi Department could do little to help the overall war effort in terms of men and material, the victory certainly represented a moral boost to the Confederate government. As J. B. Jones, the Confederate war clerk, said, "There is excitement at last … no one seems to doubt our final success." Admiral Porter feared that Federal "prestige will receive a shock" when the people of the North learned of the defeat; later, in testimony before The Joint Congressional Committee, Porter referred to Red River as "this fatal campaign." Jefferson Davis believed defense of Southern territory of critical importance to maintaining sovereignty and the ever fleeting chance for foreign recognition. Turning back the Union army had allowed Davis to keep up the appearance that the South had control of its own territory.[1]

Next, the campaign delayed full implementation of Grant's spring offensive plans indefinitely. Grant had planned "to concentrate all the force possible against the Confederate armies in the field."[2] Also, Grant wanted to direct Banks' Army of the Gulf against Mobile to close off that valuable port and prevent reinforcement of Joseph Johnston. The expedition successfully kept Grant from massing against these two armies and narrowed the long odds facing the Rebels. This turn of events played right into Confederate strategy for 1864. The Southern high command planned to maintain the status quo in the primary theaters, avoiding a major loss. In minor theaters—such as the Red River Valley—the Rebels would do their best to pin up large numbers of enemy troops and inflict as many casualties as possible. The Confederates hoped a continued stalemate, combined with a covert effort in the North, would turn the Northern electorate against

The National Cemetery at Alexandria, final resting place for hundreds of Union soldiers from the Red River Campaign.

8. "This Fatal Campaign" 121

the Lincoln administration. Kirby Smith realized the importance of what the Confederates were doing to counter the Union expedition. "We occupy a largely superior force of the enemy, which east of the Mississippi would decide the fate of the campaign," he pondered.[3] By keeping the large Union force in the Red River Valley occupied, the Confederates created an excellent chance for their strategy to succeed. At the same time, Grant's strategic designs were delayed indefinitely, so that the Union war effort might actually fail.

The diversion of the Army of the Gulf from Mobile allowed the Confederates to mass at Atlanta, which is what the Union army had intended. Rather than forcing the Confederates to defend Mobile, the expedition left Polk's Corps in southwest Mississippi idle. Using interior lines the Rebels took advantage of the Union miscue and sent Polk to Johnston's outnumbered army. The accession of over 10,000 veteran troops gave the Army of Tennessee a tangible boost in morale. At the same time, Sherman gave up 10,000 of his own troops to go on the Red River Expedition. Therefore, instead of a two-to-one advantage, Sherman would have to make do with a three-to-two margin over the Army of Tennessee, a slim margin when fighting a wily foe like Joseph Johnston.[4]

The final far-reaching effect of the campaign was the prolongation of the war. If the campaign had never occurred then a Mobile expedition would have taken place in May instead of August. A. J. Smith's men would have been available to Sherman and Polk's Corps required for the defense of Mobile. William Brooksher writes in his excellent account that the campaign postponed the outcome of the war "for some indeterminate amount of time." Ludwell Johnson, the original chronicler of the campaign, says that "two months may be a reasonable estimate."[5] Both are correct, but both dismiss the possibility that the campaign could have done anything more than prolong the war. The campaign actually could have done a great deal more than this if the Confederate high command in the Trans-Mississippi Department, principally Smith and Taylor, had made a better effort to maintain harmony.

One of the most important facets of sound military operations is a command climate that fosters cooperation and teamwork. It is the responsibility of both the leaders and subordinates to maintain such a work environment. The relationship between Kirby Smith and Richard Taylor became a huge obstacle to military success. As the campaign progressed, Taylor's surly attitude began to affect his subordinates as well as his superior. The final outcome of the bickering was that the Confederate victory was much smaller than it might have been.

There are several reasons for the ineffectual command relationship between Smith and Taylor. First, Smith and Taylor's personalities clashed because of their different backgrounds. Taylor, son of a president, was a gentleman planter who had a great disdain for pre-war military officers. Smith, the son of a circuit judge, chose a career in the same military that Taylor believed stunted mental development.[6] It is not surprising, therefore, that the two commanders rubbed each other the wrong way. Nevertheless, their mutual dedication to the cause of Southern independence should have enabled them to overcome their differences—but it did not.

Another reason for the friction between the two Confederates was Taylor's myopia. Taylor commanded a district in his home state of Louisiana where he owned a productive sugar plantation. Smith, a Floridian, had responsibility for the defense of the largest region of the Confederacy with the smallest portion of Southern resources. While Smith made plans based on the whole department, Taylor constantly badgered him about the affairs of his district and demanded the preponderance of resources. When Smith did not satisfy his requests, Taylor invariably became indignant, sometimes launching written tirades against Smith.[7]

Smith had a penchant for indecisiveness throughout his tenure in the Trans-Mississippi. Taylor's mentor in 1862 had been the self-confident and always decisive Stonewall Jackson. Stonewall never took counsel of his fears and once he made a decision never wavered in its execution. Taylor had become accustomed to that kind of leadership. In contrast, Kirby Smith often questioned himself and countermanded his own orders in the middle of their execution. Smith's leadership was a considerable source of irritation to Taylor, who took every opportunity to complain about it in official correspondence with Smith.[8]

Taylor's abrasiveness and readiness to criticize his commander no doubt alienated Smith. When Smith began the Camden Expedition in Arkansas, he purposely left Taylor in Louisiana, informing him that his "services were not required." Yet Smith took Taylor's largest division with him north to Arkansas, reducing Taylor's whole army to little more than a division-sized unit. Smith stated on more than one occasion that Taylor was his most competent district commander, and in normal circumstances he would have played a key part in the expedition. The fact that Smith specifically ordered Taylor not to accompany him is a sad testament to the dismal relationship between the two men.[9]

Taylor's openly expressed anger toward Smith destroyed the effectiveness of the Confederate army. Instead of using a diplomatic approach to influence Smith to see things his way, Taylor attacked him. Not surprisingly, Smith did the opposite of what Taylor wished. This stripped Taylor's army of its offensive punch, preventing Taylor from delivering the knockout blow to the Union army. The closer the campaign came to ending, the more Taylor directed criticism toward his subordinates. There is evidence, furthermore, that Taylor sank into depression at Alexandria. Liddell points out in his *Record* that Taylor did little more than await the arrival of Walker's division from Arkansas. He stated that Taylor expected him to disrupt work on Bailey's dam with 700 men while on the other side of the river Taylor did nothing with his 5,000.[10] The end result to all the bickering was a failure to capitalize on the success Mansfield. A little diplomacy and respect could have produced better cooperation and potentially the realization of Taylor's dream — the destruction of Banks' army and Porter's fleet.

Confederate opportunities were not all the creation of the Rebels. The Union army seemed to do all it could to deliver a spectacular victory to the enemy. The "cooperation" of the navy compounded the problems experienced by the army. When the Union high command conceived the idea for an expedition up the Red, it failed to secure a suitable command relationship between the army and navy. Instead of assigning to one service overall responsibility and authority, the high command expected the army and navy to cooperate with one another. Without unity of command the effort was doomed to go in two different directions. The navy and army became protective of their own prerogatives rather than focused on a single goal under one commander.[11]

Banks and Porter as a command team could get along no better than Smith and Taylor. Porter had a history of clashes with politicians and his relationship with Banks was no different, as Porter's correspondence to Gideon Welles amply reflects. Numerous times throughout the campaign, the two men were at odds. At Alexandria, the commanders had a spat over cotton. At Grand Ecore Porter worried that the river would dry up and the army would leave the fleet high and dry.[12] However, one critical difference made their relationship unlike Smith and Taylor's. Rather than allow their personal differences to lead to a catastrophe for the Union cause, they overcame their egos to save the force. Both the Union army and navy would fight another day, delivering decisive blows to the Confederate cause.

Conflicts also existed within the army, primarily between Banks and A. J. Smith. Smith, a career army officer, could not stomach Banks' propensity to lead by coalition, which appeared to Smith as indecisiveness. After Pleasant Hill Smith became so irritated that he began to openly speak of mutiny. The actions of W. B. Franklin diffused this situation, and for the rest of the campaign Smith's command anchored operations for the Union army.[13]

Banks' poor leadership also gave the Confederates opportunities. Banks placed Franklin and later Emory in charge of the march dispositions over the course of the campaign. For significant portions of the expedition, Banks was not even present. He delayed first at New Orleans and later at Alexandria to oversee political arrangements rather than lead the army. At Grand Ecore he lagged behind, ostensibly to look after logistic dispositions, while Franklin led the strung-out column to Mansfield. Too many times Banks did not place himself at the point of decision and the situation always overwhelmed him. It appears that Banks believed the Confederates were too weak to challenge him, so he let his guard down and became careless.[14]

Another factor contributed to Banks' carelessness in the campaign. On March 26, Banks received the letter from Grant telling him to return A. J. Smith's men as soon as possible. Closely following this letter, Banks received a letter from Sherman informing him that the loan of Smith's men to the Army of the Gulf expired on April 10. When Banks received these he was still several days' march from Shreveport and needed to get there quickly to meet the deadline. When the army reached Grand Ecore a critical decision point had been reached. Banks had to decide, with the time constraints set forth, whether to reconnoiter for a route close to the river or diverge from it and take an inland route. Reconnaissance would take time that Banks did not have, but diverging from the river would cut off Banks from critical naval support. Additionally, moving away from the river would force him to use a narrow, single-lane road that led through a howling wilderness.[15] Banks, believing the Confederates would not challenge him short of Shreveport, decided to save time and march away from the river. This gave Taylor the chance he wanted to deal with Banks on ground of his choosing.

Regardless of what the Federals did, the Confederates failed to capitalize on the opportunities given them. Taylor successfully turned back the Union tide at Mansfield and ran the Federals all the way back to Pleasant Hill. Though Taylor received a setback at Pleasant Hill, the Federal army left him in command of the field. Here the Confederates faced their critical decision point. Taylor argued vehemently to keep his army together to run Banks and Porter to ground. He argued that Frederick Steele's prong moving south to Shreveport would turn back when learning of Banks' demise. Smith disagreed, saying that "Steele is bold to rashness" and presented the greater threat to the department.[16] Therefore, he detached Churchill's, Parsons', and Walker's divisions, believing that Banks would continue retreating while he dealt with Steele. Smith had developed this Fabian defensive strategy and he believed that now was the time to put it into action. What if Smith had possessed the mental flexibility to leave Taylor's army intact to finish off Banks rather than chasing after Steele?

Taylor had three distinct opportunities to capture or destroy Banks' army after Pleasant Hill: first at Grand Ecore, then Monette's Ferry, and finally Alexandria. Had Taylor destroyed Banks this would have delivered the fleet to the Confederates by default. Taylor simply did not have the force to do this after Smith took the three infantry divisions from his army. If Smith had not taken these troops and Taylor had used them properly it is likely Taylor could have captured or destroyed Banks.

After the Army of the Gulf escaped the Red River Valley, the Union high command split it up to use as reinforcements in the East. A. J. Smith's command returned to north Mississippi under orders from Sherman to keep Forrest away from his tenuous supply line.[17] Without A. J. Smith's men Sherman would have had to detach more soldiers from his army driving on Atlanta. This would have further reduced Sherman's numerical advantage over Johnston, making it more difficult to take the city. Instead of taking Atlanta in September, Sherman would have been delayed indefinitely — possibly until after the November elections.

The long-delayed Mobile expedition finally came off in August using troops from the XIII Army Corps. The capture of this city closed a vital artery off to the Confederacy and represented the first significant boost in morale for the North in 1864.[18] If Taylor had been successful in destroying Banks, where would the troops have come from to embark on an expedition to Mobile? From Sherman? Or Meade? Any detachments would have weakened the Union forces in Georgia and Virginia while strengthening their adversary.

The XIX Army Corps with part of the XIIIth went to Virginia to strengthen the Army of the Potomac in July. Grant initially wanted the XIXth to go in line at Petersburg against Lee's besieged army there. Jubal Early's raid on Washington abruptly changed the plan and Grant diverted the corps to Washington without disembarking. Together with the VI Army Corps from the Army of the Potomac, the XIXth threw Early from Maryland and eventually played a decisive role in crushing him at Cedar Creek in October.[19] This victory became the icing on the cake for Lincoln's reelection bid in November as voters realized the North indeed was finally winning.

Grant had lost 50,000 irreplaceable men in the Overland Campaign in the spring and summer of 1864. The addition of the XIXth Corps made a welcome addition to the Army of the Potomac. Once again, if Taylor had destroyed or captured them, Grant would not have received these invaluable veterans. He would have had to detach two corps instead of one to defend Washington and chase Early back into Virginia. Lee, known for his boldness, might have taken the initiative to lunge at Meade now had the odds been improved. In any event, the non-arrival of the XIXth probably would have meant that Cedar Creek didn't happen.

Kilby Smith's division returned directly to Sherman's army operating around Atlanta. Although it was not a large accession, no general turns away a division of veteran troops. Smith's men reintegrated into the XVII Army Corps as replacements for the depleted brigades in the corps. The XVIIth had a significant role in the final capture of Atlanta.[20]

By default, defeating Banks would have made Porter's position untenable, forcing him to surrender or blow up the fleet.[21] The addition of a couple of good gunboats would have greatly improved Rebel prospects for reopening communication with the Eastern Confederacy. Mere destruction of the boats would have made patrolling the long, wide Mississippi infinitely tougher for the Federals and improved Confederate communication across the river. The loss of the fleet and the Army of the Gulf would certainly have shocked the Northern public, who had witnessed the Herculean attempts to close the Mississippi to the Confederates in 1863.

The Northern public held the key to Rebel prospects for victory in 1864. Militarily, the Confederacy simply did not have the resources to defeat the North. However, 1864 was an election year and the key to winning now was making the election a referendum on the war itself. If the Confederacy could make Northern efforts in 1864 appear too costly in the minds of the voters, then the Confederates had a chance. As Shelby Foote put it, the South "could win, in short, because the North could lose."[22] The South simply had to defend the heartland and prevent Federal armies from appearing to make any significant gains before November.

Northern morale in the summer of 1864 was at a low ebb. The failed Red River Campaign, even in its indecisive outcome, went far toward dragging Northern faith in the cause downward. Also, in the spring, the Southerners had received a boost after Major General Robert F. Hoke recaptured Plymouth, North Carolina. This threatened the Union footholds along the East Coast and blockading operations in that region. In front of Atlanta, Sherman found his offensive frustrated at every turn by the wily Johnston. Grant's offensive in Virginia similarly ground to a halt, and both threatened to drag on indefinitely with no appreciable results. Southern strategy appeared to be working as Northern voters sank into despair with late summer approaching. Then the bottom suddenly fell out.

President Davis could not adhere to a defensive strategy that put a premium on patience. He bombarded Johnston with demands for offensive action against Sherman, counter to Confederate strategy. When Davis' demands went unheeded by the contentious Johnston, Davis relieved him in favor of Lieutenant General John Bell Hood.[23] Davis got the offensive action he wanted and Sherman quickly thrashed Hood. It was now late July moving into August and the troops who had lately participated in the ill-starred Red River Campaign began arriving at locations throughout the East. This provided the main Union armies with the boost they needed in terms of personnel at a critical time. The Confederacy had no reinforcements to provide their armies and the added weight of the dismantled Army of the Gulf made a decisive difference at all points.

The biggest difference made by the trifecta of Union victories lay in the minds of the Northern electorate. Had the presidential election been held in August it is quite likely Abraham Lincoln would have lost to a Democrat with a peace platform. However, in August Farragut — with elements of the XIII Army Corps— steamed into Mobile. In September, with A. J. Smith holding down Forrest and Kilby Smith's men adding numbers to Sherman's army, the Federals captured Atlanta. In October, the XIX Army Corps assisted in permanently expelling the Confederates from the Shanandoah Valley. With each victory voter confidence in the Lincoln administration steadily soared upward. In November, the voters convincingly reelected Lincoln, sealing the Confederacy's fate. The Confederates could no longer hope for a negotiated peace. To win the war now, they had to win on the battlefield.[24]

The recognition of and then capitalization on opportunity means the difference between victory and defeat on the battlefield. Just as important is the submission of personalities by leaders to ensure cooperation on their common cause. Richard Taylor recognized vast possibilities offered by the Federal incursion into the Red River Valley, away from the main theater of the war. Smith did not see things the same way, preferring to preserve the integrity of the department. Taylor could have diplomatically pressed his commander to pursue Banks, where the great opportunity lay. Instead, Taylor foolishly attacked Smith's strategy and pushed his commander toward choosing the opposite course of action. Smith, a proud man, reacted predictably, spurning Taylor's acid-laced advice. Because of a conflict of personality they could not come to agreement and fought the entire campaign at cross-purposes. This produced a hollow victory and allowed the Army of the Gulf to tip the scales toward victory in the East.

The Union commanders had a stormy relationship as well. They were at odds with each other at every turn of the campaign. At the critical point of the expedition, however, Banks and Porter were able to subdue their personalities in favor of preserving the force. Had they not done this, the Union would have lost the services of 30,000 veteran troops and a significant chunk of the "brown water" navy. Banks and Porter's cooperation saved an army and fleet that decisively influenced the final outcome of the Civil War in favor of the Union.

Appendix 1: Campaign Chronology[1]

Date	Event
1863	
10 August	Halleck sends dispatch to Banks informing him of need "to restore the flag" to Texas soil and suggesting Red River as invasion route.
8 September	Franklin's landing force repulsed at Sabine Pass, Texas.
2 November	Banks lands small detachments along Texas coast.
7 December	Halleck writes Banks expressing displeasure over landings on Texas coast. Again suggests Red River as proper route of invasion.
1864	
23 January	Banks supports an expedition up Red River. Halleck coordinates cooperation from the navy, Sherman, and Steele.
10 March	General A. J. Smith's detachment from the Army of the Tennessee moves from Vicksburg en route to Red River. Admiral David D. Porter provides escort with boats from the Mississippi Squadron.
12 March	Smith and Porter arrive at mouth of the Red. Troops disembark at Simmesport and begin moving overland on Fort De Russy.
14 March	Troops from General Joseph Mower's Division capture Fort De Russy. General Franklin starts with Army of the Gulf from Berwick's Bay en route to Alexandria.
15 March	Union gunboats arrive at Alexandria.
16 March	Van of Smith's force arrive at Alexandria. General Nathan Bedford Forrest begins raid into west Tennessee and Kentucky.

Appendix 1: Campaign Chronology

Date	Event
18 March	General E. Kirby Smith orders reinforcements from Arkansas and Texas to Louisiana to bolster Taylor's District of West Louisiana.
20 March	Skirmish at Bayou Rapides north of Alexandria as Federal troops conduct reconnaissance. Van of Franklin's column begins arriving at Alexandria.
21 March	Mower captures most of Taylor's cavalry at Henderson's Hill on a stormy, miserable night when the Confederates posted no pickets.
23 March	Major General Frederick Steele begins advance south from Little Rock bound for Shreveport on Red River.
24 March	Franklin's column closes at Alexandria.
25 March	General Banks arrives in person at Alexandria.
28 March	Combined force consisting of the Army of the Gulf and A. J. Smith's command move forward from Alexandria.
1 April	Army arrives at Natchitoches while navy pulls in at Grand Ecore. Banks conducts elections at Alexandria. Churchill and Parsons' Divisions from Arkansas begin arriving vicinity of Shreveport.
2 April	Banks leaves Alexandria to link up with army assembling at Grand Ecore.
4 April	Banks receives letter from Grant advising him to take Shreveport as soon as possible or abandon the expedition. Churchill and Parsons ordered down to Keatchie north of Mansfield in supporting distance of Taylor.
5 April	Banks decides to diverge from river to make better time to Shreveport.
6 April	Army moves from Grand Ecore toward Pleasant Hill. Thomas Green's cavalry arrives near Pleasant Hill from Texas to reinforce Taylor.
7 April	Banks' cavalry has skirmish at Wilson's Farm vicinity Pleasant Hill. This is the first significant resistance offered by the Confederates since the start of the campaign.
8 April	Taylor turns back Army of the Gulf at Sabine Crossroads—also known as the Battle of Mansfield.
9 April	Combined Confederate Trans-Mississippi forces attack Army of the Gulf at Pleasant Hill as Taylor attempts to follow up victory of Sabine Crossroads. E. Kirby Smith arrives on battlefield initially notifying Taylor of his intent to take Churchill, Parsons, and Walker with him to Arkansas to pursue Steele.
10 April	Banks decides to withdraw back to Grand Ecore.
11 April	Banks arrives back at Grand Ecore while Admiral Porter stalls at Loggy Bayou where Confederates have obstructed the river. Couriers reach Porter, informing him of the army's reverse. Porter starts back to Grand Ecore.

Appendix 1: Campaign Chronology

Date	Event
12 April	Engagement between Green's cavalry and gunboats at Blair's Landing. Little damage to either side, but Thomas Green is killed.
13 April	Porter arrives back at Grand Ecore.
14 April	Taylor sends Churchill's, Parsons', and Walker's Divisions to Shreveport for advance into Arkansas. Meanwhile remainder of his army has Union army at Grand Ecore loosely invested.
15 April	*Eastport* strikes mine, sinking in shallow water.
18 April	Steele receives serious setback as Confederate cavalry captures a huge supply train at Poison Springs bound for his army.
21 April	Banks begins retreat from Grand Ecore back to Alexandria following route that will take him between Cane and Red Rivers. Taylor follows closely while sending a force around to cut off Federal retreat at Monette's Ferry.
23 April	Battle at Monette's Ferry. XIX Army Corps successfully forces a crossing at the Ferry, pushing Hamilton Bee's scratch force aside.
25 April	Army of the Gulf begins arriving back at Alexandria. Taylor makes dispositions to block the Red below Alexandria and lay a loose siege to the town.
26 April	Fleet suffers heavy damage at confluence of Red and Cane as Confederates successfully block river. Porter is forced to scuttle the *Eastport*. Frederick Steele turns back in Arkansas headed for Little Rock.
30 April	E. Kirby Smith fights ineffectual battle at Jenkin's Ferry in Arkansas, suffering heavy losses. Steele continues retreat to Little Rock.
1 May	Confederate cavalry blocking Red captures transport *Emma* at David's Ferry.
3 May	Frederick Steele back at Little Rock.
4 May	Rebels destroy supply steamer *Covington* while capturing gunboats *Signal* and *Warner* at Dunn's Bayou. Red is effectively blocked to Union communication. Banks gives approval to construct Bailey's dam to free boats trapped above the rapids at Alexandria.
13 May	Fleet passes falls at Alexandria. Banks resumes retreat. Alexandria destroyed by fire as Union troops pull out of town.
15 May	Skirmish at Avoyelle's Prairie.
16 May	Fighting continues along Banks' route of retreat at Mansura as Taylor makes last-ditch attempts to stop Union army.
18 May	Sharp engagement at Yellow Bayou, final engagement of the campaign.
19 May	Lieutenant Colonel Bailey constructs transport bridge so Union army can cross the Atchafalaya at Simmesport.

Appendix 1: Campaign Chronology

Date	Event
20–21 May	Union Army of the Gulf crosses the Atchafalaya, making good their escape from Red River Valley.
22 May	A. J. Smith reembarks for Mississippi.
5 June	Taylor relieved by E. Kirby Smith.
11 July	Elements of the XIX Army Corps arrive in Washington, D.C., to repulse General Jubal Early's attack on Washington.
14 July	A. J. Smith with XVI Army Corps engages Forrest at Tupelo, Mississippi. Smith has kept Forrest occupied since arriving from Red River Campaign, preventing Forrest from cutting Sherman's supply line.
2–8 August	Elements of the former XIII Army Corps with Farragut's fleet steam into Mobile Bay, cutting off port, taking Fort Gaines, and laying siege to Fort Morgan.
1–2 September	Confederates evacuate Atlanta, while Sherman — with elements of the XVII Army Corps that participated in the Red River Campaign — moves in to take the city.
19 September	XIX Army Corps, part of army commanded by General Phillip Sheridan, defeats Early at Winchester, Virginia, in the Shanandoah Valley.
22 September	Early suffers another defeat at Fisher's Hill in Shanandoah with the XIX Army Corps present.
19 October	XIX Army Corps plays decisive role in defeat of Early at Cedar Creek, representing the final break of Confederate control of the Shanandoah.
8 November	Lincoln reelected President by a margin of 494,567 votes out of 4,166,537 cast for a 55% majority. This event guarantees Union victory in the Civil War.

Appendix 2: Order of Battle[1]

UNION ARMY OF THE GULF
Major General Nathaniel P. Banks
Headquarters Troops, A and B Companies
C Company (escort)

Thirteenth Army Corps (Two Divisions Detached)
Brigadier General Thomas E. G. Ransom (wounded)

THIRD DIVISION
BRIGADIER GENERAL ROBERT A. CAMERON

First Brigade:
Lieutenant Colonel Aaron M. Flor
46th Indiana
29th Indiana

Second Brigade:
Colonel William H. Raynor
24th Iowa
28th Iowa
56th Ohio

Artillery:
A Battery, 1st Missouri Light
2d Battery, Ohio Light

FOURTH DIVISION
COLONEL WILLIAM J. LANDRAM

First Brigade:
Colonel Frank Emerson
  (wounded and captured)

Second Brigade:
Colonel Joseph W. Vance
  (killed)

Appendix 2: Order of Battle

(First Brigade cont'd)
77th Illinois
67th Indiana
19th Kentucky
23d Wisconsin

Artillery:
1st Battery, Indiana Light
Chicago Mercantile Battery

(Second Brigade cont'd)
130th Illinois
48th Ohio
83d Ohio
96th Ohio

Nineteenth Army Corps
Major General William B. Franklin (wounded)

FIRST DIVISION
BRIGADIER GENERAL WILLIAM H. EMORY

First Brigade:
Brigadier General William Dwight
29th Maine
114th New York
116th New York
153d New York
161st New York

Second Brigade:
Brigadier General James W. McMillan
13th Maine
15th Maine
160th New York
47th Pennsylvania

Third Brigade:
Colonel Lewis Benedict (killed)
30th Maine
162d New York
165th New York
173d New York

Artillery:
Captain George T. Hebard
25th Battery, New York Light
L Battery, 1st United States
1st Battery, Vermont Light

SECOND DIVISION
BRIGADIER GENERAL CUVIER GROVER

Second Brigade:
Brigadier General Henry Birge
13th Connecticut
1st Louisiana
90th New York (3 companies)
159th New York

Third Brigade:
Colonel Jacob Sharpe
38th Massachusetts
128th New York
156th New York (3 companies)
175th New York

First Brigade
  (arrived after Pleasant Hill):
Brigadier General S. F. Nickerson
133d New York
176th New York

Artillery:
Captain George W. Fox
7th Battery, Massachusetts Light
26th Battery, New York Light
F Battery, 1st United States
C Battery, 2d United States

Cavalry:
3d Maryland

Corps Artillery Reserve:
Captain Henry Closson

Appendix 2: Order of Battle 135

(Corps Artillery Reserve cont'd)
1st Battery, Delaware Light
D Battery, 1st Indiana Heavy

CAVALRY DIVISION
BRIGADIER GENERAL ALBERT L. LEE (RELIEVED)
BRIGADIER GENERAL RICHARD ARNOLD
(ASSUMED COMMAND 18 APRIL 1864)

First Brigade:
Colonel Thomas J. Lucas
16th Indiana Infantry (Mounted)
2d Louisiana Infantry (Mounted)
6th Missouri
14th New York

Second Brigade:
Colonel Harai Robinson
87th Illinois Infantry (Mounted)
1st Louisiana

Fourth Brigade:
Colonel Nathan A. M. Dudley
2d Illinois
3d Massachusetts
31st Massachusetts Infantry (Mounted)
8th New Hampshire Infantry (Mounted)

Fifth Brigade:
Colonel Oliver P. Gooding
2d New York
18th New York
3d Rhode Island

Corps D'Afrique (1st Brigade, 1st Division):
Colonel William H. Dickey
1st Infantry (73d U.S.C.T.)
3d Infantry (75th U.S.C.T.)
12th Infantry (84th U.S.C.T.)
22d Infantry (92d U.S.C.T.)

Engineer Brigade:
Colonel George D. Robinson
3d Engineers, Corps D'Afrique
5th Engineers, Corps D' Afrique

Transferred from Texas to Louisiana between dates 18–26 April 1864:
Thirteenth Army Corps
Major General John A. McClernand

1ST DIVISION, 2D BRIGADE
BRIGADIER GENERAL MICHAEL K. LAWLER

49th Indiana
69th Indiana
34th Iowa

22d Kentucky
16th Ohio
114th Ohio

Detachment from the Army of the Tennessee
Brigadier General Andrew J. Smith

FIRST DIVISION, SIXTEENTH ARMY CORPS
BRIGADIER GENERAL JOSEPH A. MOWER[2]

Second Brigade:
Colonel Lucius Hubbard
47th Illinois

Third Brigade:
Colonel Sylvester G. Hill
35th Iowa

(Second Brigade cont'd)
5th Minnesota
8th Wisconsin

(Third Brigade cont'd)
33d Missouri

Third Division, Sixteenth Army Corps

First Brigade:
Colonel William F. Lynch
58th Illinois
119th Illinois
89th Indiana

Second Brigade:
Colonel William T. Shaw
14th Iowa
27th Iowa
32d Iowa
24th Missouri (with non-veterans of the 21st Missouri attached)

Third Brigade:
Colonel Risdon M. Moore
49th Illinois
117th Illinois
178th Illinois

Artillery:
Captain James M. Cockefair
3d Battery, Indiana Light
9th Battery, Indiana Light

Provisional Division, Seventeenth Army Corps
Brigadier General Thomas Kilby Smith

First Brigade:
41st Illinois
3d Iowa
33d Wisconsin

Second Brigade:
81st Illinois
95th Illinois
14th Wisconsin

Artillery:
M Battery, 1st Missouri Light

Confederate Army
Department of the Trans-Mississippi
General Edmund Kirby Smith

District of West Louisiana
Major General Richard Taylor

Walker's Division[3]
Major General John G. Walker (wounded)

Waul's Brigade:
Brigadier General Thomas N. Waul

8th Texas
18th Texas
22d Texas

Scurry's Brigade:
Brigadier General W. R. Scurry
(killed in Arkansas)
3d Texas
16th Texas
17th Texas

(Waul's Brigade cont'd)
13th Texas Cavalry (Dismounted)

Randal's Brigade:
Colonel Horace Randal
   28th Texas Cavalry (Dismounted)
11th Texas
14th Texas
Gould's Battalion

(Scurry's Brigade cont'd)
19th Texas
16th Texas Cavalry (Dismounted)

MOUTON'S DIVISION
BRIGADIER GENERAL ALFRED MOUTON (KILLED)

Polignac's Brigade:
Brigadier General Camille J. de Polignac
15th Texas
17th Texas Cavalry (Dismounted)
22d Texas Cavalry (Dismounted)
31st Texas Cavalry (Dismounted)
34th Texas Cavalry (Dismounted)

Gray's Brigade:
Colonel Henry Gray
18th Louisiana
28th Louisiana
Crescent Regiment

Sub-District of North Louisiana
Brigadier General St. John R. Liddell

CAVALRY DIVISION
BRIGADIER GENERAL THOMAS GREEN (KILLED)
MAJOR GENERAL JOHN A. WHARTON
(ASSUMED COMMAND 19 APRIL 1864)

Bee's Brigade:
Brigadier General Hamilton Bee
1st Texas Cavalry
23d Texas Cavalry
26th Texas Cavalry
35th Texas Cavalry
36th Texas Cavalry

Major's Brigade:
Brigadier General James P. Major
1st Texas Partisan Rangers
2d Texas Partisan Rangers
2d Arizona Cavalry
3d Arizona Cavalry

Bagby's Brigade:
Brigadier General Arthur P. Bagby
4th Texas Cavalry
5th Texas Cavalry
7th Texas Cavalry
13th Texas Cavalry

Unattached Cavalry:
2d Louisiana
4th Louisiana

Detachment of Price's Army
(under Taylor's operational control from 3–14 April 1864)

ARKANSAS DIVISION
BRIGADIER GENERAL THOMAS J. CHURCHILL

Tappan's Brigade:
Brigadier General J. C. Tappan
19th and 24th Arkansas
27th and 38th Arkansas
33d Arkansas

Gause's Brigade:
Colonel L. C. Gause
26th Arkansas
32d Arkansas
36th Arkansas

Hawthorn's Brigade[4]

MISSOURI DIVISION
BRIGADIER GENERAL MOSBY M. PARSONS

First Brigade:
Brigadier General John B. Clark
8th Missouri
9th Missouri
Ruffner's Missouri Battery

Second Brigade:
Colonel S. P. Burns
10th Missouri
11th Missouri
12th Missouri
16th Missouri
9th Missouri Battalion Sharpshooters
Lesueur's Missouri Battery

Appendix 3: Maps

The maps in this appendix, most of which are reproduced from the *Official Records* and *Battles and Leaders of the Civil War*, provide a perspective of the participants' actions during the engagements of the Red River Campaign. Also included are new interpretive maps (by the author) of the primary battles, which clarify the *Official Records* maps and offer detailed analysis of unit movements and actions.

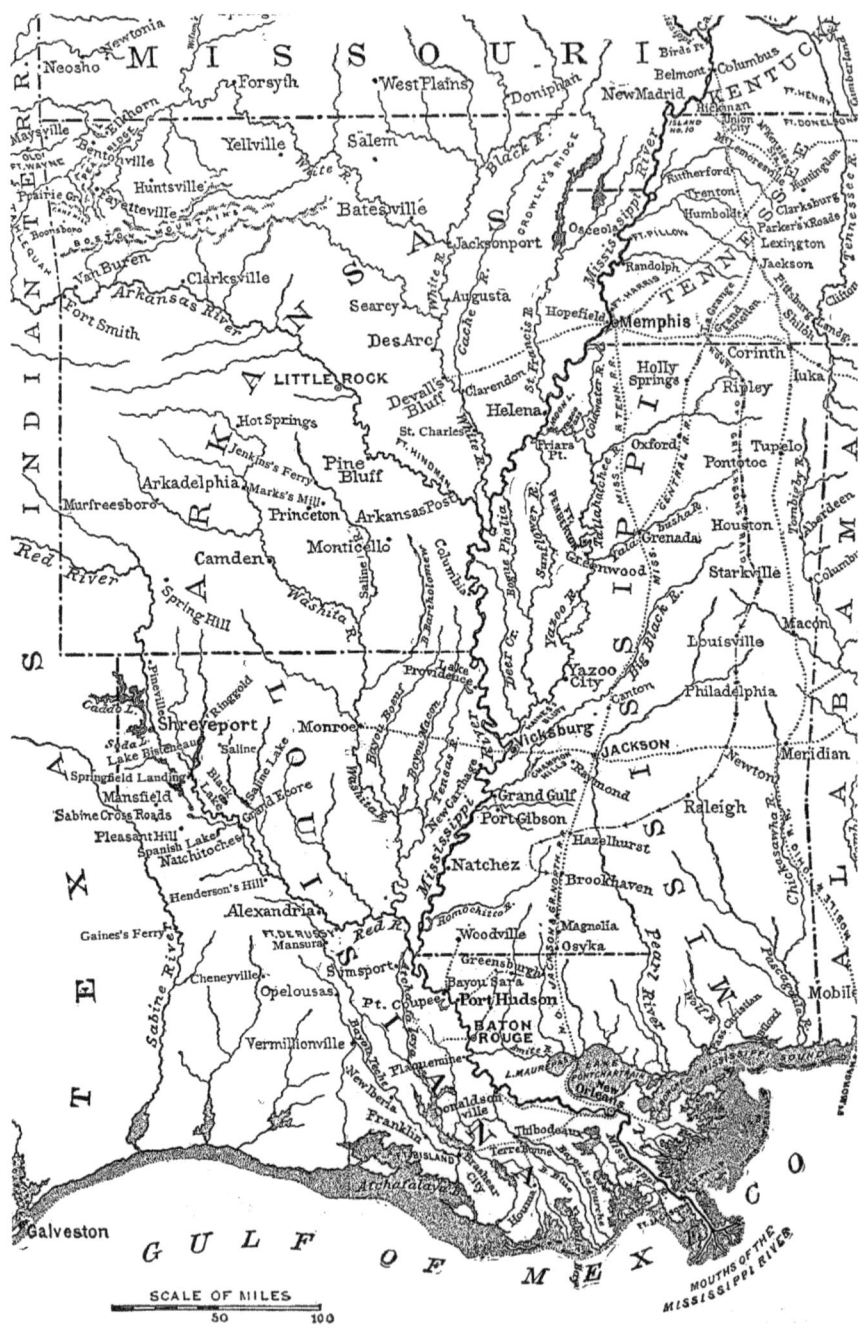

Map 1. Theater of Operations. (Source: *Battles and Leaders of the Civil War*, IV, 348.)

Appendix 3: Maps 141

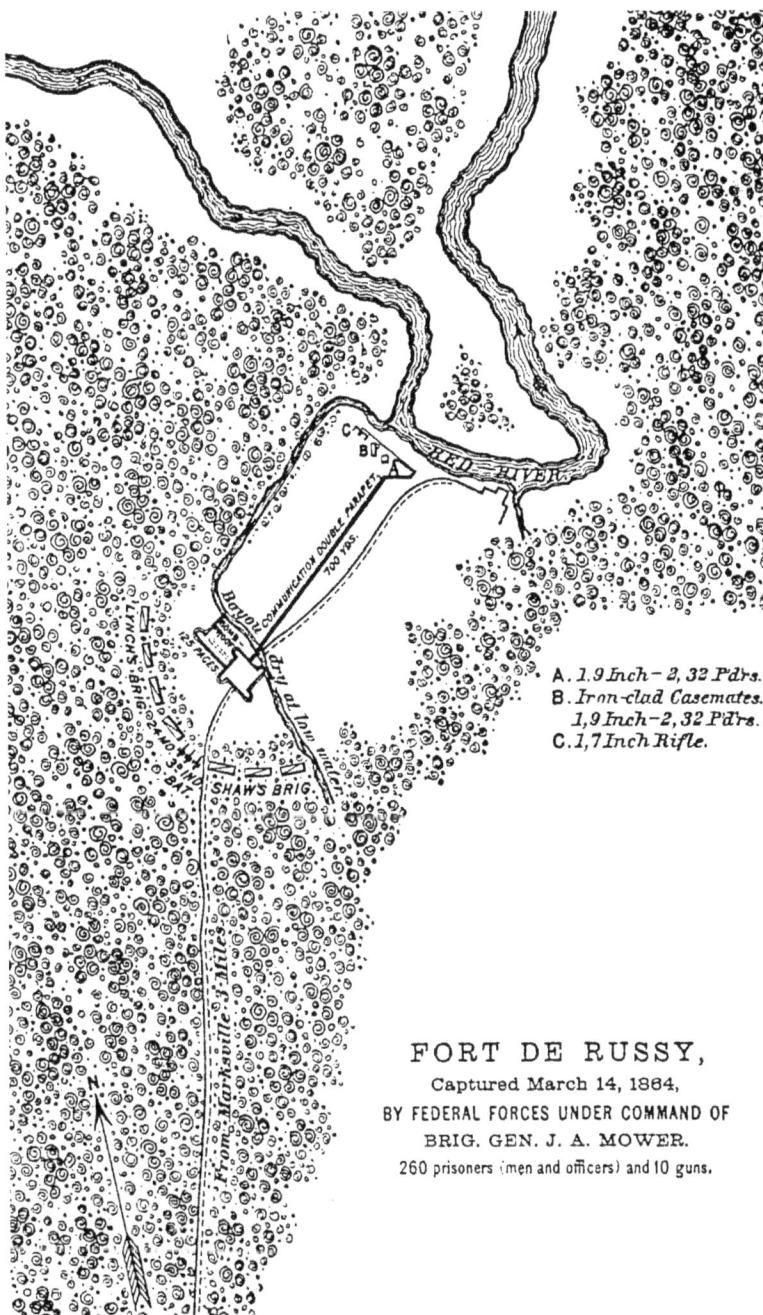

Map 2. Fort De Russy. (Source: *Official Records*, series 1, volume 34, part 1, 224.)

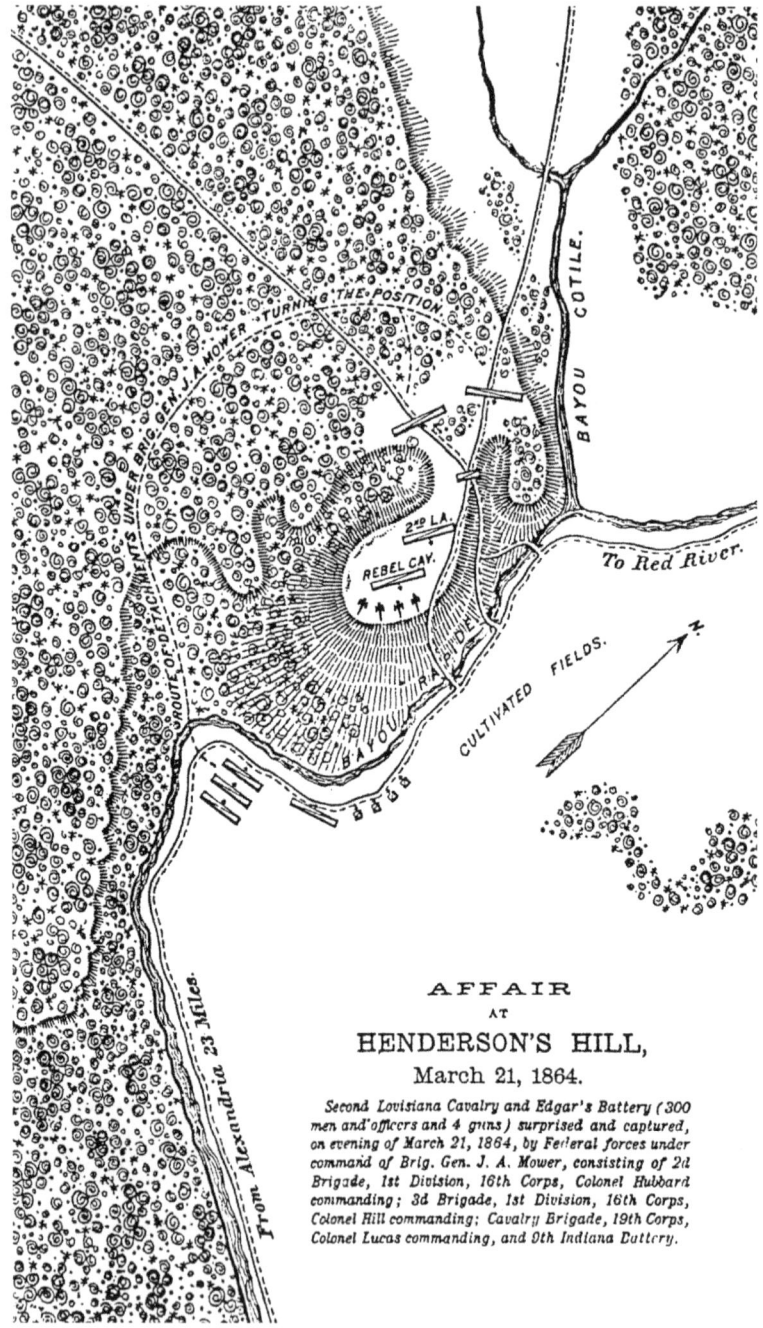

Map 3. Henderson's Hill. (Source: *Official Records*, series 1, volume 34, part 1, 225.)

Appendix 3: Maps

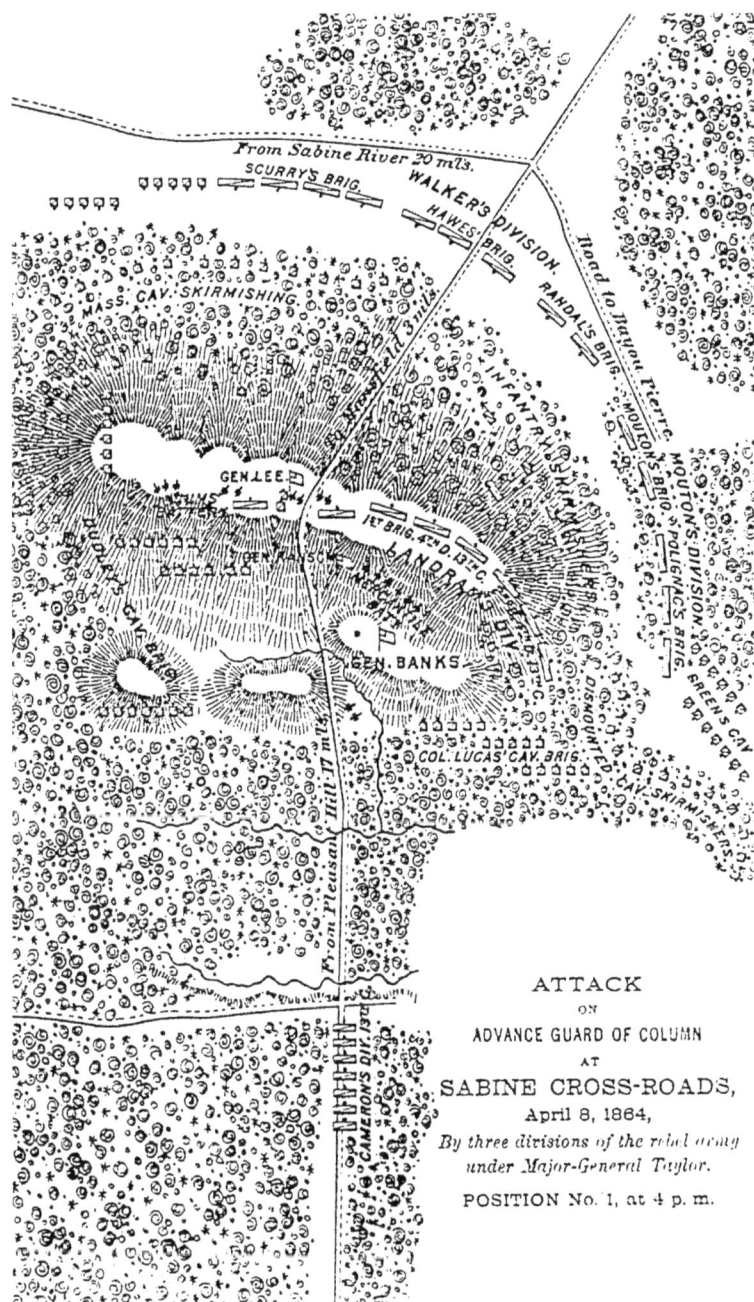

Map 4. Sabine Crossroads Phase 1— Huneycutt Hill. (Source: *Official Records*, series 1, volume 34, part 1, 227.)

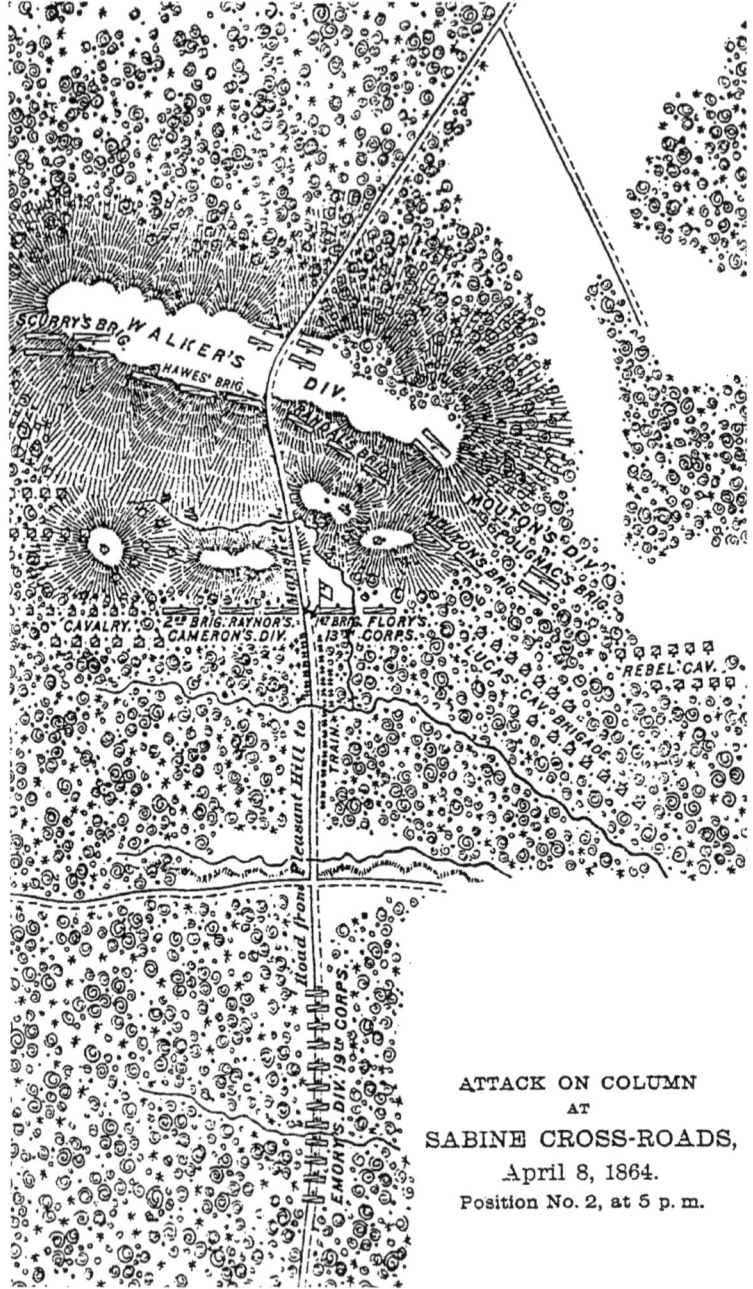

Map 5. Sabine Crossroads Phase 2 — Attack on Cameron's Division and the Cavalry Train. (Source: *Official Records*, series 1, volume 34, part 1, 228.)

Appendix 3: Maps

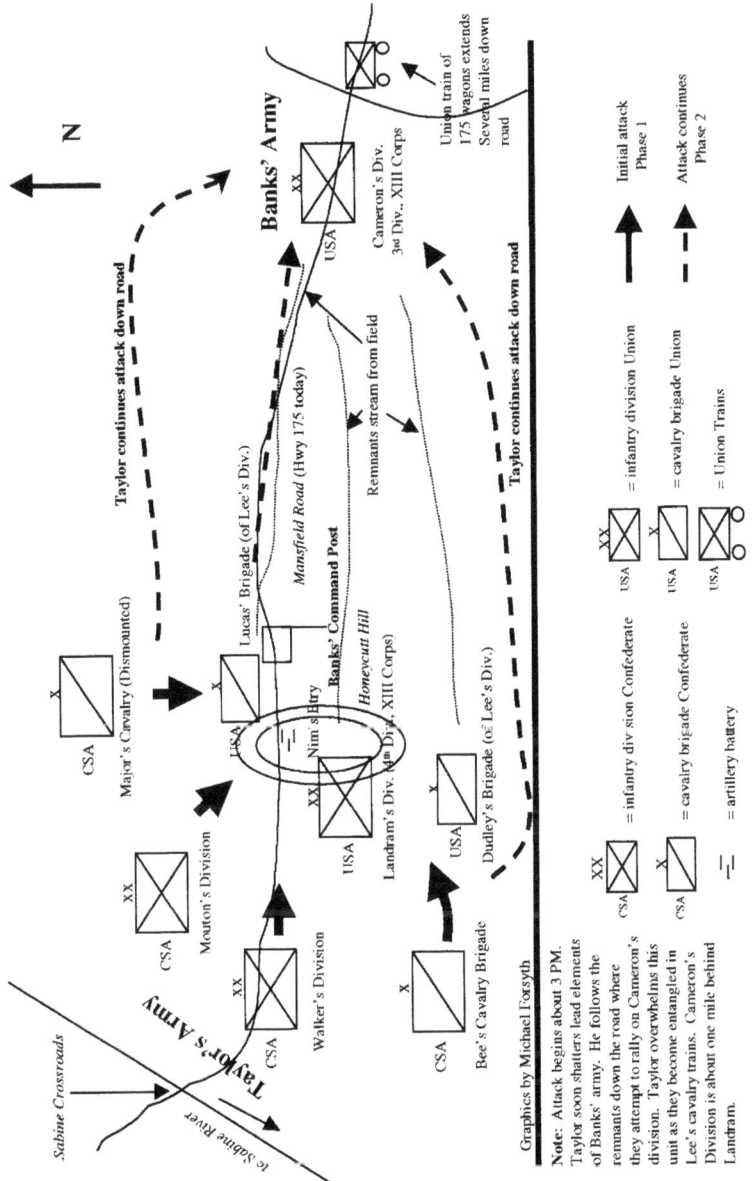

Map 5A. Battle of Sabine Crossroads – Phases 1 & 2: Supplement to Maps 4 and 5.

146   Appendix 3: Maps

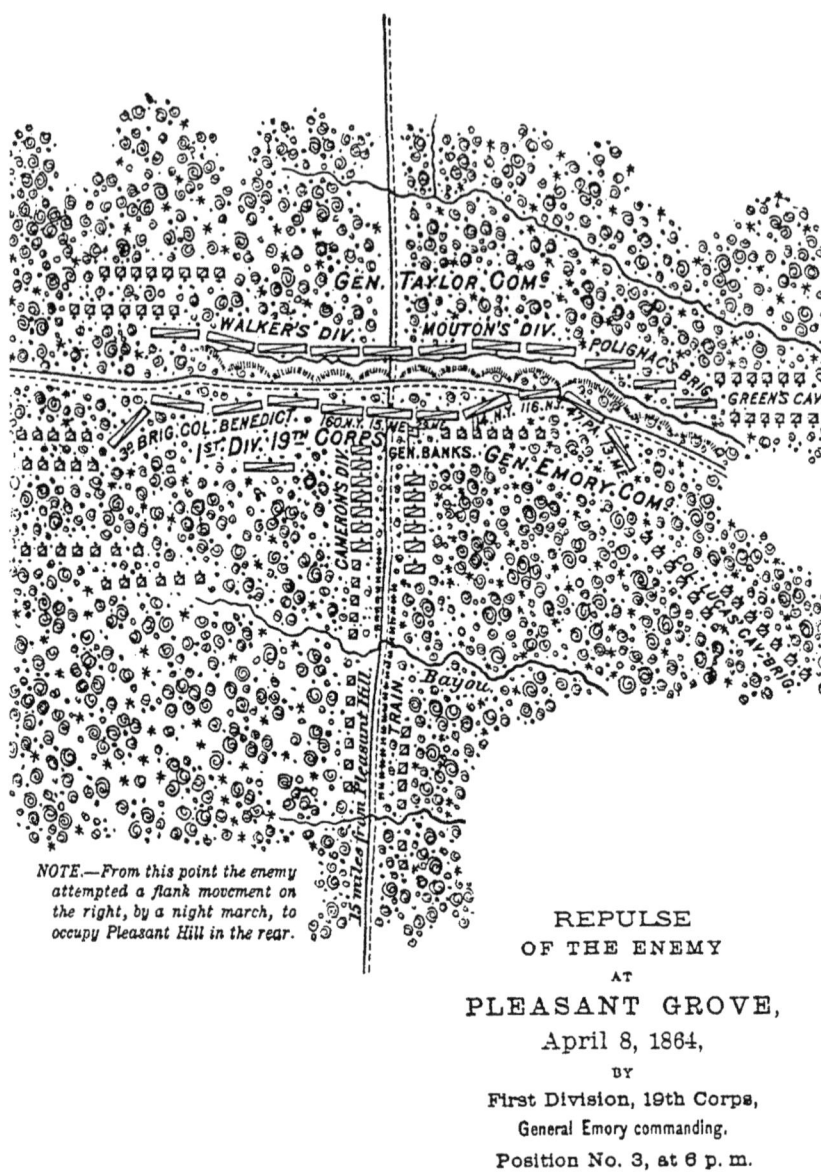

Map 6. Sabine Crossroads Phase 3 — Emory Halts Taylor. (Source: *Official Records*, series 1, volume 34, part 1, 229.)

Appendix 3: Maps 147

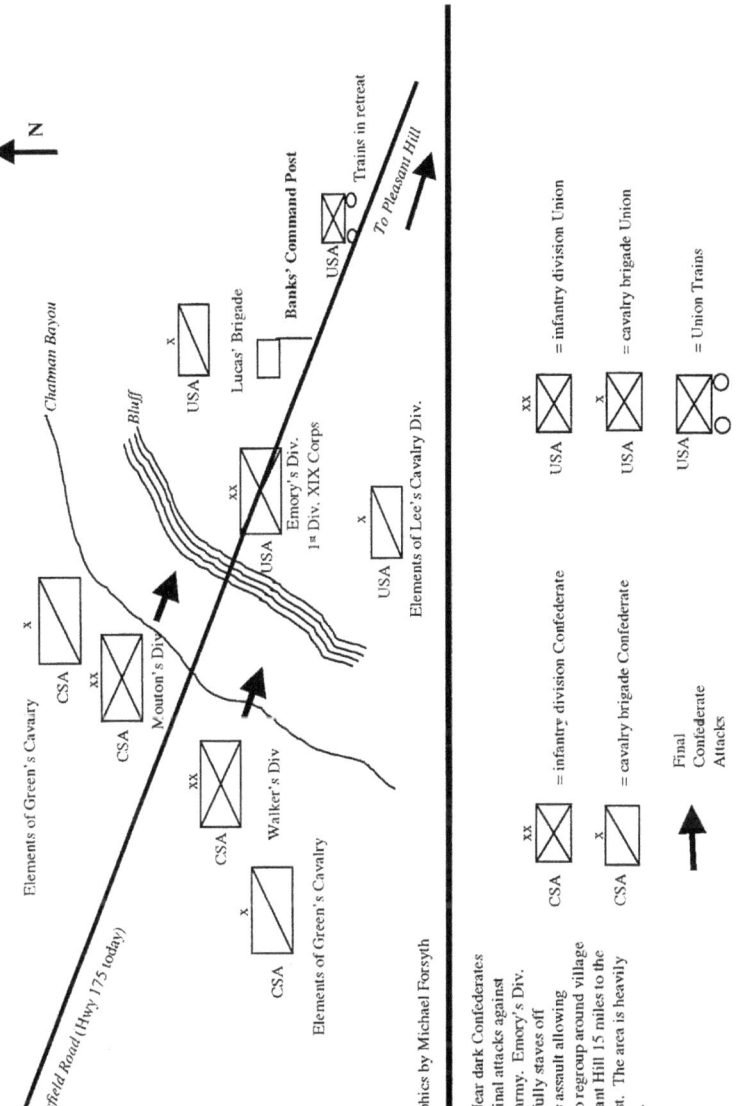

Map 6A. Battle of Sabine Crossroads – Phase 3: Supplement to Map 6.

Map 7. Pleasant Hill — Initial Confederate Attack. (Source: *Official Records*, series 1, volume 34, part 1, 230.)

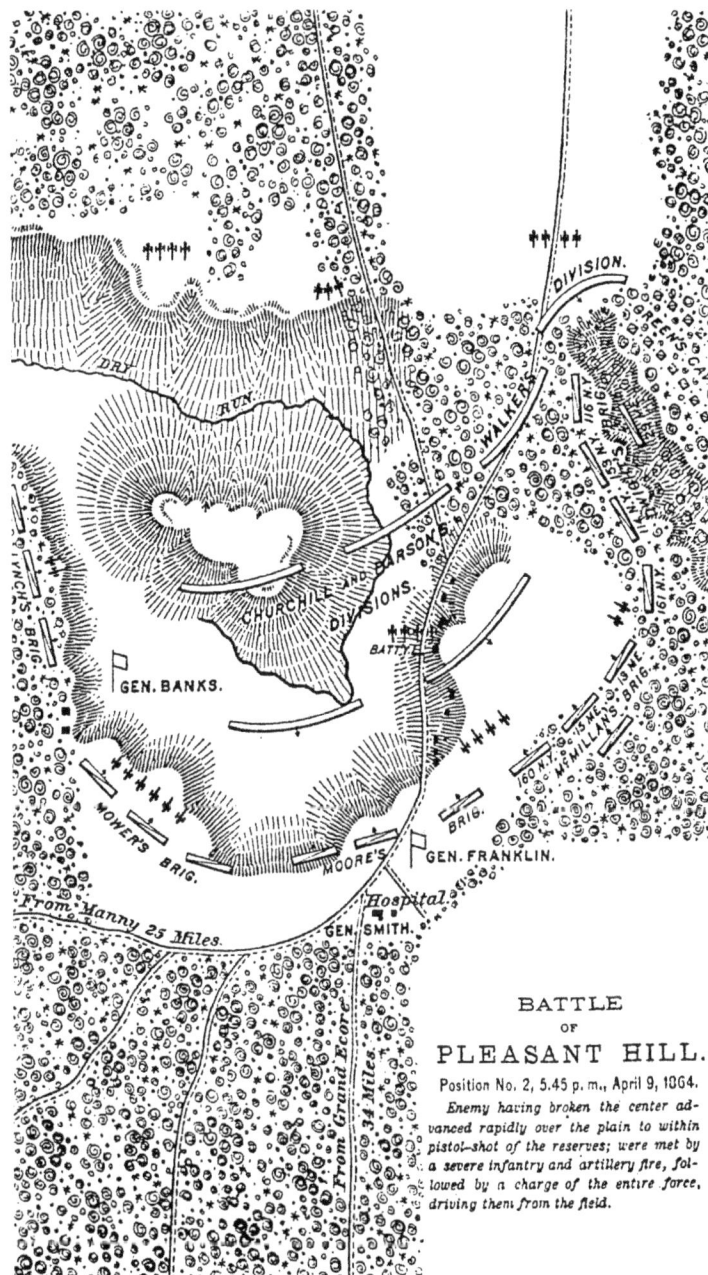

Map 8. Pleasant Hill — Farthest Confederate Advance. (Source: *Official Records*, series 1, volume 34, part 1, 231.)

150 Appendix 3: Maps

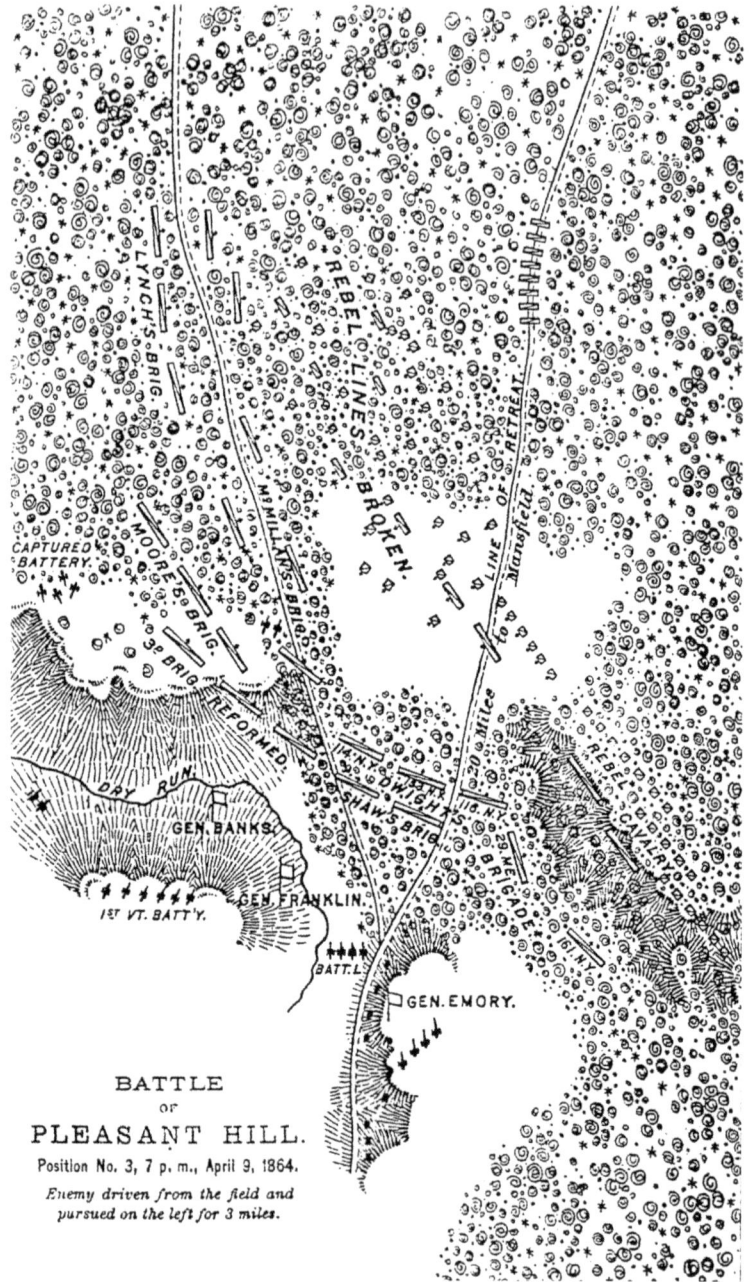

Map 9. Pleasant Hill — A. J. Smith's Counterattack. (Source: *Official Records*, series 1, volume 34, part 1, 232.)

Appendix 3: Maps

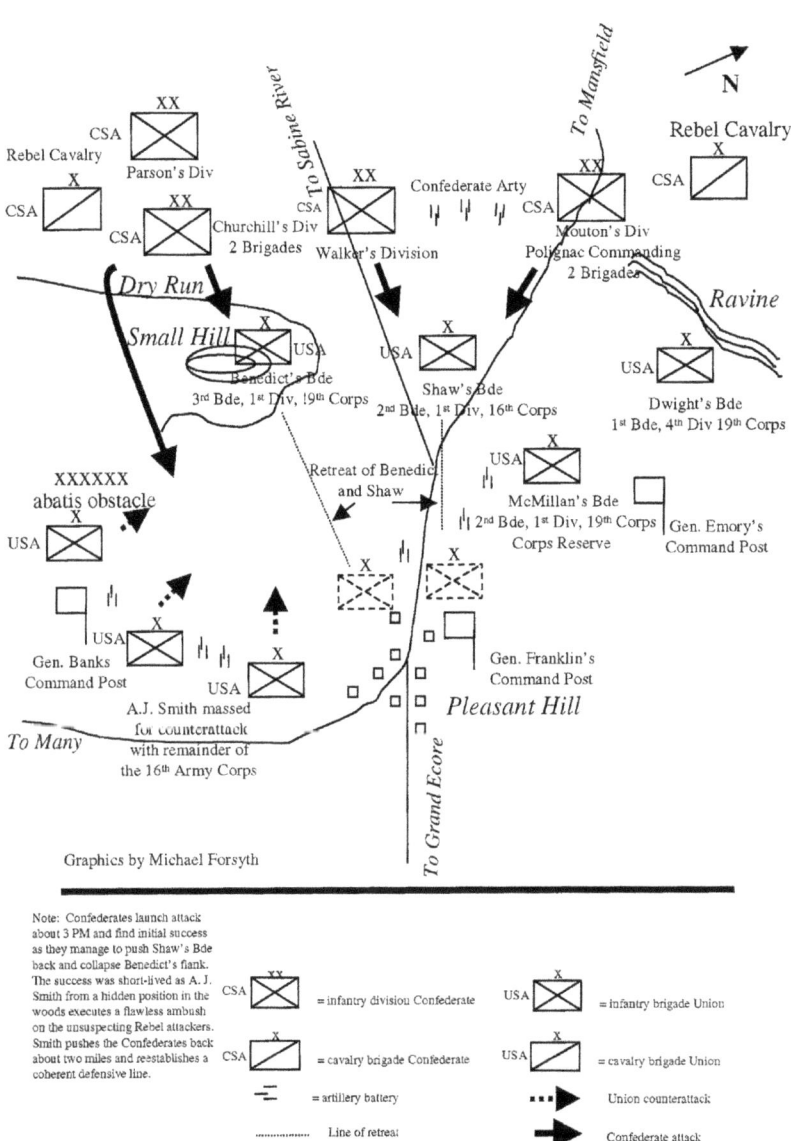

Map 9A. Battle of Pleasant Hill: Supplement to Maps 7, 8, and 9.

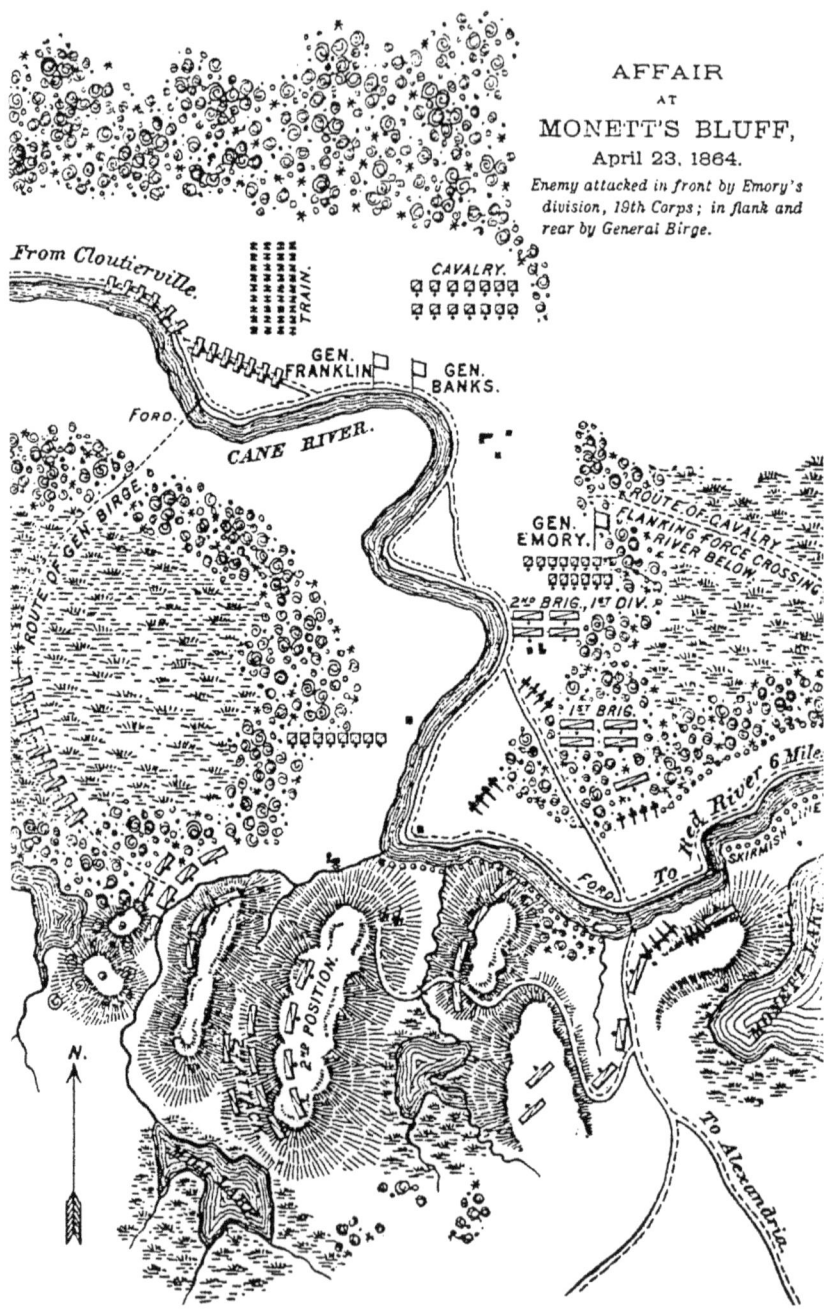

Map 10. Monette's Ferry. (Source: *Official Records*, series 1, volume 34, part 1, 233.)

Appendix 3: Maps 153

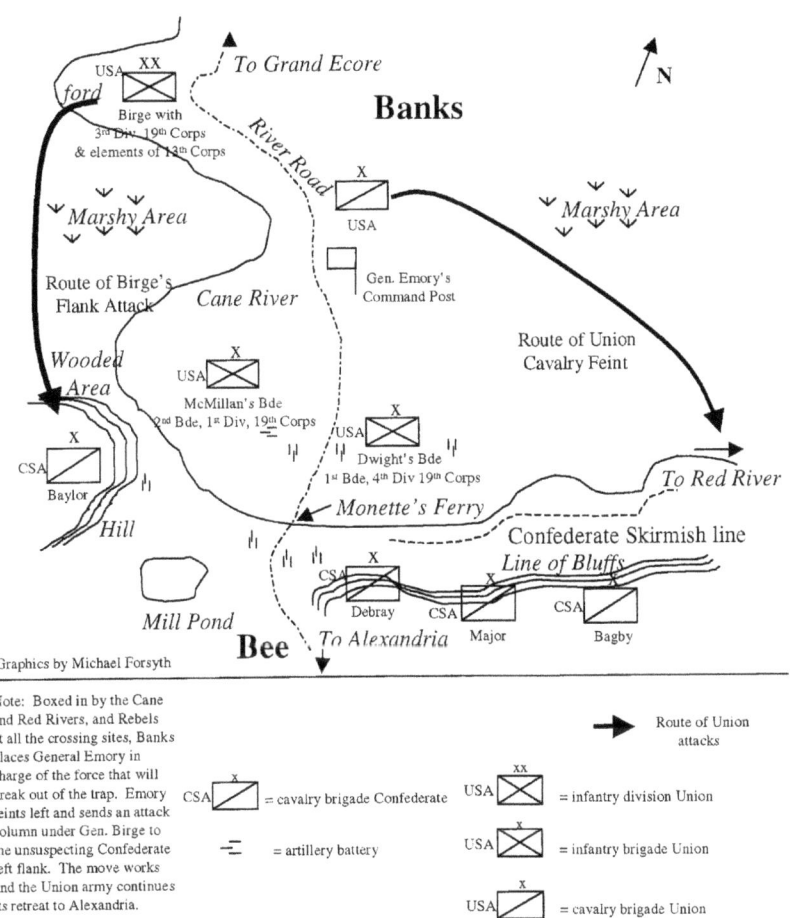

Map 10A. Battle of Monette's Ferry: Supplement to Map 10.

Notes

Chapter 1

1. Ludwell Johnson, *Red River Campaign: Politics and Cotton in the Civil War*, 280–281; William R. Brooksher, *War Along the Bayous*, 229.
2. United States War Department, *The War of the Rebellion: A Compilation of the Official Records of the Union and Confederate Armies*, series 1, vol. 34, part 1, 541–542. Hereafter cited as *OR*.
3. Jeffery S. Prushankin, "A Crisis in Command," M. A. Thesis, Villanova University, 100–101.
4. Richard Taylor, *Destruction and Reconstruction*, 224–225.
5. *Report of the Joint Committee on the Conduct of the War: Red River Expedition*, 244–245 letter from Admiral Porter to Gideon Welles dated 23 April 1864.
6. Johnson, *Red River Campaign*, 281.
7. Brooksher, *War Along the Bayous*, 234.
8. Robert L. Kerby, *Kirby Smith's Confederacy: The Trans-Mississippi South, 1863–1865*, 1–2.
9. *OR*, series 1, vol. 34, part 1, 263–264 and 258–261; Robert U. Johnson, ed., *Battles and Leaders of the Civil War*, Vol. IV, 367, hereafter cited as *B & L*. *Red River Expedition*, 332.
10. *B & L*, Vol. IV, 366 extracted from an After Action Review by Admiral David D. Porter.
11. Ludwell Johnson, *Red River Campaign*, 278; *OR*, series 1, vol. 34, part 1, 314.
12. Ibid., 236–241 and 678–681.
13. United States War Department, *Official Records of the Union and Confederate Navies in the War of the Rebellion*, Vol. 26, 63, 110, 71–77, 116, 127, 782. Hereafter cited as *ORN*.
14. *OR*, series 1, vol. 34, part 1, 236–241 and 678–681.
15. William T. Sherman, *Memoirs of W. T. Sherman*, vol. 2, 23–24 and 48.
16. Johnson, *Red River Campaign*, 277–278
17. John B. Jones, *A Rebel War Clerk's Diary*, 365, 371, and 379.

18. Johnson, *Red River Campaign*, 277–279; *OR*, series 1, vol. 34, part 1, 476–477; *B & L*, Vol. IV, 368; Taylor, *Destruction and Reconstruction*, 227.
19. Johnson, *Red River Campaign*, 41–48.
20. John C. Waugh, *Reelecting Lincoln*, 233; Prushankin, "A Crisis in Command," 118–119.
21. S. Grant, *Personal Memoirs*, Vol. 2, 479–481.
22. *Ibid.*, 478–480, a confidential letter from Gen. Grant to Gen. Sherman dated 4 April 1864.
23. *Ibid.*, same letter; *Report of the Joint Committee*, 159 and 383–384.
24. Albert Castel, *Decision in the West: The Atlanta Campaign of 1864*, 127.
25. John A. Wyeth, *That Devil Forrest*, 300 and 342.
26. Kerby, *Kirby Smith's Confederacy*, 245; Prushankin, "A Crisis in Command," 40–41.
27. *Ibid.*, 27–33; Kerby, *Kirby Smith's Confederacy*, 246–248.
28. *Ibid.*, 39; *OR*, series 1, vol. 34, part 1, 514.
29. *Ibid.*, 494; 516; Prushankin, "A Crisis in Command," 41–44.
30. *Ibid.*, 43; *OR*, series 1, vol. 34, part 1, 513–515.
31. Taylor, *Destruction and Reconstruction*, 207–208.
32. *OR*, series 1, vol. 34, part 1, 530–531.
33. Brooksher, *War Along the Bayous*, 145–149; *OR*, series 1, vol. 34, part 1, 538, 551, 599, and 784–788. Field returns are incomplete for the Confederate army and this is an estimate.
34. Shelby Foote, *The Civil War: A Narrative*, III, 33.
35. *Report of the Joint Committee*, 244–245.
36. *Ibid.*, 250–253.
37. Frank E. Vandiver, *Jubal's Raid*, vii, 18–19, 25–26.
38. Jeffry D. Wert, *From Winchester to Cedar Creek*, 9.
39. *Ibid.*, 230–233.
40. Sherman, *Memoirs*, Vol. 2, 13–14, in a letter from Sherman to Banks dated 3 April 1864; Wyeth, *That Devil Forrest*, 342; Castel, *Decision in the West*, 277.
41. *Ibid.*, 372–373, 375 & 399.
42. *OR*, series 1, vol. 34, part 1, 168.
43. *Ibid.*, 7.
44. *B & L*, "Land Operations against Mobile," by Richard B. Irwin, vol. IV, 400, 410–411.
45. *Ibid.*, "Farragut at Mobile Bay," by John C. Kinney, 391.
46. Gideon Welles, *Diary of Gideon Welles*, Vol. 2, 100–101.
47. Waugh, *Reelecting Lincoln*, 203–204.
48. *Ibid.*, 201.
49. Bruce Catton, *Never Call Retreat*, 363; Oscar A. Kinchen, *Confederate Operations in Canada*, 76, 85–86.
50. David H. Donald, ed., *Why the North Won the Civil War*, "The Military Leadership of North and South," by T. Harry Williams 46–47.
51. David D. Porter, *The Naval History of the Civil War*, 529.
52. Williams, "The Military Leadership of North and South," in Donald, ed., *Why the North Won the Civil War*, 40.

53. Taylor, *Destruction and Reconstruction*, 189.
54. *Report of the Joint Committee*, 282–284.
55. John G. Walker, "War of Secession West of the Mississippi River During the Years 1863–4 & 5," Myron Gwinner Collection, U.S. Army Military History Institute, Carlisle Barracks, 44.
56. Brooksher, *War Along the Bayous*, 142–143; Johnson, *Red River Campaign*, 164.

Chapter 2

1. Michael T. Parrish, *Richard Taylor: Soldier Prince of Dixie*, 3.
2. *Ibid.*, 10–12.
3. *Ibid.*, 13–15.
4. Richard Taylor, *Destruction and Reconstruction*, 121–124.
5. Jack Welsh, M. D., *Medical Histories of Confederate Generals*, 210–211.
6. Parrish, *Richard Taylor*, 69.
7. *Ibid.*, 69–70 & 85; Taylor, *Destruction and Reconstruction*, 6–7.
8. *Ibid.*, 8; Parrish, *Richard Taylor*, 105–107.
9. Taylor, *Destruction and Reconstruction*, in a letter from Bragg, 10.
10. *Ibid.*, 11.
11. Charles E. Fenner, "Richard Taylor," from *The Library of Southern Literature*, vol. 12, 5200.
12. Parrish, *Richard Taylor*, 131–132 and 141.
13. Taylor, *Destruction and Reconstruction*, 52.
14. Parrish, *Richard Taylor*, 162.
15. Taylor, *Destruction and Reconstruction*, 91.
16. *Ibid.*, 95–96; Welsh, *Medical Histories of Confederate Generals*, 210–211.
17. Taylor, *Destruction and Reconstruction*, 107–108; Parrish, *Richard Taylor*, 241.
18. *Ibid.*, 241; Taylor, *Destruction and Reconstruction*, 119–120.
19. Joseph H. Parks, *General Edmund Kirby Smith C. S. A.*, 1–6.
20. *Ibid.*, 9–12.
21. *Ibid.*, 15; Edmund K. Smith "Papers" from a letter to Joseph dated February 1842.
22. Parks, *Gen. E. K. Smith*, 36–41. As an aside, I also served in the 5th Infantry Regiment during my service.
23. *Ibid.*, 62.
24. Smith "Papers" in a letter to his mother dated 28 September 1852.
25. Parrish, *Richard Taylor*, 125.
26. Parks, *E. K. Smith*, 87–88 and 100.
27. Smith "Papers" in letters to his mother dated 23 November 1860 and 24 December 1860.
28. Parks, *E. K. Smith*, 121.
29. *Ibid.*, 137–140; Nina Smith Buck, "Blucher of the Day at Manassas," *Confederate Veteran*, VII, March 1889, 108.

30. *Ibid.*, 140–142.
31. *Ibid.*, 158; *OR*, vol. 5, 1072–1073 and 1078.
32. Parks, *E. K. Smith*, 167.
33. *Ibid.*, 197–199.
34. *Ibid.*, 199, 216–230; Smith "Papers" from a letter to Braxton Bragg dated 24 July 1862.
35. Parks, *E. K. Smith*, 243–251.
36. *Ibid.*, 252–256.
37. Fred H. Harrington, *Fighting Politician: Major General N. P. Banks*, 2.
38. James G. Hollandsworth, Jr., *Pretense of Glory* 4.
39. *Ibid.*, 4–5.
40. Harrington, *Fighting Politician*, 5.
41. *Ibid.*, xii, 8 and 14.
42. *Ibid.*, 8–9 and 15.
43. *Ibid.*, 18; Hollandsworth, *Pretense of Glory*, 20–21.
44. *Ibid.*, 31.
45. Hollandsworth, *Pretense of Glory*, 33–38.
46. Harrington, *Fighting Politician*, 52–53.
47. Nathaniel P. Banks to his wife in a letter dated 5 August 1862, Banks Papers.
48. Harrington, *Fighting Politician*, 66–68.
49. *Ibid.*, 69–70; Burke Davis, *They Called Him Stonewall*, 29–43.
50. Banks to Brigadier General George H. Gordon quoted in Davis, *They Called Him Stonewall*, 38.
51. Hollandsworth, *Pretense of Glory*, 62–66.
52. *Ibid.*, 67.
53. Henry K. Douglas, *I Rode with Stonewall*, 58.
54. Banks "Papers" contains an account of the accident penned by Banks for a friend written 20 January 1891 on House of Representatives stationery. Also, there is a copy of Stanton's handwritten orders to Banks telling him to prepare his expedition to the Gulf in relief of Butler dated 27 October 1862; *OR*, series 1, vol. 15, 590.
55. Harrington, *Fighting Politician*, 90–91.
56. *Ibid.*, 121–122; Hollandsworth, *Pretense of Glory*, 125–133; Edward Cunningham, *The Port Hudson Campaign: 1862–1863*, 49, 67 and 111–113.
57. *Report of the Joint Committee on the Conduct of the War*, 38th Congress, 2d Session, II, 305–310.
58. *ORN*, Vol. IV, 220–221.
59. Chester G. Hearn, *Admiral David Dixon Porter: The Civil War Years*, 1–2.
60. *Ibid.*, 2–3.
61. *Ibid.*, 5–7.
62. *Ibid.*, 7–8.
63. *Ibid.*, 11.
64. *Ibid.*, 23–24.
65. *Ibid.*, 25–26.
66. *Ibid.*, 30–35; David Dixon Porter "Papers," Library of Congress, letters dated 6 September 1854 and 8 September 1854 discuss his ship designs and attempt at having the navy adopt them.

67. Porter "Papers," Letters dated 25 August 1853, 10 September 1853 and 25 April 1857 demonstrate Porter's indebtedness and his attempts to recover compensation from the Mexican government owed to his father.
68. *Ibid.*, 40; Gideon Welles, *The Diary of Gideon Welles*, volume 1, 19.
69. David D. Porter, *Incidents and Anecdotes of the Civil War*, 13; Hearn, *Admiral David Dixon Porter*, 38–39.
70. *Ibid.*, 48–50, and 66; Welles, *The Diary of Gideon Welles*, Vol 1, 36–37.
71. Hearn, *Admiral David Dixon Porter*, 67–70.
72. *Ibid.*, 72–73.
73. Porter "Papers," Orders dated 2 December 1861 assigning Porter to command of the mortar flotilla.
74. Hearn, *Admiral David Dixon Porter*, 73–75, and 78.
75. *ORN*, vol. 18, 158.
76. *OR*, vol. VI, 505.
77. Porter "Papers," Letter to General Montgomery C. Meigs in which Porter states that Butler is not 'the man to command' at New Orleans and "For God's sake don't let us fail for want of a good military head."
78. Hearn, *Admiral David Dixon Porter*, 116–117.
79. *Ibid.*, 142.
80. *Ibid.*, 177–192; *ORN*, vol. 24, 478–479.
81. "The Vicksburg Campaign," by Ulysses S. Grant, III, 538.
82. Hearn, *Admiral David Dixon Porter*, 220–237.

Chapter 3

1. Jones, *A Rebel War Clerk's Diary*, 331.
2. *OR*, series 1, vol. 27, part 2, 329–346; Foote, *The Civil War*, 9–21 and 101.
3. Foote, *The Civil War*, 9–21 and 97–101; Waugh, *Reelecting Lincoln*, 3.
4. Stanley F. Horn, *The Army of Tennessee*, 308.
5. Sam R. Watkins, *"Company Aytch": A Side Show of the Big Show*, 171.
6. *OR*, series 1, vol. 38, part 3, 625–626; Foote, *The Civil War*, III, 117–119.
7. Joseph E. Johnston, *Narrative of Military Operations During the Civil War*, 291–298.
8. Jones, *A Rebel War Clerk's Diary*, 294.
9. Foote, *The Civil War*, Vol. 3, 104.
10. John D. Winters, *The Civil War in Louisiana*, 317–319; Kerby, *Kirby Smith's Confederacy*, 253–259.
11. Anne J. Bailey, "The Abandoned Western Theater: Confederate National Policy Toward the Trans-Mississippi Region," *Journal of Confederate History*, V, 1990, 35.
12. *Ibid.*, 36–37.
13. *Ibid.*, 37 compiled using statistics from the 1860 census.
14. *Ibid.*, 37, 46–48; Kerby, *Kirby Smith's Confederacy*, 37.
15. *Ibid.*; Bailey, "The Abandoned Western Theater," *Journal of Confederate History*, 42–48.

Notes — Chapter 3

16. *Ibid.*, 48–50; Kerby, *Kirby Smith's Confederacy*, 52–53.
17. Bailey, "The Abandoned Western Theater," *Journal of Confederate History*, 48–50; Parks, *General Edmund Kirby Smith, C. S. A.*, 257.
18. Bailey, "The Abandoned Western Theater," *Journal of Confederate History*, 53–54.
19. *OR*, series 1, vol. 34, part 2, 819.
20. *Ibid.*, 814.
21. *Ibid.*, 15–16, 55–56, & 133.
22. *OR*, series 1, vol. 34, part 1, 479, 494 and part 2, 1027.
23. Foote, *The Civil War*, Vol. 3, 97.
24. *Ibid.*, 97–98.
25. *Ibid.*, 98.
26. *Ibid.*, 98–101.
27. *Ibid.*, 101; Waugh, *Reelecting Lincoln*, 149; Donald Dale Jackson, *Twenty Million Yankees: The Northern Home Front*, 149–150; Kinchen, *Confederate Operations in Canada*, 30.
28. *Ibid.*, 149–150; Foote, *The Civil War*, Vol. 3, 101–103; Robert Garlick Hill Kean, *Inside the Confederate Government*, 143.
29. Larry E. Nelson, *Bullets, Ballots, and Rhetoric: Confederate Policy for the United States Presidential Contest of 1864*, 25–26; Kinchen, *Confederate Operations in Canada*, 219.
30. *Ibid.*, 24; Waugh, *Reelecting Lincoln*, 152, 154–158; Jefferson Davis, *Jefferson Davis, Constitutionalist: His Letters, Papers, and Speeches*, VI, 204–206, 236–238, and 324–326. Contains correspondence concerning the appointment of agents and the prospects of success in influencing the election.
31. *Ibid.*, 351. Davis reveals his aggressive side in a speech to citizens of Columbia, South Carolina. He states that "the only way to make them [the Yankees] is to whip them." Nelson, *Bullets, Ballots, and Rhetoric*, 25–27, 45 & 98; Kinchen, *Confederate Operations in Canada*, 31–32, 35–37.
32. Catton, *Never Call Retreat*, 305; *OR*, series 1, vol. 32, part 3, 468–469.
33. *OR*, series 1, vol. 34, part 1, 167–168; part 2, 15–16, 55–56, and 133; Catton, *Never Call Retreat*, 321; Kean, *Inside the Confederate Government*, 127. Kean states in his diary that Confederate newspapers treated this policy with "derision," but he considered it an "able and crafty" policy.
34. Johnson, *Red River Campaign*, 41–48.
35. *Ibid.*, 9.
36. *Ibid.*, 5–10; Foote, *The Civil War*, Vol. 3, 26–27.
37. Johnson, *Red River Campaign*, 10–11 and 45–48.
38. *Ibid.*, 13.
39. *Ibid.*, 14.
40. *Ibid.*, 14–17.
41. *Ibid.*, 34–35; John Hay, *Lincoln and the Civil War in the Diaries and Letters of John Hay*, 77. Kean, *Inside the Confederate Government*, 131.
42. *Report of the Joint Committee*, iv–v. Italics in original.
43. *Ibid.*, v; James Callaghan, "Miraculous Rebel Defense of Sabine Pass," *America's Civil War* (May 1999), 34–40.

44. *Report of the Joint Committee*, xxii–xxviii; Brooksher, *War Along the Bayous*, 27–28.
45. *OR*, series 1, vol. 34, part 2, 587.
46. Foote, *The Civil War*, Vol. 3, 25–29; Johnson, *Red River Campaign*, 40.
47. *Report of the Joint Committee*, xxvii–xxxi; *OR*, series 1, vol. 34, part 1, 168.
48. *Report of the Joint Committee*, xxiv–xxv.
49. Hearn, *Admiral David Dixon Porter*, 243–244.
50. Banks, "Papers" in a letter from Porter to Banks dated 26 February 1864.
51. Grant, *Personal Memoirs of U. S. Grant*, 469–477; Catton, *Never Call Retreat*, 281–290.
52. *Ibid.*, 290–291; Grant, *Personal Memoirs*, 478–484.
53. *Ibid.*; Catton, *Never Call Retreat*, 290–291.
54. Johnson, *Red River Campaign*, 278–279.
55. Johnson, *Red River Campaign*, 44–45; Grant, *Personal Memoirs*, 484.
56. Johnson, *Red River Campaign*, 86; *OR*, series 1, vol. 34, part 2, 819.
57. *Ibid.*, series 1, vol. 34, part 1, 494.
58. *Ibid.*, 516
59. Prushankin, "A Crisis in Command," 40.
60. *OR*, series 1, vol. 34, part 1, 515.

Chapter 4

1. Walker, "The War of Secession West of the Mississippi," 42–43.
2. *Ibid.*, description derived from a handwritten preface to his essay and an excerpt from *Frank Leslie's Magazine* attached to the paper.
3. Taylor, *Destruction and Reconstruction*, 180.
4. *Ibid.*, Brooksher, *War Along the Bayous*, 36
5. William Arceneaux, *Acadian General: Alfred Mouton and the Civil Wa*r, 23, 44–45 and 53.
6. Taylor, *Destruction and Reconstruction*, 178.
7. Sherman, *Memoirs*, Vol. 2, 333.
8. Joseph P. Blessington, *The Campaigns of Walker's Texas Division*, 167.
9. Felix Pierre Poche, *A Louisiana Confederate: Diary of Felix Pierre Poche*, 93.
10. Walker, "War of Secession West of the Mississippi," 44.
11. *Report of the Joint Committee*, 232, copy of report of Lieutenant Commander Phelps dated 16 March 1864.
12. *Ibid.*, 231–232; Brooksher, *War Along the Bayous*, 44.
13. *Report of the Joint Committee*, 235; Richard B. Irwin, *History of the Nineteenth Army Corps*, 287; Porter, *The Naval History of the Civil War*, 497–498.
14. Taylor, *Destruction and Reconstruction*, 181.
15. *Report of the Joint Committee*, 154–155, in a 6 March 1864 dispatch from Banks to Halleck describing campaign plans.
16. Harrington, *Fighting Politician*, 144–147.

17. *Sherman, Memoirs*, Vol. 1, 425–426.
18. *OR*, series 1, vol. 34, part 1, 378.
19. Poche, *A Louisiana Confederate*, 95.
20. Taylor, *Destruction and Reconstruction*, 181–182.
21. Prushankin, "A Crisis in Command," 39.
22. Brooksher, *War Along the Bayous*, 36 and 54.
23. Walker, "The War of Secession West of the Mississippi," 45.
24. *OR*, series 1, vol. 34, part 1, 561.
25. W.F. Beyer, ed., *Deeds of Valor*, "10,000 Damned Gorillas," by John H. Cook, 313.
26. *Report of the Joint Committee*, 81.
27. *Ibid.*, 271.
28. Brooksher, *War Along the Bayous*, 51.
29. Taylor, *Destruction and Reconstruction*, 183.
30. *Ibid.*, 184; *OR*, series 1, vol. 34, part 1, 315–316, 323–324, 334–335, 463–464, and 501.
31. Blessington, *The Campaigns of Walker's Texas Division*, 177.
32. *B & L*, "The Defense of the Red River," by E. K. Smith, Vol. IV, 370; Castel, *General Sterling Price and the Civil War in the West*, 173; *OR*, series 1, vol. 34, part 1, 516–517.
33. William R. Boggs, *Military Reminiscences of General William R. Boggs, CSA*, 75–76; Prushankin, "A Crisis in Command," 45.
34. *OR*, series 1, vol. 34, part 1, 510, 513–514.
35. *Report of the Joint Committee*, 383–384.
36. *Ibid.*, 8 and 275.
37. Johnson, *Red River Campaign*, 106; Irwin, *History of the Nineteenth Army Corps*, 292.
38. *Report of the Joint Committee*, 280–282.
39. Harrington, *Fighting Politician*, 153–154.
40. *Report of the Joint Committee*, 277, 280–281 and 335.
41. Poche, *A Louisiana Confederate*, 102.
42. Blessington, *Walker's Texas Division*, 179.
43. Banks "Papers," 2 April 1864 letter to General Halleck.
44. Brooksher, *War Along the Bayous*, 68.
45. Johnson, *Red River Campaign*, 113–116.
46. *Report of the Joint Committee*, 286.
47. *Ibid.*, 286–287.
48. *Ibid.*, 35.
49. Banks "Papers," in a 4 April 1864 letter to his wife.
50. *Report of the Joint Committee*, 323.
51. *Ibid.*, 10.
52. Johnson, *Red River Campaign*, 117.
53. *Report of the Joint Committee*, 32 and 58.
54. *OR*, series 1, vol. 34, part 1, 522.
55. *Ibid.*, 523–526.
56. *B & L*, "The Defense of the Red River," by E. Kirby Smith, Vol. IV, 370–371.

57. Taylor, *Destruction and Reconstruction*, 186–187.
58. Walker, "War of Secession Beyond the Mississippi," 49.
59. Taylor, *Destruction and Reconstruction*, 187.
60. *Ibid.*, 188.
61. Rangers at the Mansfield State Commemorative Area dispute this number which until now has been the one most often cited — as too low — and are currently conducting a study to ascertain from the spotty Confederate reports the actual numbers available. The park personnel completed a study concerning Union troop strength in 1998. It is included in the bibliography and I will refer to it later when discussing the events at Mansfield.
62. Taylor, *Destruction and Reconstruction*, 189; *OR*, series 1, vol. 34, part 1, 526.
63. *Ibid.*; J. E. Sliger, "How General Taylor Fought the Battle of Mansfield, La." *Confederate Veteran*, Vol. 31, 457; Prushankin, "A Crisis in Command," 56–58.
64. Poche, *A Louisiana Confederate*, 105; Sliger, "How General Taylor Fought The Battle of Mansfield, La." Blessington, *The Campaigns of Walker's Texas Division*, 182.

Chapter 5

1. *Report of the Joint Committee*, 10, 32, and 58; Foote, *The Civil War*, Vol. 3, 40.
2. Taylor, *Destruction and Reconstruction*, 187.
3. Foote, *The Civil War*, Vol. 3, 40.
4. *Report of the Joint Committee*, 58 from Brigadier General Albert L. Lee's testimony before the committee.
5. *Ibid.*, 58–59.
6. *Ibid.*, 29, 59, and 194; Brooksher, *War Along the Bayous*, 85.
7. J. E. Sliger, "How General Taylor Fought the Battle of Mansfield, La.," *Confederate Veteran*, 457.
8. Taylor, *Destruction and Reconstruction*, 189.
9. Norman C. Delaney, "The Diary and Memoirs of Marshall Samuel Pierson," *Military History of Texas and the Southwest*, XIII, 1975, 33–34.
10. *OR*, series 1, vol. 34, part 1, 528.
11. *Report of the Joint Committee*, 29, 195; Richard B. Irwin, *History of the Nineteenth Army Corps*, 298; *OR*, series 1, vol. 34, part 1, 290.
12. *Ibid.*, 60.
13. Taylor, *Destruction and Reconstruction*, 190.
14. Sarah A. Dorsey, *Recollections of Henry Watkins Allen*, 261; Taylor, *Destruction and Reconstruction*, 191.
15. W. W. Heartsill, *Fourteen Hundred and 91 Days, in the Confederate Army*, 199.
16. Blessington, *The Campaigns of Walker's Texas Division*, 183.
17. Poche, *A Louisiana Confederate*, 105.

18. *Report of the Joint Committee*, 37 and 60; OR, series 1, vol. 34, part 1, 291.
19. *Report of the Joint Committee*, 61.
20. Ibid.
21. Taylor, *Destruction and Reconstruction*, 191.
22. Poche, *A Louisiana Confederate*, 107; Arceneaux, *Acadian General*, 132.
23. Ibid.; J. E. Hewitt, "The Battle of Mansfield, Louisiana," *Confederate Veteran*, 172–173.
24. Blessington, *The Campaigns of Walker's Texas Division*, 188.
25. Brooksher, *War Along the Bayous*, 95–98; Irwin, *History of the Nineteenth Army Corps*, 304.
26. *Report of the Joint Committee*, 61; OR, series 1, vol. 34, part 1, 462–463.
27. Ibid., 273.
28. *Report of the Joint Committee*, 61; OR, series 1, vol. 34, part 1, 279–280; Brooksher, *War Along the Bayous*, 99–101.
29. Taylor, *Destruction and Reconstruction*, 192; Irwin, *History of the Nineteenth Army Corps*, 309; Hewitt, "The Battle of Mansfield, La.," *Confederate Veteran*, 198.
30. Irwin, *History of the Nineteenth Army Corps*, 307.
31. Ibid., 308.
32. Ibid.
33. Scott Dearman, Jr., "Statistical Report of Union Troop Strength at the Battle of Mansfield, Louisiana April 8, 1864," study held at the Mansfield State Commemorative Area, 8.
34. OR, series 1, vol. 34, part 1, 258–261.
35. Taylor, *Destruction and Reconstruction*, 192–195; OR, series 1, vol. 34, part 1, 527.
36. Dorsey, *Recollections of Henry Watkins Allen*, 263.
37. Walker "Papers," letter from Taylor to Walker dated 9 April 1864 1:30 AM.
38. Taylor, *Destruction and Reconstruction*, 193–194.
39. *Report of the Joint Committee*, 179, from the testimony of Brigadier General William Dwight.
40. Irwin, *History of the Nineteenth Army Corps*, 310. Irwin, as Banks' AAG, was intimately familiar with the interworkings of the army during the campaign. His duty position is a rough equivalent to a modern day operations officer.
41. Taylor, *Destruction and Reconstruction*, 194–195.
42. Ibid.
43. Ibid., 195–196.
44. Brooksher, *War Along the Bayous*, 112; Report of the Joint Committee, 176; Irwin, *History of the Nineteenth Army Corps*, 317–318.
45. Taylor, *Destruction and Reconstruction*, 196–197.
46. *Report of the Joint Committee*, 92, from the testimony of Colonel Francis Fessenden who succeeded Benedict as brigade commander; Blessington, *The Campaigns of Walker's Texas Division*, 195.
47. Walker, "The War of Secession West of the Mississippi," 54–55; David H. and Jane Harris Johansson, "Two 'Lost' Battle Reports: Horace Randal's and Joseph L. Brent's Reports of the Battles of Mansfield and Pleasant Hill 8 & 9 April

1864," *Military History of the West*, 180; Taylor, *Destruction and Reconstruction*, 198–199.

48. *Report of the Joint Committee*, 188 and 218–219; Irwin, *History of the Nineteenth Army Corps*, 319–320.

49. Ibid., 219; Brooksher, *War Along the Bayous*, 132.

50. Taylor, *Destruction and Reconstruction*, 198–199.

51. OR, series 1, vol. 34, part 1, 309.

52. Ibid., 167–168, 258–261, 313, 398, 476, and 604–605; Johnson, *Red River Campaign*, 168–169. Both armies engaged on roughly equal terms at Pleasant Hill, but Taylor suffered higher losses in his assault.

53. *Report of the Joint Committee*, 13, 77, 195–196, and 326–327; Irwin, *History of the Nineteenth Army Corps*, 323; Harrington, *Fighting Politician*, 157–158.

54. Parrish, *Richard Taylor*, 369.

55. OR, series 1, vol. 34, part 1, 309; Brooksher, *War Along the Bayous*, 143.

56. Foote, *The Civil War*, Vol. 3, 50.

57. Brooksher, *War Along the Bayous*, 143–144; Johnson, *Red River Campaign*, 206.

58. OR, series 1, vol. 34, part 1, 526–527.

59. *B & L*, "Defense of the Red River," by E. K. Smith, IV, 372.

60. Taylor, *Destruction and Reconstruction*, 200–201.

61. *B & L*, "Defense of the Red River," by E. K. Smith, IV, 372.

62. Sliger, "How General Taylor Fought the Battle of Mansfield, La.," *Confederate Veteran*, 458; Taylor, *Destruction and Reconstruction*, 207.

63. *B & L*, "Defense of the Red River," by E. K. Smith, IV, 372.

64. Taylor, *Destruction and Reconstruction*, 207–208.

65. OR, series 1, vol. 34, part 1, 531.

66. Walker, "The War of Secession West of the Mississippi," 56–57.

67. Prushankin, "A Crisis in Command," 80.

68. OR, series 1, vol. 34, part 1, 530; St. John R. Liddell, *Liddell's Record*, 178–179.

69. Irwin, *History of the Nineteenth Army Corps*, 324; Report of the Joint Committee, 203

70. Ibid., 203–204, 237; Porter, *Incidents and Anecdotes of the Civil War*, 233.

71. *Report of the Joint Committee*, 239–243.

Chapter 6

1. Taylor, *Destruction and Reconstruction*, 200–201.

2. Ibid., 208–209; OR, series 1, volume 34, part 1, 530.

3. *B & L*, "The Navy in the Red River," by Thomas O. Selfridge, IV, 363; *Report of the Joint Committee*, 204; Liddell, *Liddell's Record*, 179.

4. Taylor, *Destruction and Reconstruction*, 209; Brooksher, *War Along the Bayous*, 154–155.

5. H. Allen Gosnell, *Guns on the Western Waters*, 250.

6. *Ibid.*, 251; *B & L*, "The Navy in the Red River," Selfridge, IV, 363–364; *ORN*, volume 26, 49 and 52; Porter, *The Naval History of the Civil War*, 513.

7. Gosnell, *Guns on the Western Waters*, 249.

8. Taylor, *Destruction and Reconstruction*, 209 and 211; Brooksher, *War Along the Bayous*, 157.

9. Irwin, *History of the Nineteenth Army Corps*, 323 and 326.

10. *OR*, Series 1, volume 34, part 1, 530 and 532.

11. Taylor, *Destruction and Reconstruction*, 212–213; *OR*, Series 1, volume 34, part 1, 533–534.

12. Taylor, *Destruction and Reconstruction*, 213.

13. *Ibid.*

14. *Ibid.*, 212.

15. Boggs, *Military Reminiscences of General William R. Boggs*, C. S. A., 78–79.

16. Welsh, *Medical Histories of Confederate Generals*, 210–211; I have in my possession several xerox copies of letters Taylor wrote to various persons over the course of the campaign. As the campaign wore on there is a noticeable decline in his penmanship, probably due to flare-ups of rheumatoid from the stress. For example, two letters written to Walker are contained in the Walker Papers from the University of North Carolina. One is dated 12 March 1864—the beginning of the campaign—and another was written late at night on 9 April 1864 after Pleasant Hill. Taylor by my judgement had poor handwriting to begin with, but the letter of 9 April is barely readable—the writing is comparable to that of a physician writing a prescription.

17. Porter, *Incidents and Anecdotes*, 235.

18. *Ibid.*, 236–238.

19. *Report of the Joint Committee*, 239–242.

20. Welles, *Diary of Gideon Welles*, II, 18.

21. *Report of the Joint Committee*, 31 and 385.

22. Porter, *Incidents and Anecdotes of the Civil War*, 238–239; Porter, *The Naval History of the Civil War*, 518–519; *Report of the Joint Committee*, 242, 244–245.

23. Banks "Papers" in a letter to his wife dated 17 April 1864.

24. Irwin, *History of the Nineteenth Army Corps*, 327; Johnson, *Red River Campaign*, 219–220.

25. Welles, *The Diary of Gideon Welles*, II, 19–20.

26. Taylor "Papers," in a letter to Walker dated 26 April 1864. Taylor's assistant adjutant general, Eustace Surget, penned this letter for his commander. Surget might have done this because Taylor's rheumatism prevented him from writing it himself.

27. Taylor, *Destruction and Reconstruction*, 213.

28. Liddell, *Liddell's Record*, 179–180.

29. Taylor, *Destruction and Reconstruction*, 214–215.

30. Irwin, *History of the Nineteenth Army Corps*, 328; *Report of the Joint Committee*, 31.

31. Irwin, *History of the Nineteenth Army Corps*, 328; Brooksher, *War Along the Bayous*, 173.

32. Blessington, *The Campaigns of Walker's Texas Division*, 266.
33. Poche, *A Louisiana Confederate*, 113.
34. Irwin, *History of the Nineteenth Army Corps*, 329.
35. Ibid., 330; *Report of the Joint Committee*, 219.
36. *OR*, series 1, volume 34, part 1, 402.
37. Johnson, *Red River Campaign*, 227–228; Irwin, *History of the Nineteenth Army Corps*, 330.
38. Ibid., 330–331; *Report of the Joint Committee*, 219; *B & L*, "Opposing Forces in the Red River Campaign," IV, 367.
39. Irwin, *History of the Nineteenth Army Corps*, 330; Taylor, *Destruction and Reconstruction*, 214; Brooksher, *War Along the Bayous*, 176–177.
40. Irwin, *History of the Nineteenth Army Corps*, 331–333; Taylor, *Destruction and Reconstruction*, 215; *OR*, series 1, volume 34, part 1, 406–407; Parrish, *Richard Taylor*, 375–377.
41. Irwin, *History of the Nineteenth Army Corps*, 331; *Report of the Joint Committee*, 97, from the testimony of Colonel Frances Fessenden.
42. Ibid.
43. Ibid.; *OR*, series 1, volume 34, part 1, 407; Irwin, *History of the Nineteenth Army Corps*, 332–333; Taylor, *Destruction and Reconstruction*, 215.
44. Taylor, "Confederate District of West Louisiana Record Book," Louisiana Historical Association Collection, Tulane University, in a letter to Bee dated 29 April 1864.
45. *OR*, series 1, volume 34, part 1, 534–535.
46. Eustace Surget (for Taylor) to Walker, 26 April 1864, Walker "Papers." Emphasis in original.
47. United States Army, Student Text 101-5: Command and Staff Decision Processes, U. S. Army Command and General Staff College, 3–4 and 3–5.
48. *OR*, Series 1, volume 34, part 1, 541–543.
49. Ibid., 543.
50. Walker, "Operations West of the Mississippi," 69.
51. Gosnell, *Guns on the Western Waters*, 253; *Report of the Joint Committee*, 243.
52. *B & L*, "The Navy in the Red River," Selfridge, IV, 364; Gosnell, *Guns on the Western Waters*, 253; *Report of the Joint Committee*, 246.
53. Porter, *The Naval History of the Civil War*, 521. Interestingly when Porter speaks of himself in this book it is always in the third person.
54. Porter, *Incidents and Anecdotes*, 239; *Report of the Joint Committee*, 247.
55. *Report of the Joint Committee*, 244–245.
56. Ibid., 248–249; Porter, *Incidents and Anecdotes*, 241–245; Taylor, *Destruction and Reconstruction*, 217.
57. Ibid., 219 and 221; Liddell, *Liddell's Record*, 181–183.
58. Dorsey, *Recollections of Henry Watkins Allen*, 279.
59. Walker, "The War of Secession West of the Mississippi," 57.
60. Eustace Surget (for Taylor) to Walker, 26 April 1864, Walker "Papers."
61. Dorsey, *Recollections of Henry Watkins Allen*, 265.
62. Eustace Surget (for Taylor) to Walker, 26 April 1864, Walker "Papers."
63. Taylor, *Destruction and Reconstruction*, 224.

64. *Report of the Joint Committee*, 250–253.
65. Irwin, *History of the Nineteenth Army Corps*, 334.
66. George J. Castille III and Steven D. Smith, *Bailey's Dam, A Louisiana Anthropological Study #9*, 9.
67. *Ibid.*, 9–10.
68. *OR*, series 1, volume 34, part 1, 403; *Report of the Joint Committee*, 15, 35, and 279; Porter, *Incidents and Anecdotes*, 246–247; Porter, T*he Naval History of the Civil War*, 525.
69. *Ibid.*, 527.
70. Smith and Castille, *Bailey's Dam*, 14–19
71. *Ibid.*, 20; *Report of the Joint Committee*, 16; Porter, *Incidents and Anecdotes*, 248.
72. Gosnell, *Guns on the Western Waters*, 264; Castille and Smith, *Bailey's Dam*, 20–22.
73. *Report of the Joint Committee*, 82–83.
74. Castille and Smith, *Bailey's Dam*, 22–23; Porter, *Incidents and Anecdotes*, 249–250.

Chapter 7

1. Taylor, *Destruction and Reconstruction*, 221; *ORN*, vol. 26, 102.
2. Taylor, *Destruction and Reconstruction*, 221; *Report of the Joint Committee*, 267; *ORN*, vol. 26, 113–119; *B & L*, "The Navy in the Red River," by Thomas O. Selfridge, 365.
3. *Ibid.*; *Report of the Joint Committee*, 259–260 and 267–268; Porter, *Naval History of the Civil War*, 528–529.
4. Taylor, *Destruction and Reconstruction*, 221.
5. Liddell, *Liddell's Record*, 173, 178, and 180.
6. *Ibid.*, 181–183; Brooksher, *War Along the Bayous*, 206.
7. Liddell, *Liddell's Record*, 183; Taylor, *Destruction and Reconstruction*, 224; *OR*, series 1, vol. 34, part 1, 478, 584, and 635–636.
8. Liddell, *Liddell's Record*, 183; H. T. Douglas, "The Trans-Mississippi Department," *Confederate Veteran*, XXV, 153; Prushankin, "A Crisis in Command," 105.
9. Taylor, *Destruction and Reconstruction*, 225; *OR*, series 1, vol. 34, part 1, 592.
10. *Report of the Joint Committee*, 266.
11. Irwin, *History of the Nineteenth Army Corps*, 344.
12. *Report of the Joint Committee*, 335; *Official Report Relative to the Conduct of Federal Troops*, 79–89.
13. Dorsey, *Recollections of Henry Watkins Allen*, 279; *Report of the Joint Committee*, 335; *Conduct of Federal Troops*, 79–89; Porter, *Incidents and Anecdotes*, 258–259.
14. Taylor, *Destruction and Reconstruction*, 226; Blessington, *The Campaigns of Walker's Texas Division*, 261.

15. *OR*, series 1, vol. 34, part 1, 591.
16. Taylor, *Destruction and Reconstruction*, 229–231. Emphasis in original.
17. *OR*, series 1, vol. 34, part 1, 325 and 593; Irwin, *History of the Nineteenth Army Corps*, 344–345.
18. Johnson, *Red River Campaign*, 273–274.
19. Irwin, *History of the Nineteenth Army Corps*, 345–346; Taylor, *Destruction and Reconstruction*, 226.
20. Ibid.; Johnson, *Red River Campaign*, 275.
21. *OR*, series 1, vol. 34, part 1, 320–321, 329–330, 337–338, 347–348, 357–358, 363–367, 594, 624, and 631; Taylor, *Destruction and Reconstruction*, 226–227.
22. Irwin, *History of the Nineteenth Army Corps*, 346–347; Porter, *Naval History of the Civil War*, 533.
23. Irwin, *History of the Nineteenth Army Corps*, 346–347.
24. Taylor, "Confederate District of West Louisiana Record Book," in a letter to Smith dated 14 May 1864.
25. Taylor, *Destruction and Reconstruction*, 225; *OR*, series 1, vol. 34, part 1, 593–594.
26. *OR*, series 1, vol. 34, part 1, 543–545.
27. *Ibid.*, 545–546.
28. *Ibid.*, 546–548.
29. *Ibid.*, 540–541.
30. Liddell, *Liddell's Record*, 181; Walker, "The War of Secession West of the Mississippi," 56; H. T. Douglas, "The Trans-Mississippi Department," *Confederate Veteran*, XXV, 153–154.
31. Taylor, *Destruction and Reconstruction*, 224.

Chapter 8

1. Jones, *A Rebel War Clerk's Diary*, 365, 371; *Report of the Joint Committee*, 252; Foote, *The Civil War*, III, 101–103; Kean, *Inside the Confederate Government*, 150–151.
2. Grant, *Personal Memoirs*, II, 129.
3. *OR*, series 1, volume 34, part 1, 526.
4. Sherman, *Memoirs*, II, 13–14, 23–24; Johnston, *Narrative*, 574–575; Johnson, *Red River Campaign*, 279.
5. *Ibid.*, 279–281; Brooksher, *War Along the Bayous*, 234–235.
6. Parks, *Edmund Kirby Smith*, 1–6, 77; Parrish, *Richard Taylor*, 121–125.
7. Kerby, *Kirby Smith's Confederacy*, 245–251.
8. *OR*, series 1, vol. 34, part 1, 514–515, 541–548, 592–594. These letters are representative of Taylor's constant criticism of Smith.
9. *Ibid.*, 546.
10. Liddell, *Liddell's Record*, 183.
11. *Report of the Joint Committee*, 370.
12. *Ibid.*, 244–245, 271.

13. Brooksher, *War Along the Bayous*, 142–143.
14. *Report of the Joint Committee*, 10; Banks "Papers." In his 2 April letter to Halleck, Banks expresses "my fear is that they may not be willing to meet us."
15. *Report of the Joint Committee*, 35, 383–384; Sherman, *Memoirs*, II, 13–14.
16. *OR*, series 1, vol. 34, part 1, 531.
17. Sherman, *Memoirs*, II, 12–13; Castel, *Decision in the West*, 277–278.
18. Waugh, *Reelecting Lincoln*, 295.
19. Vandiver, *Jubal's Raid*, 143, 157; Wert, *From Winchester to Cedar Creek*, 9–10, 249–250.
20. *OR*, series 1, vol. 34, part 1, 168.
21. *Report of the Joint Committee*, 245.
22. Foote, *The Civil War*, III, 101–103.
23. Johnston, *Narrative*, 349, 355; Nelson, *Bullets, Ballots, and Rhetoric*, 98; Davis, *Jefferson Davis, Constitutionalist: Letters, Papers, and Speeches*, VI. This volume — from his 1864 correspondence — is rife with dispatches to military officials, including Johnston (pp. 283, 288, 295), but contains few references to the operations to sway the election. Davis failed to capitalize on this opportunity and follow his own strategy, instead choosing to focus his energies on military affairs, which he believed were his forte.
24. James M. McPherson, *Battle Cry of Freedom*, 769, 774–780, 806; Nelson, *Bullets, Ballots and Rhetoric*, 118–120; Kinchen, *Confederate Operations in Canada*, 96–97.

Appendix 1

1. Compiled from *OR*, series 1, vol. 34, part 1, 162–163; E. B. Long and Barbara Long, *The Civil War: Day by Day*, 474–594; *Report of the Joint Committee*.

Appendix 2

1. Compiled from the *OR* and *B & L*. Confederate field returns are incomplete for the District of West Louisiana and the data contained here is based on scanning several reports from the commanders. Data concerning Confederate artillery units is almost entirely incomplete. The Arkansas and Missouri commanders kept better returns and the order of battle is more complete.
2. Mower commander both the First and Third Divisions, Sixteenth Army Corps, during the Red River Campaign.
3. Confederate Units at the Division and Brigade levels generally took the name of their commanding officers and did not have number designations. Most of the Regiments were numbered; however, in some cases these units took on the name of their commander as the designation.
4. Incomplete records exist in the *OR* to list its subordinate units.

Bibliography

Unpublished Sources

Banks, Nathaniel P. Papers. Charles Ramsdell Microfilm Collection, reels 786.1, 786.7, 786.9, 786.16, University of Texas at Austin.
Confederate District of West Louisiana Record Book, April 11–May 23, 1864. Louisiana Historical Association Collection 55-B, volume 7, Special Collections, Howard Tilton Memorial Library, Tulane University, New Orleans, La.
Porter, David Dixon. Papers. Containers 17 and 22 General Correspondence and Journal, Library of Congress, Washington, D.C.
Smith, Edmund Kirby. Papers. Southern Historical Collection, University of North Carolina, Chapel Hill, N.C.
Taylor, Richard. Papers. Louisiana Adjutant General's Office, Jackson Barracks, New Orleans, La.
Walker, John G. "The War of Secession West of the Mississippi River During the Years 1863–4 & 5." Mss. Myron Gwinner Collection, United States Army History Institute, Carlisle Barracks, Carlisle, Pa.
_____, Papers. Southern Historical Collection, University of North Carolina, Chapel Hill.

Published Sources

"The Battle of Yellow Bayou." *Confederate Veteran* XXV (1917): 94–95. Reprint. Wilmington, N.C.: Broadfoot Publishing Company, 1987–88.
Beyer, W. F. and Keydel, O. F., eds. *Deeds of Valor: How America's Civil War Heroes Won the Congressional Medal of Honor*. Detroit: Perrien-Keydel Co., 1903. Reprint. Stamford, Conn.: Longmeadow Press, 1992.
Blessington, Joseph P. *The Campaigns of Walker's Texas Division*. New York: Lange, Little and Co., 1875.
Boggs, William R. *Military Reminiscences of General William. R. Boggs, C. S. A.* Durham, N.C.: Seeman Printery, 1913.

Buck, Nina Smith. "Blucher of the Day at Manassas." *Confederate Veteran* VII (March 1889): 108. Reprint. Wilmington, N.C.: Broadfoot Publishing Company, 1987–88.

Callaghan, James. "Miraculous Rebel Defense of Sabine Pass." *America's Civil War* XII (May 1999): 34–40.

Davis, Jefferson. *Jefferson Davis, Constitutionalist: His Letters, Papers, and Speeches*, Volume VI. Edited by Roland Dunbar. New York: Press of J. J. Little & Ives Company for the Mississippi Department of Archives and History, 1923.

Dorsey, Sarah A. *Recollections of Henry Watkins Allen, Brigadier-General Confederate States Army, Ex-Governor of Louisiana.* New York: M. Doolady, 1866.

Douglas, H. T. "The Trans-Mississippi Department." *Confederate Veteran* XXV (April 1917): 153–155. Reprint. Wilmington, N.C.: Broadfoot Publishing Company, 1987–88.

Fenner, Charles E. "Richard Taylor." *The Library of Southern Literature* 12 (1907): 5199–5203. Atlanta: The Martin and Hoyt Company, 1954.

Grant, U. S. *Personal Memoirs of U. S. Grant.* Edited by E. B. Long. Cleveland: World Publishing, 1952. Reprint with an introduction by William S. McFeely. New York: DaCapo Press, 1982.

Hay, John. *Lincoln and the Civil War in the Diaries and Letters of John Hay.* New York: Dodd, Mead & Company, 1939.

Hazewell, C. C. "The Twentieth Presidential Election." *Atlantic Monthly* 14 (November 1864): 633–641.

Heartsill, W. W. *Fourteen Hundred and 91 Days, in the Confederate Army.* Jackson, Tenn.: McCowat-Mercer Press, 1953.

Hewitt, J. E. "The Battle of Mansfield, La." *Confederate Veteran* XXXIII (May 1925): 172–173, 198. Reprint. Wilmington, N.C.: Broadfoot Publishing Company, 1987–88.

Irwin, Richard B. *History of the Nineteenth Army Corps.* New York: 1892. Reprint with an introduction by Lawrence L. Hewitt. Baton Rouge, La.: Elliot's Book Shop Press, 1985.

Johnson, Robert U., and Clarence C. Buell, eds. *Battles and Leaders of the Civil War.* 4 vols. New York: 1887. Reprint. N.J.: Castle Company, 1989.

Johnston, Joseph E. *Narrative of Military Operations During the Civil War.* Indianapolis: Indiana University Press, 1959. Reprinted in paperback. New York: De Capo Press, 1990.

Jones, John B. *A Rebel War Clerk's Diary.* 2 vols. Philadelphia: Lippincott & Co., 1866. Reprint, edited by Earl Schenck Miers in one volume. New York: Sagamore Press, Inc., 1958.

Kean, Robert Garlick Hill. *Inside the Confederate Government: The Diary of Robert Garlick Hill Kean.* Edited by Edward Younger. New York: Oxford University Press, 1957.

Liddell, St. John R. *Liddell's Record.* Edited by Nathaniel C. Hughes: Dayton: Morningside, 1985.

Lowell, James Russell. "The Next General Election." *North American Review* 99 (October 1864): 557–72.

Official Report Relative to the Conduct of Federal Troops in Western Louisiana, During the Invasions of 1863 and 1864. Compiled from Sworn Testimony Under

Direction of Governor Henry W. Allen. Shreveport, April 1865. Shreveport, La.: News Printing Establishment-John Dickinson, Proprietor, 1865.

Poche, Felix Pierre. *A Louisiana Confederate: Diary of Felix Pierre Poche.* Edited by Edwin C. Bearss. Natchitoches, La.: Northwestern State University, Louisiana Studies Institute, 1972.

Porter, David D. *Incidents and Anecdotes of the Civil War.* New York: D. Appleton and Company, 1885. Reprint. Harrisburg, Pa.: The Archive Society, 1997.

———. *The Naval History of the Civil War.* New York: Sherman Publishing Company, 1886.

Report of the Joint Committee on the Conduct of the War, Red River Expedition: 1863–1865; Thirty-Eighth Congress, Second Session. Millwood, N.Y.: Kraus Reprint Co., 1977.

Ryan, Frank T. "The Kentucky Campaign and Battle of Richmond." *Confederate Veteran* XXVI (April 1918): 158–160. Reprint. Wilmington, N.C.: Broadfoot Publishing Company, 1987–88.

Shaw, William T. "The Red River Campaign." *Confederate Veteran* XXV (March 1917): 116–118. Reprint. Wilmington, N.C.: Broadfoot Publishing Company, 1987–88.

Sherman, William T. *Memoirs of General W. T. Sherman.* 2 vols. New York: D. Appleton and Company, 1875. Reprint. Harrisburg, Pa.: The Archive Society, 1997.

Sliger, J. E. "How General Taylor Fought the Battle of Mansfield, La." *Confederate Veteran* XXXI (December 1923): 456–458. Reprint. Wilmington, N.C.: Broadfoot Publishing Company, 1987–88.

Taylor, Richard. *Destruction and Reconstruction: Personal Experiences of the Late War.* New York: D. Appleton and Company, 1879. Reprint with an introduction by Edwin C. Bearss. New York: Bantam Books, 1992. This reprint does not follow the same pagination as the original text.

United States War Department. *Official Records of the Union and Confederate Navies in the War of the Rebellion.* 31 vols. Washington, D.C.: Government Printing Office, 1894–1927.

———. *The War of the Rebellion: A Compilation of the Official Records of the Union and Confederate Armies.* 127 vols. Washington, D.C.: Government Printing Office, 1880–1901.

Watkins, Sam R. *"Company Aytch": A Side Show of the Big Show.* New York: Macmillan Publishing Company, 1962 and 1985.

Welles, Gideon. *The Diary of Gideon Welles, Secretary of Navy Under Lincoln and Johnson.* 3 vols. Boston: Houghton Mifflin, 1911.

Secondary Sources

Anders, Curt. *Disaster in Damp Sand: The Red River Expedition.* Indianapolis: Guild Press of Indiana, 1997.

Arceneaux, William. *Acadian General: Alfred Mouton and the Civil War.* Lafayette: Center for Louisiana Studies, University of Southwestern Louisiana, 1981.

Bailey, Anne J. "The Abandoned Western Theater: Confederate National Policy Toward the Trans-Mississippi Region." *Journal of Confederate History* V (1990): 35–54.

_____. "Edmund Kirby Smith." Edited by William C. Davis. *Confederate General* V, 162–171. Harrisburg, Va.: National Historical Society, 1991.

Bartlett, Napier. *Military Record of Louisiana*. 1874. Reprint. Baton Rouge: Louisiana State University Press, 1964.

Bearss, Edwin C. *Steele's Retreat from Camden and the Battle of Jenkin's Ferry*. Little Rock, Ark.: Pioneer Press, 1961.

Bergeron, Arthur W., Jr. *Guide to Louisiana Confederate Military Units*. Baton Rouge: Louisiana State University Press, 1989.

Borbitt, Gabor S. ed. *Why the Confederacy Lost*. New York: Oxford University Press, 1992.

Bragg, Jefferson Davis. *Louisiana in the Confederacy*. Baton Rouge: Louisiana State University Press, 1941.

Brooksher, William R. *War Along the Bayous: The 1864 Red River Campaign in Louisiana*. Washington and London: Brassey's, 1998.

Castel, Albert. *Decision in the West: The Atlanta Campaign of 1864*. Lawrence: The University of Kansas Press, 1992.

_____. *General Sterling Price and the Civil War in the West*. Baton Rouge: Louisiana State University Press, 1968; paperback edition, 1993.

Castille, George J., III and Steven D. Smith. *Bailey's Dam*. Department of Culture, Recreation and Tourism, Archaeological Survey and Antiquities Commission, Anthropological Study No. 8, Baton Rouge, La.: Bourque Printing, Inc., March 1986.

Catton, Bruce. *Grant Takes Command*. Boston: Little, Brown and Company, 1968.

_____. *Never Call Retreat*. New York: Doubleday and Company, 1965.

Connelly, Thomas L. *Army of the Heartland: The Army of Tennessee 1863–1865*. Baton Rouge: Louisiana State University Press, 1967; reprint 1993.

Cunningham, Edward. *The Port Hudson Campaign: 1862–1863*. Baton Rouge: Louisiana State University Press, 1963.

Davis, Burke. *They Called Him Stonewall: A Life of Lt. General T. J. Jackson, C. S. A.* Chapel Hill: The University of North Carolina Press, 1954. Reprint. New York: Fairfax Press, 1988.

Dearman, Scott, Jr. "Statistical Report of Union Troop Strength at The Battle of Mansfield, Louisiana April 8,1864." Submitted to the Louisiana Park Service, Baton Rouge, 1997.

Delaney, Norman C. "The Diary and Memoirs of Marshall Samuel Pierson; Company C, 17th Regiment, Texas Cavalry." *Military History of Texas and the Southwest* 13 (1975): 35–37.

Donald, David H., ed. *Why the North Won the Civil War: Six Authoritative Views on the Economic, Military, Diplomatic, Social, and Political Reasons Behind the Confederacy's Defeat*. New York: Simon and Schuster, 1996.

Dougan, Michael B. *Confederate Arkansas*. Tuscaloosa: University of Alabama Press, 1976; reprint 1991.

Duke, Kevin. *Why Brice's Crossroads*. Memphis, Tenn.: WordMagic Press, 1984.

Foote, Shelby. *The Civil War: A Narrative. Volume III, Red River to Appomattox*. New York: Random House, 1974.

"The Forgotten March: The Red River Campaign." Produced by James Kilcoyne, Henry Maggio and Daniel Graves. 35 mins. The Museum of Historic Natchitoches, 1994. Videocassette.
Glatthaar, Joseph T. *Partners in Command: The Relationships Between Leaders in the Civil War*. New York: The Free Press, 1994.
Gosnell, H. Allen. *Guns on the Western Waters*. Baton Rouge: Louisiana State University Press, 1949; reprint 1993.
Harrington, Fred H. *Fighting Politician: Major General N. P. Banks*. Philadelphia: University of Pennsylvania Press, 1948.
Hearn, Chester G. *Admiral David Dixon Porter: The Civil War Years*. Annapolis, Md.: Naval Institute Press, 1996.
Henry, Robert Selph. *"First With the Most" Forrest*. New York: Mallard Press, 1991.
Hewitt, Lawrence Lee. *Port Hudson: Confederate Bastion on the Mississippi*. Baton Rouge: Louisiana State University Press, 1987.
Hollandsworth, James G. *Pretense of Glory: The Life of General Nathaniel P. Banks*. Baton Rouge: Louisiana State University Press, 1987.
Horn, Stanley F. *The Army of Tennessee*. Norman: The University of Oklahoma Press, 1952. Reprint. Wilmington, N.C.: Broadfoot Publishing Company, 1987.
Jackson, Donald Dale. *Twenty Million Yankees: The Northern Home Front*. Civil War Series. Alexandria, Va.: Time-Life Books, 1985.
Johansson, David H. and Jane Harris. "Two 'Lost' Battle Reports: Horace Randal's and Joseph L. Brent's Reports of the Battles of Mansfield and Pleasant Hill 8 and 9 April 1864." *Military History of the West* 23, (Fall 1993): 169–178.
Johnson, Ludwell H. *Red River Campaign: Politics and Cotton in the Civil War*. Kent, Ohio: Kent State University Press, 1993.
Jones, Archer. *Civil War Command and Strategy*. New York: The Free Press, 1992.
Kennedy, Paul. *The Rise and Fall of the Great Powers*. New York: Vintage Books, 1987.
Kerby, Robert L. *Kirby Smith's Confederacy: The Trans-Mississippi South, 1863–1865*. New York: Columbia University Press, 1972. Reprint. Tuscaloosa: The University of Alabama Press, 1991.
Kinchen, Oscar A. *Confederate Operations in Canada and the North: A Little Known Phase of the American Civil War*. Quincy, Mass.: Christopher Publishing House, 1970.
Long, David E. *The Jewel of Liberty: Abraham Lincoln's Re-Election and the End of Slavery*. Mechanicsburg, Pa.: Stackpole Books, 1994.
Long, E. B. and Barbara Long. *The Civil War Day By Day: An Almanac 1861–1865*. With Foreword by Bruce Catton. New York: Doubleday and Co., 1971. Reprint in paperback. New York: Da Capo Press, 1971.
McPherson, James M. *Battle Cry of Freedom: The Civil War Era*. New York: Oxford University Press, 1988.
Nelson, Larry E. *Bullets, Ballots, and Rhetoric: Confederate Policy for the United States Presidential Contest of 1864*. University, Ala.: University of Alabama Press, 1980.
Parks, Joseph H. *General Edmund Kirby Smith C. S. A*. Baton Rouge: Louisiana State University, 1954 and 1982.

Parrish, T. Michael. *Richard Taylor: Soldier Prince of Dixie*. Chapel Hill: The University of North Carolina Press, 1992.
Prushankin, Jeffery S. "A Crisis in Command: Richard Taylor and Edmund Kirby Smith in Confederate Louisiana During the Red River Campaign." M. A. Thesis, Falvey Memorial Library: Villanova University, 1996.
Savas, Theodore P., and David A. Woodbury, eds. "The Red River Campaign." *Civil War Regiments: A Journal of the American Civil War*. IV, 2. Campbell: Regimental Studies Inc., 1994.
United States Army. *Student Text 101–5 Command and Staff Decision Processes*. Fort Leavenworth, Kans.: Command and General Staff College, 1995.
Vandiver, Frank E. *Jubal's Raid: General Early's Famous attack on Washington in 1864*. New York: McGraw-Hill, 1960. Reprint. Lincoln: University of Nebraska Press, 1992.
Warner, Ezra J. *Generals in Blue: Lives of the Union Commanders*. Baton Rouge: Louisiana State University Press, 1964; reprint 1992.
_____. *Generals in Gray: Lives of the Confederate Commanders*. Baton Rouge: Louisiana State University Press, 1959; reprint 1992.
Waugh, John C. *Reelecting Lincoln*. New York: Crown Publishers Incorporated, 1997.
Welsh, Jack, M. D. *Medical Histories of Confederate Generals*. Kent, Ohio: Kent State University Press, 1995.
Wert, Jeffry D. *From Winchester to Cedar Creek*. South Mountain Press, 1987. Reprint with new material. Mechanicsburg, Pa.: Stackpole Books, 1997.
Winters, John D. *The Civil War in Louisiana*. Baton Rouge: Louisiana State University Press, 1963.
Woodworth, Steven E. *Jefferson Davis and His Generals: The Failure of Confederate Command in the West*. Lawrence: University of Kansas Press, 1990.
Wyeth, John Allan. *That Devil Forrest: Life of General Nathan Bedford Forrest*. With a new Foreword by Albert Castel. Reprint. Baton Rouge: Louisiana State University Press, 1989.

Index

Alexandria, Louisiana: burning 112, 113; dam 106–108; falls description 17, 61, 104; mentioned 15–16, 48, 54, 56, 57, 58, 59, 61, 94, 95, 96, 100, 102, 122, 125, 129, 131; National Cemetery 120; ship transloading 61; Union elections 62
Anderson, William 35
Andres, Captain 87
Andrew, John 46
Arkansas, CSS 18
Arkansas, District of 15
Army Corps, Union: 6th 19, 125; 7th 48; 13th 8, 19, 53, 59, 61, 65, 68, 71, 75, 96, 98, 125, 127, 132, 133; 16th 8, 14, 19, 53, 65, 81, 97, 112, 132, 135; 17th 14, 19, 53, 65, 97, 112, 126, 132, 136; 19th 8, 18, 19, 53, 59, 61, 65, 68, 76, 96, 98, 99, 112, 125–126, 127, 131, 132, 134
Army of Northern Virginia 18, 40, 45, 50
Army of Tennessee, CSA 12, 19, 41, 45, 50 121
Army of the Cumberland 41, 45
Army of the Gulf: friction within 23, 84, 87–88, 105–107, 127; mentioned 12, 16, 18, 21, 49, 50, 53, 59, 97, 104, 120, 121, 126
Army of the James 50
Army of the Ohio 45
Army of the Potomac 19, 40, 45, 50, 125
Army of the Tennessee, USA 45
Arnold, Richard 96
Atchafalaya River: "floating bridge" 115, 131–132; level of 114–115; mentioned 53, 55, 89
Atlanta 8, 12, 19, 21, 121, 125, 126, 132

Bagby, Arthur 69, 90, 98, 104, 112, 113, 137
Bailey, Joseph: bridge over the Atchafalaya 115, 131; description 106; mentioned 111; plans for dam 106; receives thanks of Congress 108; recon of Monette's Ferry 98; work on dams 107–108, 110
Bailey's Dam 123,131
Banks, Nathaniel P.: agrees to launch Red River Campaign 48, 129; assignment to Department of the Gulf 33; at Cedar Mountain 33; command style 3, 22, 32, 34, 64–65, 84, 97, 123–124; congratulates A. J. Smith 82; countermands Franklin concerning cavalry 70–71; decision to diverge from Red River 63–64; decision to retreat from Pleasant Hill 78–79, 80; dispute over cotton 59; does not accompany troops at start of campaign 57; entry into politics 31; House Speaker 31; indecision at Mansfield 72, 75; intent to save fleet 105–106, 107, 111–112; Lincoln offers commission 32; Massachusetts governor 31; mentioned 5, 7, 8, 11–12, 14–16, 26, 35, 38, 45, 49, 52, 54, 60, 68, 85, 86, 91, 93, 102, 114, 117, 120, 125, 126, 130, 131, 133; opinion on Red River Campaign 48; party affiliation 31; plans continuation of campaign 93–94; Pleasant Hill council of war 83–84; preparations for and retreat from Pleasant Hill 78–79, 80; pressure to finish campaign 61, 63; pressure to initiate Red River

Campaign 47–48; relations with A. J. Smith 23, 123; relations with Porter 3, 21–22, 23, 24, 61, 88, 105–107, 111, 118, 123, 125, 127; relieves Albert Lee and Charles Stone 95; retreat to Grand Ecore 89; role in Ten Percent Plan 46, 62; siege of Port Hudson 33–34; sketch of 30–34; soldier's opinion of 84; in Valley Campaign 32–33
Baylor, George 98, 99
Bayou Pierre 90
Beasley's Depot 100
Bee, Hamilton: at Mansfield 71, 72; mentioned 69, 86, 102, 137; at Monette's Ferry 96, 98–100, 131; pursuit to Grand Ecore 89; relieved of command 100–101
Benedict, Lewis 78, 80–81, 99, 134
Berwick's Bay 10, 53, 54, 55, 57, 129
Birge, Henry 97, 98, 99 134
Blair's Landing 90–91, 131
Blessington, Joseph P. 63, 67, 71, 74, 82, 97
Boggs, William 93
Bragg, Braxton 26, 29–30, 41
Brent, Joseph L. 81, 82
Brooksher, William R. 7, 8, 121
Bull Run: First Battle of 26; Second Battle of 33
Butler, Benjamin 33, 37
Byrd, Lieutenant Colonel, commander at Fort De Russy 55–56

Camden Expedition: mentioned 122; origins 48
Cameron, Robert A. 75, 76, 98, 133
Cane River: description 96; mentioned 16, 98, 104
Carondelet USS 108
Cedar Creek, Battle of 8, 19, 125–126, 132
Chattanooga, Battle of 1, 20, 41
Chicago Mercantile Battery 76, 134
Chickamauga, Battle of 41
Churchill, Thomas: Division 16, 60, 66, 71, 77, 81, 86, 92, 124, 130, 138; mentioned 116; at Pleasant Hill 79–80, 82
Closson, Henry 99, 134
Cloutierville, Louisiana 97, 98
Command Climate: Confederate 87–88, 90, 101, 110–111, 115–118, 121; Union 84, 87–88, 105–107, 111, 118
Compromise of 1850 31
Corps D'Afrique 106–107, 135
Cotile Landing 62
Covington USS 109–110, 131

Cricket USS 104
Crump's Corners 68–69
Cushing, Caleb 31

David's Ferry 104, 109–110, 113, 131
Davis, Jefferson President CSA: endorses relief of Taylor 117; on foreign recognition 43–44, 120; influencing 1864 election 44–45, 51, 120; mentioned 26–27, 28, 29, 51; military planning 45; on negotiated peace 44; relieves Joseph Johnston 126; strategic planning 41–45, 120, 126–127
Debray, Xavier B. 71, 98
Democratic Convention of 1860 25
Department of the Gulf 45
Dunn's Bayou 109, 131
Dwight, William 78, 81, 134

Early, Jubal A.: mentioned 8, 20; Shenandoah Raid 18, 125, 132
Eastport USS: at Fort De Russy 56; mentioned 62, 63, 64, 102, 104, 119; sinking and destruction 103, 131
Emma USS 109, 131
Emory, William H.: assumes command of retreat to Alexandria 97, 123; at Chatman's Bayou 76–77; description 76; at Mansura 113; mentioned 78, 112, 134; at Monette's Ferry 99–100; plan at Monette's Ferry 98; at Pleasant Hill 81

Fabian defensive policy 14–16, 21, 51, 60, 86, 115, 122, 124
Farragut, David G. USN 20, 37, 127, 132
Fessenden, Francis 81, 99, 100
Foote, Shelby 44, 126
Forrest, Nathan B. 14, 19, 125, 127, 129, 132
Fort De Russy: description 54; destruction of 57; engagement 55–57; mentioned 4, 53, 113, 119, 129
Fort Jackson 37
Fort Jesup Road 79, 80, 81
Fort St. Phillip 37
Franco-Confederate Alliance 47
Franklin, William B.: advises reconnaissance of river routes 63; command of retreat from Pleasant Hill 94, 97; description 53; march dispositions 64–65, 68–69; mentioned 57, 58, 72, 129, 134; rebukes A. J. Smith 23, 84, 123; rebukes Albert Lee 70; relinquishes command 97; wounded at Mansfield 76, 97
Free-Soil Germans 46–47

Index

Gettysburg, Battle of 1, 20, 34, 40
Grand Bayou Landing 90
Grand Ecore 4, 16, 61, 62, 63, 65, 68, 69, 78, 80, 84, 85, 89, 90, 91, 92, 93, 95, 96, 101, 102, 112, 124, 125, 131
Grant, Ulysses S.: campaign plan for 1864 2, 11–12, 49–50, 120; command of the Union armies 2, 11, 46, 49; considers calling off Red River Campaign 50–51; mentioned 18, 19, 41, 47, 117; pressures Banks 22, 61, 63, 94, 124, 130; relieves Banks 106; at Vicksburg 38
Gray, Henry 85, 137
Green, Thomas: actions at Mansfield 69–71, 74, 76; actions at Pleasant Hill 77, 79, 81; attempt to cut off fleet 86, 90; death of 91, 131; description 70; mentioned 61, 65, 67, 80, 95, 13, 137; plan for Blair's Landing 90
Grover, Cuvier 61, 112, 134

Hahn, Michael, Union governor of Louisiana 57
Halleck, Henry W.: command style 48; conceives Red River Campaign 12, 45, 47–48, 129; mentioned 3, 49, 63, 64
Hallowell, Ben 27
Henderson's Hill 4, 59–60, 130
Hoke, Robert F. 126
Holmes, Theophilus 30, 42, 43
Homefront morale: Northern 2, 3, 5, 7–8, 11, 20, 40, 101, 119, 125, 126; Southern 11, 40, 42–43
Honeycutt Hill 72
Hood, John B. 28, 126–127
Hooker, Joseph 63
Hunter, David 106

Illinois Infantry Regiments: 77th 73; 130th 73
Irwin, Richard B. 78, 97

Jackson, Thomas J. "Stonewall": mentioned 22, 66; mentor of Richard Taylor 26, 122; in Valley Campaign 32
Jenkin's Ferry 105, 113, 116, 131
Johnson, Andrew 20
Johnson, Ludwell 7, 8, 121
Johnston, Albert S. 28
Johnston, Joseph E. 2, 8, 19, 29, 41, 45, 50, 120, 121, 125, 126
Joint Congressional Committee on the Conduct of the War 90, 119

Jones, Carroll Plantation 59
Jones, John B. 11, 40, 41, 119

Kansas-Nebraska Act 31
Kenner, Duncan 60–61
Kentucky Campaign, 1862 29

Landram, William J.: at Mansfield 72; mentioned 71, 133
Lee, Albert G. USA: at Carroll's Mill 70; at Mansfield 72, 74–75; march to Mansfield 65, 70, 71; mentioned 53, 57, 62, 68, 78, 135; relieved of command 95; requests change to order of march 65; at Wilson's Farm 69
Lee, Robert E. CSAL on assumption of offense in 1864 44; dispatches Jubal Early to the Valley 18–19; mentioned 2, 8, 28, 40, 50, 125; opinion of E. Kirby Smith 30
Lexington USS 107
Liddell, St. John R.: at Alexandria 104, 109–110; description 95–96; harassment of the fleet 86, 90–91; at Monette's Ferry 96; opinion of Red River Campaign 118; opinion of Taylor's generalship 123; relations with Richard Taylor 96, 110–111; relieved of command 111
Lincoln, Abraham, President of the United States and Administration: approves Grant's campaign plans 50; on Banks' bravado 63; Blind Memorandum 20; call for volunteers 32; Emancipation Proclamation 44; endorsement of plan to take New Orleans 36; on French in Mexico 47; gives U. S. Grant command of Union armies 49; mentioned 2, 10, 11, 21, 34, 37, 38, 51, 62, 94, 125; reelected 127, 132; Ten-Percent Plan 46; on textile interests 46–47
Loggy Bayou 68, 87
Lord, George 110
Louisiana Cavalry 2nd 55, 58, 59–60
Louisiana Infantry 9th 26

Magruder, John B. 52, 58
Major, James P.: at David's Ferry 104, 109–110; mentioned 69, 71, 90, 98, 112, 113, 137
Mansfield, Louisiana: Battle of 5, 72–77, 116, 117, 118, 130; description 66; disposition of forces 71; mentioned 4, 15, 63, 66, 68, 81, 86, 87, 89, 123, 124; numbers and losses 77; as a turning point 77

Index

Mansura, engagement at 113, 131
McClellan, George B. 32, 46
McMillan, James 81, 134
McPherson, James 45
Meade, George G. 45, 50, 125
Meigs, Montgomery 36
Mississippi River Squadron, USN: mentioned 17, 102, 130; runs the dam 107–108, 131
Mobile, Alabama 8, 12, 20, 22, 41, 45, 47, 50, 52, 120, 121, 125, 127, 132
Monette's Ferry: Battle of 98–100, 131; description 96; mentioned 16, 101, 125
Moore, Thomas Confederate Louisiana Governor 26, 27, 104
Morgan, Edward 110
Moss Plantation 76
Mound City, USS 108
Mouton, Alfred G.: death of 73; description 55; at Mansfield 71, 74; mentioned 67, 137
Mower, Joseph: at Fort De Russy 55–57; Henderson's Hill 59–60, 130; mentioned 135; at Pleasant Hill 81; at Yellow Bayou 114

Napoleon III 47
New England textile interests 11, 46–47
New Falls City 87
New Orleans 33, 36–37
New York World, opinion of Lincoln 20
Nims, Ormand 72, 73, 75
9th Louisiana Infantry 26

Osage, USS 91
Overland Campaign 18, 20, 125

Parsons, Mosby M.: Division 16, 60, 77, 81, 92, 124, 130, 131, 138; at Pleasant Hill 79–80 Peninsula Campaign 26
Perryville, Battle of 30
Phelps, S. L. USN 56–57, 103
Pittsburg, USS 108
Pleasant Grove 76, 78
Pleasant Hill: Battle of 7, 16, 80–82, 118, 130; Confederate conference 85; description 79; dispositions 78–79; Federal Council of War 83–84; mentioned 63, 69, 78, 87, 89, 94, 124, 125
Plymouth, North Carolina 126
Poche, Felix Pierre 56, 57–58, 67, 71, 73, 97
Poison Springs 131
Polignac de, Camille J.: at Alexandria 104;
at Mansfield 71, 76; at Mansura 113; mentioned 86, 92, 96, 112, 137; at Pleasant Hill 80, 81–82; at Yellow Bayou 114
Polk, Leonidas K. and Polk's Confederate Corps 11, 12, 45, 50, 121
Pope, John 63
Porter, David, Captain, USN (father of David Dixon Porter) 34–35
Porter, David D., Rear Admiral, USN: advocate of iron steam ships 35–36; ambush of *Cricket* 104; assists his mother 36; commands Mississippi River Squadron 37; concerns over Red River water level 17, 87; controversy with Benjamin Butler 37; cotton gathering activities 58–59; decides to destroy the *Eastport* 103; departs Vicksburg 53, 129; destruction of fleet 18, 87, 106; fears army will abandon fleet 95, 105; feelings for father 34; at Fort Pickens 36; on joint operations 38; loyalty to the Union 36; mentioned 7, 8, 86, 91, 112, 126, 131; in Mexican Navy 35; in Mexican War 35; objects to continuing the Campaign 93; opinion of Banks 103; opinion of politicians 3, 22, 34–35; opinion of Red River Campaign 49, 87, 94, 119–120; on passing up the Red 62; plan for New Orleans 36; receives word of army's defeat at Mansfield 87, 130; relations with Banks 3, 21–22, 24, 61, 87–88, 106–107, 111, 118, 123–125, 127; sketch of 34–39; supports scheme to build Bailey's dam 106; at Vicksburg Campaign 38
Port Hudson, Louisiana 18, 33–34, 41, 106
Presidential election of 1864 1–5, 11, 19, 20, 44, 45, 46, 51, 101, 120–121, 125, 126, 127
Price, Sterling 52, 60, 101, 117

Randolph, G. W. CSA Secretary of War 30
Ransom, Thomas E. G.: at Mansfield 72, 74–75, 76; mentioned 53, 71, 133; wounding 75
Rantoul, Robert Jr. 31
Red River: as an avenue of invasion 3, 10, 45, 48, 53, 89, 129; level of water 4, 17, 51, 61, 86, 87, 89, 90, 106, 107
Red River Campaign: begins 53; command arrangements 49; Confederate army strength 10; end of 115, 118, 132; losses 5, 10–11; maps 139–153; objectives

of Federal army 11, 46–50; origins 3, 45–50, 123; short-term effects 20–21, 119–120; significance 7, 9, 12, 21, 115, 119–121, 125, 126; Union army strength 10
Rhett, Barnwell 25
Richmond, Kentucky, Battle of 29
Ruffin, Edmund 25

Sabine Pass 48, 129
Sabine Road 79, 80, 82
Schofield, John M. 45
Scott, Winfield 35
Scurry, William R. 56, 81, 136
2nd Louisiana Cavalry 55, 58, 59–60
Selfridge, Thomas O. 90–91
Seward, William H. 36
Shaw, William T.: at Fort De Russy 56–57; mentioned 136; at Pleasant Hill 78, 80–81
Sherman, William T. 9–10, 12, 14, 19, 21, 22, 38, 41, 45, 48, 55, 57, 83, 94, 113, 117, 121, 124, 125, 126, 127, 129, 132
Shreveport, Louisiana 10, 12, 15, 17, 48, 60, 61, 63, 65, 70, 78, 83, 86, 92, 124
Signal, USS 109–110, 131
Simmesport, Louisiana 10, 43, 49, 53, 54, 55, 89, 104, 113, 114, 115, 129, 131
Smith, Andrew J. Major General, USA: burns Alexandria 112; commander, 16th & 17th Corps 14, 53; departs Vicksburg 53, 129; at Fort De Russy 54–57; Henderson's Hill 59; launches assault at Pleasant Hill 81–82; makes dispositions at Pleasant Hill 78; at Mansura 113; march to Alexandria 57–58; march to Mansfield 69; mentioned 22, 48–49, 57, 61, 68, 78, 83, 94, 121, 124, 125, 135; oversees destruction during retreat 97; proposes mutiny 23, 84; sends support to fleet 91; Tupelo, Battle of 19, 132; at Yellow Bayou 114
Smith, Edmund Kirby, Lieutenant General, CSA: appointment to command of the Trans-Mississippi Department 30, 43; at Bull Run, First Battle of 29; decision to purse Steele 86; defeat at Jenkin's Ferry 105; defense of the Red River Valley 55, 121; Fabian Policy 14–16, 21, 51, 60, 86, 115, 122, 124; Kentucky Campaign 29–30; at Mansfield recommends against fight 70, 77; meets with Taylor in Mansfield 66; mentioned 7, 9, 17, 26, 45, 48, 58, 67, 68, 93, 111, 113, 125, 136; Mexican War service 28; opinion of service 28; plans to counter Federal offensive 52, 60; Pleasant Hill conference with Taylor 85; preparation for West Point 27; prepares for the Red River Campaign 51, 130; relations with Richard Taylor 3–5, 14–15, 21, 24, 61, 65, 87–88, 90, 92, 101–102, 113, 115–118, 121–123; relieves Taylor 117, 132; on secession crisis 28; sketch of 27–30; stands by decision to pursue Steele 92
Smith, Frances (sister of E. Kirby Smith) 27
Smith, Joseph (father of E. Kirby Smith) 27
Smith, Sol (E. Kirby Smith's medical director) 15, 60
Smith, Thomas Kilby, Brigadier General, USA: accompanies Porter's fleet 68; destruction of Fort De Russy 57; mentioned 19, 65, 127; receives word of Mansfield 87; return to Sherman's army 126
Southard, Samuel 34
Steele, Frederick, Major General, USA: mentioned 12, 15–16, 49, 52, 60, 61, 64, 65, 68, 83, 92, 93, 101, 116, 130; ordered to support Banks 48, 129; retreat from Jenkin's Ferry 105, 131; threat to the Trans-Mississippi Department 86, 117, 124
Steele, William 104
Stephens, Alexander 31
Stone, Charles P. 63, 64, 95
Stuart, James E. B. 33

Taylor, Richard, Major General CSA: compliments Thomas Green 70; on death of Green 91; decision to fight at Mansfield 66–67, 72–73; dominance of Banks 22, 84, 119; evacuates Alexandria 58; feelings for Louisiana 14–15, 21, 52, 104–105; at Fort De Russy 54–56; health of 25, 26, 93, 102, 116; meeting with Smith in Mansfield 66; mentioned 10, 12, 19, 30, 33, 43, 51, 54, 64, 68, 81, 97, 108, 136; military training 26; objection to pursuit of Steele 86, 92; opinion of secession 25–26; opinion of the Fabian Policy 60; opinion of the Red River Forts 55; orders pursuit of Banks 86, 90, 95–96; plans for Monette's Ferry 96, 98; plans for Pleasant Hill 77, 79–80; plans trap at Alexandria 104, 109–110; Pleasant Hill conference with E. Kirby Smith

85; political affiliation 25; preparations for Mansfield 69, 71, 130; pursuit at Mansfield 76–77; pursuit to Simmesport 112–115; relations with Edmund Kirby Smith 3–4, 14, 21, 24, 28, 61, 65, 87–88, 90, 92, 93, 102, 115–118, 121, 123; relations with Liddell 110–111; relieved of command 117, 132; relieves Bee 100–101; requests relief from command 102, 115, 116–117; sketch of 24–27; social attitudes 25; vision of opportunity 7, 8, 17, 89, 101–102, 125, 127

Taylor, Zachary (father of Richard Taylor): mentioned 24, 27; relationship with Richard 24–25

Teche Offensive 14, 53–54, 61

Ten-Percent Plan 46

Texas, District of 52

Thomas, George 45

Trans-Mississippi Department: Confederate National Policy 21, 41–45, 119; description 9–10, 42; mentioned 5, 11, 14, 86

Tupelo, Battle of 19, 132

Valley Campaign, 1862 26, 32–33, 34

Van Dorn, Earl 28

Vicksburg, Mississippi 1, 2, 10, 20, 33–34, 36, 38, 40, 41, 42, 43, 49

Vincent, William G. 55, 58, 59–60

Virginia, CSS 18

Walker, John G. Major General, CSA: description 55; Division 15–16, 56, 63, 67, 72, 74, 76, 80, 86, 92, 101, 115, 116, 123, 124, 130, 131, 136; at Fort De Russy 55–56; at Jenkin's Ferry 113; at Mansfield 71; mentioned 58, 66, 77, 101, 104, 105, 107, 111; opinion of pursuing Steele 86, 102; opinion of Red River Campaign 118; at Pleasant Hill 81; wounded 81

Warner, USS 109, 131

Webster, Daniel 31

Welles, Gideon, US Secretary of the Navy: describes Porter 34, 36, 38; mentioned 18, 37, 49, 87, 93, 103; news of Mobile 20; opinion of Banks 94

West Louisiana, District of: description 54; mentioned 15, 27, 52, 136

Wharton, John A. 95, 112, 114, 137

Williams, T. Harry 21, 22

Williams, T. J. 80

Wilson, J. G. 59

Wilson's Farm, skirmish of 69–70, 130

Withenbury, Wellington W. 62, 63

Yancey, William 25

Yellow Bayou, engagement of 114, 131

www.ingramcontent.com/pod-product-compliance
Ingram Content Group UK Ltd.
Pitfield, Milton Keynes, MK11 3LW, UK
UKHW042013140426
5217IPUK00015B/1156